What's Past is Prologue

"Ferdy"

What's Past is Prologue

A Collection of Essays in Honour of

L. J. WOODWARD

edited by

SALVADOR BACARISSE
BERNARD BENTLEY
MERCEDES CLARASÓ
DOUGLAS GIFFORD

SCOTTISH ACADEMIC PRESS
EDINBURGH

Published by
Scottish Academic Press Ltd,
33 Montgomery Street
Edinburgh EH7 5JX

SBN 7073 0344 3

© 1984 Scottish Academic Press Ltd

British Library Cataloguing in Publication Data

What's past is prologue.
1. Spain—Study and teaching—addresses, essays, lectures.
I. Bacarisse, S.   II. Woodward, L. J.
946'.007   DP4

Printed by The Universities Press (Belfast) Ltd

Contents

Foreword

This collection of essays by L. J. Woodward's students and colleagues of former days tries to mark out our appreciation of over a third of a century's teaching and warmth. The contributors are now teachers in University or Polytechnic departments of Spanish. Because of the limited space available the present editors restricted their activity to the gathering and presentation of material, thus joining those who, from so many other walks of life, would have liked to contribute to this volume as well.

One sad note. Kemlin Lawrence, who worked under Ferdy in 1958–60, was to have sent us an article. Her untimely death meant that it remained unfinished though not unmourned.

Douglas Gifford
St Andrews, 1983

Dedication—Leslie James Woodward

Most friends, and probably all former students of the above-named will have raised their eyebrows at those two Christian names, for nobody has ever known Woodward by any other name than Ferdy. Only when I was asked to write an introduction to this volume did I think of asking how he had been christened. I learnt then that his nickname was given him by his fellow students at Cambridge because his abundant and curly hair recalled to them Ariel's description of the survivors of the shipwreck in *The Tempest:*

> "... The King's son, Ferdinand
> with hair up-staring,—then like reeds, not hair,—"

Subsequently, his own students must have been equally awed by the exuberant *melena*, just as they must have been constantly over-awed by the loudness and resonance of his bass voice. Convention has never been a characteristic of the Woodwards and so universal has been his wife's nickname with friends and students alike, that it might be safe to wager that none have ever known her real name, which is Joan. She was apparently given her nickname when in the early years of marriage, she had to act as a buffer between her disputatious husband and brother. The nickname itself must not, however, be given the dignity of print for it does not befit so gracious and witty a lady.

Woodward was born on 9th July 1916 in Liverpool, but spent most of his childhood in the Isle of Man, where his mother had been born. He has always considered himself a Manxman, suitably a more unconventional place of origin than Liverpool. When one visited the Woodward household, one always saw a cat without a tail, in fact, several over the years. Only on one of his visits to my home did I learn of Woodward's Manx origin, for he found that my children were delighting in a collection of folk-tales from the Isle of Man, and he proceeded to put us all right on the proper pronounciation of the various mythical monsters, such as the Buggane.

Woodward was educated at Oulton School in Liverpool where he was appointed Head Boy, a post that kept him there until 1936. He then went up to Downing College, Cambridge where he read Spanish and graduated in 1939. I was still at Cambridge until after the declaration of war in that year, but I have no recollection of meeting him or seeing the famous *melena*. Woodward joined the Navy in 1941, serving at sea until commissioned in the R.N.V.R. in 1942. He was given a temporary shore post with the Polish Navy which was stationed in Britain, until he was transferred to Naval Intelligence at Bletchley Park. It was there that I first became aware of our paths crossing, when someone pointed to a young naval officer and said: "Did you know that man at Cambridge? He read Spanish". In 1945 Woodward was promoted to Acting Lieutenant Commander and sent to the Gairloch as C.O. of a tank-landing ship. The following year he was demobilised.

The War had prevented the academic career he would have embarked on in Cambridge, where he was awarded a *beca* by the Spanish Government which he was unable to take up. He taught for a year at Midhurst School, until the Spanish Government offered to renew the *beca* they had awarded him earlier.

While at Cambridge, Woodward had met his future wife, Joan Bradshaw who was a student at Bedford College and was evacuated with the College to Cambridge. They were married in 1942, and when Woodward was transferred to Bletchley Park he found his wife already working in the same section. Joan accompanied him to Madrid when he took up his research scholarship, making ends meet for the two of them by teaching English to the nephews and niece of General Franco. The unconventionality that has invariably accompanied the Woodwards' domestic and professional lives manifested itself in Madrid. Some friends sent him the announcement for the new post of lecturer in Spanish at St Andrews in order to start a new department. Seated in the Café Gijon, husband and wife discussed the advisability of applying for the post. Woodward succumbed to Joan's urging after a good deal of hesitation. The waiter was asked to bring pen and paper, and the application for the lectureship was posted to St Andrews written with a scratchy pen on café notepaper. On leaving Madrid in 1948, Woodward received an invitation to an interview at St Andrews and was offered the post. He resumed school teaching until the start of the academic year in September 1948 when he took up his duties at the University. During that year, or perhaps the following, I was appointed External Examiner for St Andrews. I was then at Aberdeen, holding the corresponding post to Woodward's, but in a Department that had been in existence, though unenergetically, since 1919. I commenced a succession of annual visits to St Andrews and had the privilege of the Woodwards' hospitality and of a friendship that has endured.

By then, the Woodwards had three daughters and were shortly to have a fourth. Nothing, it should be emphasized, was ever conventional about the Woodwards. I think it was on my second visit that as I walked from the station to the Woodward home, I saw my host dressed in a large white apron hanging up sheets on a washing-line in the front garden. Life was not easy for young men starting a professional career in those first years after the War. It was difficult to make ends meet and food rationing was probably still in force. Furthermore, Joan had gone to the South of France to visit a sick relative, so I found Woodward not only doing all the laundry but also, all the cooking, including the baking of bread. I do not remember if he was also coping uncomplainingly with the care of the three small children. Some of them may have been left with a grandparent, but I do remember that on the last day of my visit, before taking the train back to Aberdeen, I suggested that the family might lunch out with me, and I do remember at least one little girl. Some time later Woodward casually remarked that my invitation to lunch had been a timely one, for he had no cash with which to offer me lunch. This memory has been for me the most typical revelation of the man. Looking after a house and family single handedly, the laundry, the cooking and the baking, always cheerful and uncomplaining but too poor to give his External Examiner the customary range of hospitality and giving no inkling of his difficulty—that sums up "Ferdy".

The Department grew rapidly and it is worth mentioning that Ferdy appointed a series of Assistant Lecturers, all of whom, in due course came to hold Chairs—R. O. Jones, G. W. Ribbans, V. F. Dixon, J. S. Cummins and Arsenio Pacheco. I think this would deserve to be an entry in an academic Guinness Book of Records. Permanent posts were added, and the first of these appointments,

Douglas Gifford, helped to set a lasting seal on the unconventionality of the Department's life and activity. It has become a by-word among academic departments for its complete lack of formality and the originality of its ventures. The exclusive use of Christian names between Staff and students is no longer a novelty anywhere, but I first met it in St Andrews where not only Christian names were in force, but also the nicknames of the Professor and his wife. Woodward himself was a partial exception to this custom, for whenever I heard him address a girl student it was invariably by her surname unprefixed by "Miss". Indeed, one of his most engaging habits is the absence of the pronoun "I" from his conversation ("when Woodward left home this morning . . ."; "You must not expect Woodward to agree with that"), which is paralleled by his addressing his wife as "Woman!". Parties always seemed to be about to take place, or actually taking place whenever I visited the Department, with sausages frying in all sorts of unexpected places and most people sitting on the floor. Picnics for the whole Department seemed to be of frequent occurrence with food cooked on the sea shore.

Gifford added to the international fame of the Department, not only by persuading the University to found a Centre for Latin American Linguistic Studies, but by taking students off to camp in the Andes in order to learn Quechua. Gifford also founded a choir, The Renaissance group, which specialized in sixteenth century religious music and travelled around Britain giving public concerts. With his winning ways he also gained access for his choir's performances in cathedrals and monasteries on the Continent. Woodward added his powerful bass voice to the choir; but what is more typical of him is that he took out a bus driver's licence in order to transport the choir around Europe.

Woodward himself contributed to the international reputation of his Department, not only by his publications, but also by his periods of lecturing across the Atlantic. He was invited four times to the United States, three times as Andrew Mellon Visiting Professor to the University of Pittsburgh, and once to the University of Montana. This last appointment added one more, and not the least significant, to his list of unusual accomplishments and qualities, for he entered on his duties at the University of Montana with the official title of "Thinker in Residence". During these visits he also gave lectures at other universities in the United States and Canada.

In between parties, expeditions and choral concerts, teaching presumably took place in the Department. Doubtless, this was as excitingly unconventional as all its other activities, though I have not much evidence to support this assertion. I do know that Woodward had little use for "history of literature" and a special flair for interpretative analysis. The first paper I heard him read was at Pittsburgh, Pennsylvania, when I was astonished by what he could extract from a Góngora *romance;* the last paper I heard him read was in Wolfenbüttel where I was even more astonished by the brilliance of his analysis of a Calderonian *loa sacramental.* His teaching clearly stimulated the minds of his students in what seems to have been a very special way. I was invited on one occasion to read a paper to the Department and chose for my subject an analysis of Calderón's use of the metaphor "life is a dream" which I thought I had at last been able to relate to the actions of all the characters, thus arriving at a unified interpretation of the theme of the play. A lively discussion ensued with the students but not (much to my surprise) on the subject I had developed, but only on incidental remarks I had made about the motives of some of the characters for some of their particular actions. The unified "philosophy" which I prided myself on having extracted from the dramatic technique peculiar to Calderón, did not seem to interest the students, but they were passionately interested in the living human experience which they had extracted from their understanding of the characters. When we withdrew to another room for refreshments, I remember one student saying with the utmost conviction "I cannot imagine that Basilio could possibly have thought such a thing...". Clearly, the academic life in the Department, under Woodward's direction and with his example, gave the students an active experience of living and not just of learning. This experience of living was as much a part of the social relationship fostered between teachers and taught, as it was of the exciting exploration of literature. Woodward will always be remembered by all of his friends outside St Andrews for the kindness, generosity, friendliness and helpfulness of his character, as well as by the liveliness and good humour of his personality. Unfailingly benevolent and tolerant, he gave voice to only one aversion, a hatred of smoking, which led to the apocryphal rumour that no smoker could ever by appointed to the Department. No student and no friend will ever have been in difficulties without Woodward gently and unassumingly offering his help. It is fitting, indeed, that the contributions to this volume of essays offered as a tribute to his academic life and work, should all be written by former students and colleagues who will all have benefited most directly from the warmth and generosity which he has always spread around him.

Alexander A. Parker

1. Sin and Grace in *El Casamiento engañoso y el coloquio de los perros*—STEPHEN BOYD

The aim of this contribution is to sketch a possible theological ground plan for the most complex and enigmatic of Cervantes' *Novelas ejemplares*.

The *Casamiento engañoso* is essentially the story of a sinner's conversion.[1] It is a conversion wrought by apparently miraculous means—the experience of hearing the nocturnal conversation of two dogs in a hospital, called appropriately, the *Hospital de la Resurrección*. Before turning attention to the *Coloquio de los perros*, which is the record of that conversation, it may be helpful to reflect on the language which the *alférez* Campuzano uses to describe the culminating moment in the story of his disastrous marriage. This comes when he returns to the lodging which he had shared with his 'wife', doña Estefanía, and finds that she has rifled the chest which contained his jewels:

> Fuí a ver mi baúl, y nalléle abierto, y como sepultura que esperaba cuerpo difunto, y a buena razón había de ser el mío, *si yo tuviera entendimiento para saber sentir y ponderar tamaña desgracia.* (p. 195–196).[2]

Estefanía's triumph at this moment is only apparent, for, as Campuzano admits to his friend, Peralta, the jewels and chains were artificial and almost valueless. The moral which Peralta draws from this story is the trivial one of 'tit for tat', except that he makes it more impressive by quoting Petrarch:

> Che chi prende diletto di far frode,
> Non si de' lamentar s'altri l'inganna. (p. 198)[3]

The *Alférez*, however, seems to have learned more profound lessons than this which allow him, in retrospect, to 'sentir y ponderar

1

tamaña desgracia'. The image of the empty trunk as a "sepultura" suggests that he now appreciates his misfortune, not as an exterior, material one, but as an interior death. Obviously something must account for this attainment of a superior moral vantage point. Equally obviously, that 'something' can only be the experience of hearing the *Coloquio de los perros*. A helpful way of approaching the *Coloquio* would be to ask why it should have had a transforming effect on Campuzano.

The *Coloquio de los perros* consists of Berganza's oral autobiography interspersed with Cipión's comments and criticisms. In a manner reminiscent of the picaresque novel Berganza describes his experiences with a succession of masters who are representative of almost the entire range of seventeenth century Spanish society. It emerges as a society riddled with lies and deceit. The case of Berganza's second masters, the shepherds, is typical. The flocks which they tend are ravaged by wolves, but the 'wolves' turn out to be human:

> Pasméme, quedé suspenso cuando vi que los pastores eran los lobos, y que despedazaban el ganado los mismos que le habían de guardar. (p. 232)

Cipión draws a predictable lesson from this experience:

> ... pero el daño está en que es imposible que puedan pasar bien las gentes en el mundo si no se fía y se confía.
> (p. 232–233)

The theme of deceit in the service of concupiscence is an important link between both parts of the *novela*. But if each episode in the *Coloquio* only provides yet another illustration of the same truth: "all men deceive and are deceived", it would seem that it is nothing more than a rhetorical amplification of the *Casamiento*. This is not to deny the subjective effectiveness of the insistence on human malice. It is persuasive and depressing. The *Coloquio* convinces the reader of the fact of sinfulness but does it help him to understand it or see a way out of it?

A traditional Christian understanding is offered explicitly at various points in the dogs' conversation. Berganza is evidently refering to the doctrine of original sin when he says:

> ... vuelvo a decir lo que otra vez he dicho: que el hacer y decir mal lo heredamos de nuestros primeros padres y lo mamamos en la leche. (p. 240)

His attempts to find some trace of pre-lapsarian virtue in the world meet with frustration. Among the shepherds where he had hoped to find 'alguna reliquia de aquella felicísima vida' (p. 229), full of harmony and order, described in pastoral literature, he is confronted instead with the discord and confusion of a fallen world in which men are scarcely distinguishable from animals. The crude music-making of the shepherds, in which singing is replaced by grunting ('que no cantaban, sino que gritaban o gruñían.' [p. 228]) is an image of their distorted humanity. The evangelical associations of the pastoral world also arouse expectations which are disappointed:

> . . . creí que habia hallado en él el centro de mi reposo,
> pareciéndome ser propio y natural oficio de los perros guardar
> ganado, que es obra donde se encierra una virtud grande,
> como es amparar y defender de los poderosos y soberbios los
> humildes y los que poco pueden. (p. 221)[4]

With few exceptions (notably the Jesuit fathers and the young captain who is 'muy buen caballero y gran cristiano' [p. 279].) the world which Berganza experiences is one in which *la soberbia* triumphs.

These references to original sin are scattered and not consistently developed. The reader has to wait for the central episode of the witch, la Cañizares, for an extensive, explicit discussion of the nature of sin. The witch explains in quite sophisticated theological language that sin is a habit which consists in the enslavement of the will to disordered appetite and that it results in the disintegration of the self:

> . . . la costumbre del vicio se vuelve en naturaleza, y éste de ser
> brujas se convierte en sangre y carne, y en medio de su ardor,
> que es mucho, trae un frío que pone en el alma, tal, que la
> resfría y entorpece aun en la Fe, de donde nace *un olvido de sí
> misma*, y ni se acuerda de los temores con que Dios la
> amenaza, ni de la gloria con que la convida; y en efeto, como
> es pecado de carne y de deleites, es fuerza que amortigüe todos
> los sentidos, y los embelese y absorte, sin dejarlos usar sus
> oficios como deben: y así, quedando el alma inútil, floja y
> desmazalada, no puede levantar la consideración siquiera a
> tener algún buen pensamiento: y asi dejándose estar sumida
> en la profunda sima de su miseria, no quiere alzar la mano a

> la de Dios, que se la está dando por sola su misericordia, para
> que se levante. Yo tengo una destas almas que te he pintado:
> todo lo veo y todo lo entiendo: y como el deleite me tiene
> echados grillos a la voluntad, siempre he sido y seré mala.
> (p. 301–302).

The witch not only discourses on the nature of sin; she is a living
image of its ugliness and futility, an image to which other
characters in the *novela* conform more or less closely. The supreme
image of that futility is the devil, whose angelic knowledge of the
nature of God and of the inevitability of his ultimate defeat is of no
use to him. Cañizares consciously acknowledges Satan as her 'amo
y señor' (p. 295) perhaps suggesting that all men who lie and cheat
pay unconscious homage to the 'father of lies'. In the devil, as in
his votary, self-knowledge, ignorance and malice co-exist in a
supremely paradoxical manner. Berganza (perhaps echoing the
reader's reaction) finds this paradox incomprehensible.

> En esto, me preguntaba yo a mí mismo: '¿Quién kizo a esta
> mala vieja tan discreta y tan mala? ¿De dónde sabe ella cuáles
> son males de daño y cuáles de culpa? ¿Cómo entiende y
> habla tanto de Dios, y obra tanto del diablo? ¿Cómo peca tan
> de malicia, no excusándose con ignorancia?' (p. 305–306)

Ironically Cañizares anticipates this question and its exact
formulation:

> Dirás tú ahora, hijo, si es que acaso me entiendes, que quién
> me hizo a mí teóloga, y aún quizá dirás entre ti: '-¡Cuerpo de
> tal con la puta vieja! ¿Por qué no deja de ser bruja, pues sabe
> tanto, y se vuelve a Dios, pues sabe que está más prompto a
> perdonar pecados que a permitirlos?' (p. 301).

These passages open up interesting perspectives for the
understanding of sin. Far from having 'un olvido de sí misma'
(p. 301), Cañizares seems to have an extraordinary degree of
self-knowledge. but it is knowledge of something which is
progressively disintegrating, an awareness of the loss of self. This
pseudo-knowledge is self-consuming and self-invalidating. Cervantes was evidently interested in sin as a failure in awareness; as
springing from and resulting in a lack of vision. In the *Coloquio* this
theme is given extensive treatment. In fact it is a central

preoccupation, and it is not just a matter of the explicit content of the episodes but of the very structure of the story. The interlocutors are, after all, dogs, not men. This is obviously not a merely whimsical device. Cervantes uses it to explore the question of self-knowledge in considerable depth and to suggest that it involves much more than an awareness of one's personal idiosyncrasies.

When the dogs receive the 'divino don de la habla' they are amazed and confused. They are faced with the question of self-knowledge in a very urgent manner. Cipión comments:

> . . . y viene a ser mayor este milagro en que no solamente
> hablamos, sino en que hablamos con discurso, como si
> fuéramos capaces de razón, estando tan sin ella, que la
> diferencia que hay del animal bruto al hombre es ser el
> hombre animal racional, y el bruto, irracional. (p. 210)

Neither Cervantes nor his dogs, of course, knew that Wittgenstein wrote: 'If a lion could talk, we could not understand him'.[5] Yet the problem implied here is faced by the dogs. They are not quite sure what they are. Neither is the reader. For the moment they are quite literally 'rational animals' and, therefore, according to Cipión's definition they are men. Yet they are dogs. Berganza's life story is the story of a dog's life, except that he retrospectively attributes rational motives to his behaviour in the past as though he had always been capable of reasoning and always had a moral sense. Cervantes appears to be casting a sceptical eye on man as 'rational animal' by asking us to ponder on what happens when animals become rational.

Berganza admits at the beginning of his narration that he is uncertain about his origins:

> *Paréceme* que la primera vez que vi el sol fué en Sevilla, y en su
> Matadero, que está fuera de la puerta de la Carne; por donde
> *imaginara* (si no fuera por lo que después te diré) que mis
> padres debieron de ser alanos . . . (p. 215)

Later he gives la Cañizares's account of his birth:

> . . . estando tu madre preñada, y llegándose la hora del parto,
> fué su comadre la Camacha, la cual recibió en sus manos lo
> que tu madre parió, y mostróle que había parido dos perritos:
> y así como los vió, dijo:—'¡Aquí hay maldad; aquí hay

> bellaquería! . . . no te dé pena alguna este suceso; que ya sabes
> tú que puedo yo saber que si no es con Rodríguez, el ganapán
> tu amigo, días ha que no tratas con otro; así que este perruno
> parto de otra parte viene, y algún misterio contiene.'
> (p. 292–293)

Berganza, then, was born of a witch and an unidentified father. It
sounds very much like a parody, or, an inverted version of the
Virgin Birth. The religious echoes grow yet louder when la
Cañizares informs Berganza that la Camacha, on her death bed,
prophesied the restoration of the dogs' human nature:

> . . . que ellos volverían a su ser cuando menos lo pensasen; mas
> que ne podía ser primero que ellos *por sus mismos ojos viesen* lo
> siguiente:
>
> 'Volverán en su forma verdadera
> Cuando *vieren* con presta diligencia
> Derribar los soberbios levantados,
> Y alzar a los humildes abatidos,
> Con poderosa mano para hacello.'

As Pamela Waley has pointed out, this prophecy is a version of
part of the *Magnificat:*[6]

> Fecit potentiam in brachio suo;
> Dispersit superbos mente cordis sui.
> Deposuit potentes de sede,
> Et exaltavit humiles (Luke 1:51–52).

The dogs can become men once more by understanding a text. The
reference to the *Magnificat* suggests a possible allegorical pattern:
creatures who should be men are changed into dogs at birth but
can recover their original nature. This looks like an allegory of the
fall and restoration of man: men created in the image and likeness
of God are born as mere 'men' (higher than the animals but lower
than the angels) because of the loss of the *imago Dei* at the Fall, but
they have the opportunity of becoming 'Sons of God' once more.[7]

The dogs' recovery of their human nature depends on a double
act of seeing: seeing the prophetic text itself and then seeing the
mighty cast down and the humble exalted. The dogs fail to
understand the prophecy. They seem to have seen the type of
inversion of which it speaks taking place but yet they do not

become human. L. J. Woodward has pointed out that because they are dogs they can only interpret the text literally and allegorically but fail to appreciate its anagogical and tropological senses.[8] There is a great irony at work here. Because the dogs 'see' the text, in the sense of understanding the words, they *are* men ('rational animals') and the prophecy has indeed been fulfilled. They do not realize this because the interpretation of the text in the theological senses is dependent on faith and faith is a distinctively human perception and act. In terms of the overall allegory the implication is that unregenerate man is indeed rational but not fully human. The dogs do not see the text as having an interior reference. That is, they do not associate the 'humildes' or the 'soberbios' with themselves. Cervantes implies that understanding the prophecy, or the *Magnificat*, requires that one experience the abasement of the proud and the exaltation of the humble in an interior way. That is to say: the act of repentance, of seeing oneself as a sinner is the same as, and dependent on, the act of seeing oneself as a 'Son of God'. It is a single act of self-knowledge. This may be the real meaning of the phrase: 'por sus propios ojos viesen'; 'when they see with their own eyes', or 'when they see *for* themselves'. This paradoxical act of seeing also brings about a transformation in one's nature: if one is humble enough to recognize one's dog nature, one recovers one's human nature, 'con poderosa mano para hacello'.

It may be possible at this stage to make some generalization about the complex function of the dog/men, Berganza and Cipión. They represent both 'l'homme moyen sensuel' who has a dual nature—sensual/animal, and, rational/human; and semi-regenerate man who experiences a tension between his renewed spiritual nature and his 'adamic' nature. The justification for seeing the dogs as images of semi-regenerate man lies in the fact that they do appear to have some measure of faith. Berganza commends himself to Jesus and invokes God on many occasions. They also have 'works', since they help with the collection of alms for the hospital. Yet they have to keep struggling with their canine tendency to bark and to bite.[9] In their largely unsuccessful attempt to avoid *murmuración*, which they 'know' is sinful, they are continually reliving the truth of the vulgar proverb, cited by Berganza: 'del dicho al hecho hay gran trecho' (p. 255).

Through the experience of hearing or dreaming the *Coloquio* Campuzano has been changed and he is able to interpret his behaviour in the past as due to a failure of self-knowledge. He speaks of his understanding having been fettered by the prospect of sensual gratification: 'el gusto que me tenía echados grillos al entendimiento' (p. 184). This phrase recalls la Cañizares's words on the same subject: 'el deleite me tiene echados grillos a la voluntad' (p. 302). Such exact echoing suggests that he has learned to interpret his past through hearing her voice at the heart of his vision or dream. His description of himself in his days as a 'lady-killer' is also revelatory. It was a pose by which he himself was deceived:

> Estaba yo entonces bizarrísimo, con aquella gran cadena que vuesa merced debió de conocerme, el sombrero con plumas y cintillo, el vestido de colores, a fuer de soldado, y tan gallardo *a los ojos de mi locura,* que me daba a entender que las podía matar en el aire. (p. 180)

It is not difficult to see why the dogs' conversation should have had such a profound effect on Campuzano. It has presented him with a world full of people like himself and yet it has not driven him to despair, but rather to a renewal of his mind. The name of the hospital is obviously symbolic in this regard. One must also remember that like the dogs he is given the opportunity to reflect on the prophecy which points towards hope in the darkest episode of the *Coloquio.* For Campuzano, then, the experience of suffering has been redemptive and he is grateful for it: 'que doy por bien empleadas todas mis desgracias, nor haber sido parte de haberme puesto en el hospital . . .' (p. 201). This does not seem to have been the first intervention of grace in his life. He tells Peralta that his first reaction on finding out that Estefanía had absconded was to despair:

> . . . y sin duda lo hiciera si tantico se descuidara el ángel de mi guarda en socorrerme, acudiendo a decirme en el corazón que mirase que era cristiano, y que el mayor pecado de los hombres era el de la desesperación, por ser pecado de demonios . . . (p. 194)

Then followed a desire for revenge but 'la suerte, que no sabré decir si mis cosas empeoraba o mejoraba, ordenó que en ninguna parte donde pensé hallar a doña Estefanía la hallase' (p. 195). Later, and even more significantly, he went into a church and fell into a deep sleep after commending himself to the Virgin. This seems to prefigure his experience in the Hospital especially if one bears in mind that the *Magnificat* is the Virgin's song of joy in the Incarnation. It also reinforces an interpretation of Campuzano's dream/vision as an act of Divine grace.[10]

For Campuzano the *Coloquio de los perros* has been truly *ejemplar* because he is forced to recognize himself in Berganza's masters and in la Cañizares. For the reader (Peralta is representative) such identification is not so easy and yet Cervantes's elaborate structure of fictional speakers and listeners seems to be designed to nudge him into an awareness that he is 'listening' also, or simply that he is alive and employing his time in a certain way. He is linked to a chain of characters who listen and judge just as he is doing. The recognition of that point of identity may reveal that there are others. The creator of la Cañizares could scarcely have expected the exemplary force of his *novela* to lie in the ready-formulated teaching about sin and virtue included in the text. Rather he helps the reader to understand that truth cannot be grasped because it is not an object of knowledge but a process in which he is involved even as he reads.

2. The Lover as Icarus: Góngora's 'Qué de invidiosos montes levantados'—R. P. CALCRAFT

Of the classical myths which remain current in our time, that of Icarus maintains an acknowledged place only slightly less familiar than those of the universally recognised figures of Hercules, Mars or Venus. The essential details of his story are quickly recalled, and the allegorical significance of his ambitious flight and subsequent death has not lessened with time. The dramatic legend of the man who disobeys his father's warnings and the voice of prudence, who flies too near the sun and perishes in the sea when that sun's heat loosens the wax fastenings of his wings, has exercised a fascination for successive nations and societies, and for the artists who have worked within them.

In the ancient world interpretations of the myth normally showed Icarus, and indeed his father Daedalus also, in a negative light. From the earliest writers to Ovid's *Metamorphoses*, the story and its moral lessons remain clear. In order to escape from the captivity of King Minos on the island of Crete, Daedalus invents a means of flight for himself and his son. Before they depart the father advises Icarus to fly a middle course between the dangerous extremes of sun and sea. The young man, however, exulting in a double freedom from both captivity itself and from the normal constraints upon man, soars towards heaven, his wings loosen and he falls to his death in the sea that will take his name. His death has been caused both by pride and by the ignoring of sensible advice, but in some sources Daedalus is also seen as responsible for the tragedy, in that his unnatural invention shows the extent to which ambition may lead man into mortal danger.

In the late Middle Ages and early Renaissance Icarus begins to be seen in alternative ways, often as the aspiring lover; and with

10

this the investment of his figure with heroic attributes begins. From the troubadours to Sannazaro and Ariosto the daring of Icarus comes. to be admired, symbol for a lover's striving towards the bright perfection of a lady's beauty, even though such boldness may bring about downfall or destruction. These varied ways of looking at a familiar myth and its significance were of course fully understood in Spain, where numerous translations of Ovid were published during the sixteenth century, often with moralising commentaries, and where an enthusiasm for the chief poets of the Italian Renaissance was widespread. The subject of Icarus seems to have exercised a particular fascination upon Spanish writers in the Golden Age, above all upon Luis de Góngora.

John Turner's book on the diffusion of the Icarus myth in Spanish Renaissance literature devotes an entire chapter to its many and varied uses in the works of the Cordoban poet.[1] Generous though this would appear, Góngora's subtle and complex use of even this one myth is so far-reaching that the guidance we are offered as to its significance in individual poems is of only the most general kind. The works in which references to the Icarus myth are found range in style and subject matter across the whole of Góngora's poetry, from the Sonnets to the *Soledades*. Amongst the finest of such works is the *canción* of 1600, 'Qué de invidiosos montes levantados', a major poem included in Dámaso Alonso's *Góngora y el Polifemo*, and referred to by Robert Jammes as 'l'un des chefs-d'oeuvre de la poésie gongorine'.[2]

The subject of the poem is the passion of jealousy and its resolution in the mind of a lover who has lost the object of his affections. The implied narrative makes clear that the woman desired has taken refuge from her erstwhile suitor behind the ostensibly impregnable barriers of marriage to another. The lover's continuing and unrepentant longing for her is answered by the imposition of banishment from her presence, expressed in a series of dramatic metaphors:

> ¡Qué de invidiosos montes levantados,
>   de nieves impedidos,
>   me contienden tus dulces ojos bellos!
>   ¡Qué de ríos del yelo tan atados,
>   del agua tan crecidos,
>   me defienden el ya volver a vellos! (11. 1–6)[3]

These barriers, symbolising the hostility of her attitude to him, as
well as the state of marriage behind which she is shielded,
comdemn him to a sense of permanent exile. Rather than accept
his fate, however, the lover seeks to outwit his mistress. Physically
he may be denied her presence; his mind, however, need be subject
to none of the barriers which separate them. His Thought, which
can go where it will, can be the means to overcome his banishment.
He will regain her presence without difficulty within the confines of
his imagination; more than this, her most intimate experiences can
be revealed to him by Thought's daring flights. The rejected lover
clearly believes his revenge can be almost total. What his mistress
now enjoys with his rival will not be allowed to remain secret. The
guardians of her new state of marriage will be outwitted and
Thought, freed from the physical constraints upon its master, will
now exact for him a prurient and savage revenge:[4]

> el noble pensamiento
> por verte viste plumas, pisa el viento! (8-9)
> no hay guardas hoy de llave tan segura,
> que nieguen tu persona,
> que no desmienta con discreta maña;
> ni emprenderá hazaña
> tu esposo, cuando lidie,
> que no la registre él, y yo no invidie. (13-18)

It is important to study the tenses of the verbs by which
Góngora suggests this narrative outline in the poem. From the
initial description of Thought's activation by desire, 'el noble
pensamiento/por verte viste plumas, pisa el viento', and the sense
that his invention is certain to succeed, 'ni a los yelos perdona,/y a
la mayor dificultad engaña', the narrator goes on to suggest that
the essential victories are not yet won: 'ni emprenderá hazaña/tu
esposo, cuando lidie,/que no la registre él, y yo no invidie'. The
invention of Thought as palliative for the lover's jealous rage is
already accomplished, but what it will achieve for him is still being
anticipated. Thought is therefore dispatched to perform its master's
wishes, 'Allá vueles, lisonja de mis penas', while the latter makes
clear his pleasure that there will be an intruder at his mistress's
marriage-bed:

> Ya veo que te calas
> donde bordada tela
> un lecho abriga y mil dulzuras cela (25-27).

Thought, however, arrives too late to witness the lovers' passion, as its creator confesses:

> Tarde batiste la invidiosa pluma,
>   que en sabrosa fatiga
> vieras (muerta la voz, suelto el cabello)
> la blanca hija de la blanca espuma, . . . (28-31)

Having in mind the emotional pattern already established in the poem, the reader must be surprised at this turn in the implied narration. As has been seen, the lover's intellectual revenge on his mistress was to have found its culmination in this singular act of intrusion on the intimacy of the lovers. The arrival of Thought just too late to achieve what its creator intended invites us to speculate further on both the stratagem itself, and the poet's purposes.[5]

The use of tense to create a disconcerting narrative pattern is continued in the following lines. The anticipation of 'ya veo que te calas', having become the apparently disappointed 'Tarde batiste la invidiosa pluma', is now followed by the firm conviction of 'podrás verla dormida,/y a él casi transladado a nueva vida', and the unexpected imperative 'entre templada nieve/evaporar contempla un fuego helado'. Thought is clearly not as potent as had earlier been implied, and would appear to be subject now to other impulses from the lover's mind. Thought, we recall, was first presented as 'el noble pensamiento', though its role as *burlador* of the lady and her husband indicates that the epithet was merely ironic. That the heights and depths of experinece can be penetrated 'con igual licencia' suggests, in similar vein, that the lover is well aware of the true nature of his stratagem. However, a balance of tone is struck in other details. Sarcastic references to the husband—'tu esposo, cuando lidie',[6] 'no sé si en brazos diga/de un fiero Marte, o de un Adonis bello'—can be set against the unsullied portrait of the bride as Aphrodite herself, 'la blanca hija de la blanca espuma'. And the culminating vision of the married couple lying asleep is expressed in language of touching simplicity:

>   ya anudada a su cuello
>   podrás verla dormida,
>   y a él casi trasladado a nueva vida. (34-36)

Thought is here instructed to contemplate the lovers, awesome in their beauty and their resemblance to death itself:

> Desnuda el brazo, el pecho descubierta,
>   entre templada nieve
> evaporar contempla un fuego helado,
> y al esposo, en figura casi muerta,
>   que el silencio le bebe
> del sueño con sudor solicitado. (37-43)

This is a point of fundamental change in the structure of the poem, to which Góngora's control of our reactions to his carefully chosen language has been leading. Thought, unable for whatever reason to witness the act of love, is left passive and powerless at the scene, no longer a possible instrument for its creator's revenge. The new emotion that has overtaken the latter's mind is revealed here, as Thought's original mission is forgotten. In place of that intruder the narrator visualizes the presence of another winged figure, the God of Love himself, as guardian and protector of the lovers' noble passion. The beauty of the scene before him leads to the narrator pronouncing a murmured blessing upon his erstwhile mistress and her husband:

> Dormid, que el dios alado,
>   de vuestras almas dueño,
> con el dedo en la boca os guarda el sueño.
>   Dormid, copia gentil de amantes nobles,
>   en los dichosos nudos
> que a los lazos de amor os dio Himeneo; (43-48)

This in its turn forces a recognition from him of the true nature both of his own ignoble jealousy and his attempted revenge. He thus begs for mercy from those same harsh elements which initially he mocked as powerless to obstruct him:

> mientras yo, desterrado, de estos robles
>   y peñascos desnudos
> la piedad con mis lágrimas granjeo. (49-52)

Several figures from classical mythology are referred to directly in this poem. The most important, however, are two whose story and names are not alluded to specifically, but whose experiences and significance form the thematic substructure of the work— Daedalus and Icarus. The clear identification of Thought with the latter is made as early as line nine, and the role of Thought's creator, or father, is of course Daedalus. Reading the Icarus myth as a hidden subtext throughout 'Qué de invidiosos montes levantados' is to become aware of the moral implications that lie within the poem's range of aesthetic effects.

From his prison of grief and banishment the rejected lover, Daedalus, invents a means whereby he may escape, in spite of his mistress's aversion to him. His Thought is given wings, like Icarus, and takes flight towards the region where both happiness and the consolations of revenge are believed to lie. In the original myth Icarus was instructed to avoid the extremes of both sun and sea, and Thought here exults in its new-found powers in an identical way:

> . . . con igual licencia
> penetras el abismo, el cielo escalas; (20-21)

In the context of the poem this *abismo* represents the disreputable nature of Thought's mission, but in traditional symbolism the *abismo* also of course suggests Hell. Here, as in the heavens, is to be found a fire that melts, consumes and destroys. If the mythological Icarus flew too near the sun, fell and perished in the depths, Thought here follows a parallel destiny. This Icarus too flies towards an imagined freedom, but the beauty of the lovers, their 'icy fire' of passion and death-like repose, together with the realization of the psychological abyss into which jealousy has led him, bring about the inevitable destruction of Thought in this form. The Daedalus figure averts his gaze and turns away from his now fallen creation, his ignoble jealousy destroyed by exposure to the noble passion of love. Warfare has become peace, both for the lovers and for the now penitent narrator:

> sea el lecho de batalla campo blando. (54)[7]

Daedalus has finally escaped from dread imprisonment, for as L. J. Woodward has written, referring to another use of the Icarus myth in Góngora, 'This prison was not of walls of stone, but of the human emotions'.[8] Now serene, the narrator draws a curtain between the marriage-bed and his mind, voluntarily separating himself from the lovers and their happiness, and acknowledging the inevitability of exile. His Thought, now no longer a creature of lurid fantasy, can return whence it came—to a mind tempered by grief and matured by experience.

In this poem Góngora has taken the essential elements of a familiar myth and put them to new and imaginative use. Both classical and Renaissance views of the Icarus story are present here, for this Daedalus and his Icarus are symbols both of defeat and of victory, surviving ignoble passion and its destruction to attain a wiser understanding of the processes of love. Contemporaries of the poet would have appreciated not only Góngora's imaginative utilization of the different forms in which the myth can be interpreted; they would also have admired the skill with which references to Italian writers and Renaissance conventions in love poetry are subtly introduced and developed throughout the poem.[9] A concluding comment can be illustrative of this. It has been seen how the narrator of the poem turned finally from his creature, Thought, to pronounce a blessing on the sleeping lovers. In the last lines of the *canción*, Góngora puts the traditional *envoi* to new and moving effect, as the narrator addresses the poem itself:

> Canción, di al pensamiento
>   que corra la cortina,
> y vuelva al desdichado que camina. (55-57)

The work has revealed a gradual but eventually total change in the attitudes of its protagonist, from jealous hostility to serene resignation. These concluding lines suggest in addition that it was the composition of the song which suceeded in extinguishing Thought in its baser form. The full expression in poetry of the emotions experienced became the means, Góngora seems to imply, by which the poet-lover's resolution of his passion was finally accomplished.[10]

3. Peribáñez: Disorder Restored—ROBIN CARTER

Recent critical studies of Lope de Vega's *Peribáñez* have offered considerable modifications of the previously conventional view that Peribáñez is a worthy underdog who overcomes a superior adversary and is commended for his action by the King.[1] It has been noted that Peribáñez is imprudent in asking favours of the Comendador in the first place, that he can be criticised for his pride, and that the demeanour of King Enrique III in Act III is slightly odd. However there remain, in my view, some outstanding problems as the play draws to a close, its eponymous hero kills not one, but three, of the four people implicated in the attempted disruption of his marriage;[2] following a perfunctory trial, Peribáñez is granted a Royal Pardon for one of these killings, but not for the others; and the survivor of the conspiracy (Leonardo) remains free. Rather than disregard these as 'loose ends', I shall try to restore them to the overall design of the play.

To have reservations about the judgement on Peribáñez at the end of the play logically implies reservations about the rationale of Peribáñez's actions leading up to the killings. The aforementioned critics have selected scenes such as the wedding scene, the preparations for Toledo scene, and the ennoblement scene, to suggest that Peribáñez was not altogether sensible in his approach to marriage and his own status. These criticisms seem well founded, and are ably summed up by Mary Randel: 'the bull, the *galas*, the cart, the portrait all lure Peribáñez to the brink of folly as much as they do Don Fadrique' (art. cit., p. 157). In the text, it is Peribáñez's rejection of the suggestion that he borrow a noble's hat that focuses attention on his imprudence in the face of dangers (compromise and gossip) of which he seems well aware.[3] It is

17

reasonable to propose that what is true of a hat will also be true of borrowed noble decorations for his cart, but Peribáñez avoids consideration of this—presumably, because the tapestries are part of keeping up with the Brases, while a hat is not: Bras has no hat with which Peribáñez must compete. Nevertheless, Peribáñez is walking a tightrope, and it is not unfair to suggest that he really ought to know better: it is surely indicative of his latent awareness that, when he sees the portrait of Casilda in scene 15 of Act II, he suspects the Comendador immediately. At this point, to which we shall return, he begins to contemplate the state of his 'honour'. For our present purposes, however, we need to look at the questions raised against Peribáñez' notions of honour by the end of Act II.

The Act closes with Peribáñez's words, 'iAy honra, al cuidado ingrata!/Si eres vidrio, al mejor vidrio/cualquiera golpe le basta' (2083-85). The interested spectator has time to ponder the implications of that little word 'si'. If *honra* is like glass, it is certainly fragile; but suppose it is not? What sort of honour is it that is fragile? What sort could there be that is not? Vast amounts of scholarly endeavour (including some of mine) have been devoted to attempts to define this concept, in social terms, in dramatic terms, in Lope's terms, etc., etc., and it would be beyond the scope of this article to go over the ground again.[4] Fortunately, it is not really necessary, since the answers to most of the questions are there in the text, from which we can deduce that Peribáñez's notion of honour resides in *opinión*, and that this, almost by definition, is fragile.

Peribáñez's preoccupation with *opinión* is evident in scenes 16, 20, 21 and 23 of Act II. In scene 20 he refers to his 'perdida opinión' (1896), and, even when the song of the peasants allays his fears about Casilda's role, he still insists that 'pena tengo con razón,/porque honor que anda en canciones/tiene dudosa opinión' (941-943); it is revealing that Peribáñez should take this attitude even though he has been proved wrong. Back in his house, he takes down the Comendador's tapestries, so that 'no murmuren en Ocaña . . .' (2041). It seems a pointed comment on the notion of *honor = opinión* that Peribáñez should now be getting rid of these tapestries for the same reason that he had for acquiring them in the first place. It is, in fact, a fine dramatic illustration of the ultimate futility of concern about *opinión* as expressed by Peribáñez himself in scene 16:

> Retirarme a mi heredad
> es dar puerta vergonzosa
> a quien cuanto escucha glosa,
> y trueca en mal todo el bien . . . (1780–83)

The phrase 'quien cuanto escucha glosa/y trueca en mal todo el bien' reveals both the fragility and the absurdity of concern with *opinión*. Peribáñez, though, does not seem to perceive that, so long as there is such a thing as human malice, there will be someone to speak ill of the most convincing representatives of personal rectitude; neither does he seem to realise that killing those who threaten his 'honour' may give rise to offensive *murmuración* just as easily as not doing so. He is 'on a hiding to nothing'.[5]

Since Peribáñez' thoughts turn to murder immediately upon learning about the portrait, it behooves us to consider the rationale presented for this extreme response ('extreme' because, as Bryans explains, there *are* alternatives—see art. cit.), especially as this rationale is conveyed direct to the audience *via* the soliloquy of scene 16 (Act II). Not unnaturally, Peribáñez is considerably shocked by his discovery of the portrait, but, by the time his soliloquy begins, Lope has made us aware of three important factors: 1) that Casilda is totally unmoved by the Comendador's advances (we have just seen her effect his total humiliation, in scene 12); 2) that the other peasants witnessed her rejection of the Comendador; and 3) that Peribáñez knows that Casilda knows nothing of the portrait (1713–1721).

Peribáñez begins his soliloquy by acknowledging his wife's innocence. He goes on to assert that the Commendador, by abusing his position, has forfeited his life; Peribáñez is not, we should note, dealing with any offence that has actually been committed (he is not even aware of the Comendador's attempted entry in scenes 9–12), but is reacting to what is implied:

> si en quitarme el honor piensa
> quitaréle yo la vida;
> que la ofensa acometida
> ya tiene fuerza de ofensa. (1752–1755)

Peribáñez asks us to accept that a person should be killed (by a private citizen outside judicial processes) for an *intention*, because the intention is as culpable as the deed. This seems a rather doubtful principle. Presumably, the key to his attitude is to be found in 1766–69:

> Don Fadrique me retrata
> a mi mujer: luego ya
> haciendo debujo está
> contra el honor, que me mata.

Peribáñez feels as if he has been 'killed', therefore he will physically kill his opponent. Questions are begged here which have filled many pages of juridicial literature,[6] and further questions are begged by the following proposition:

> Si pintada me maltrata
> la honra, es cosa forzosa
> que venga a estar peligrosa
> la verdadera también. (1770–1773)

Whether a painting of his wife is likely to lead to a real besmirching of his 'honour' depends entirely upon the meaning of *honra*; meanwhile, the audience knows that Casilda's marital fidelity is beyond question.

When we summarise Peribáñez's argument we find that the steps are as follows: the portrait is a threat to Peribáñez's honour (*opinión*), a threat to honour is equal to a threat to life, an attempted offence (murder) is as dangerous as a real crime (murder), so that the punishment (death) should be the same as that for a crime (murder) actually committed. Although such thoughts are probably the natural and realistic response of a man in Peribáñez's predicament, an impartial observer may reasonably decline to give such an argument full assent, especially as Peribáñez abdicates proper judgement at the beginning of the soliloquy ('celos de marido/no se han de dar a entender', 1744–45), and avoids awkward objections by his initial presentation of the issue:

> Basta que el Comendador
> a mi mujer solicita;
> basta que el honor me quita,
> debiéndome dar honor. (1746–1749)

In addition, we may feel challenged to respond critically because the constant refrain '¡Mal haya el humilde, amén,/que busca mujer hermosa!' invites us to decide either that Peribáñez is overreacting or that he should have thought of that before he married her. Indeed, the soliloquy is 'realistic' precisely because it mirrors the chaotic jumble of vengeful thoughts which a Peribáñez might harbour. Today, we talk about 'temporary insanity' and 'crimes of passion' as if we understood these things, but we do not pretend to infer rational principles therefrom.

We observe, thus, the disposition to kill, as an angry Peribáñez takes stock of his position after discovering proof of the Comendador's interest in his wife (and proof that his previous reservations about accepting gifts were well-founded). At this juncture it is worth asking whether Peribáñez actually has a *right* to kill in defence of his *honra*. Rights, presumably, are constituted in law, and the law on murder—valid in both 1406 and the seventeenth century—makes no reference to 'honour' as an extenuating circumstance. Here is what the law actually says:

> Todo hombre que matare a otro a sabiendas, que muera por ello: salvo si matare a su enemigo conocido, o defendiendose, o si lo hallare yaziendo con su muger do quier que lo halle, o si lo hallare en su casa yaziendo con su hija o con su hermana, o si le hallare llevando mujer forzada para yazer con ella, o que haya yazido con ella, o si matare ladrón que hallare de noche en su casa, hurtando o foradandola, o si le hallare con el hurto huyendo, y no se quisiere dar a prisión, o si lo hallare hurtandole lo suyo y no lo quisiere dexar, o si lo matare por ocasión, no queriendo matarlo, ni aviendo malquerencia con él, o si lo matare acorriendo a su señor, que lo vea matar, o a padre o a hijo, o a abuelo o a hermano, o a otro hombre que debe vengar por linage, o si lo matare en otra manera que pueda mostrar que lo mató con derecho.[7]

Thus, in the circumstances of Act II, Peribáñez cannot really be said to have any convincing legal support for his intention to kill.

The circumstances of the actual killing are, of course, different (Act III, scene 17), and it is possible that these circumstances would provide Peribáñez with a reasonable legal case for killing the Comendador: his explanation to the King is designed to show that 'lo mató con derecho', it being demonstrable (*via* the villagers' testimony) that Fadrique had entered the house unbidden by

Peribáñez or Casilda, and also that Fadrique had certainly had no encouragement from Casilda, since he had made a previous approach to Casilda which she had rebuffed. Given the vagueness of the phrase 'lo mató con derecho', a court would be well advised to find more precise guidelines, in the proper manner, by recourse to the *Siete partidas*, where they would find that

> Fallando un home á otro que trababa de su fija, ó de su hermana ó de su muger con quien estuviese casado segunt manda santa iglesia, por yacer con alguna dellas por fuerza, si lo matase estonce quandol fallase quel facia tal deshonra como esta, non cae en pena ninguna por ende. (*Partida* VII, *Tít.* 8, *ley* 3).

By the terms of this law, Peribáñez would appear to have a strong defence for his killing of the Comendador.

Thus, we may summarise the legal aspects as follows: in Act II, Peribáñez' thoughts of murder have no justification in law; in Act III, the actual circumstances of the killing do provide grounds for exoneration. However, the law-books do *not* seem to condone the killing of Inés, 'por traidora', and Luján, 'por falso segador'. I should add that, while it is probably advisable to check the possible legal objections before we start assassinating people, I do not seek to make an issue of these legal niceties (Lope might be aware of them, but he could hardly expect as much from his audience). As it happens, there is no need to do so, since the text of the play should make the audience look askance at the events at court, which must now be examined.

Several critics have commented upon Lope's unflattering presentation of Enrique III, drawing attention, in particular, to the peremptory 'Matalde, guardas, matalde' of v. 3022.[8] It is certainly difficult to reconcile the King's 'Justiciero' agnomen with this instant condemnation, or, indeed, with such comments as 'no me acordaba/que las partes se han de oir,/y más cuando son tan flacas' (3029–31), 'Yo le hago gracia/de la vida ... Mas, ¿qué digo?/Esto justicia se llama' (3109–11), or even with the influential interventions of the Queen (3023–29, 3101–04). Furthermore, all this is preceded by a sequence of scenes in which the King anticipates an expedition (2912–26) that he will not live to see, is misinformed about the nature of Peribáñez' motives ('Por celos', 2962), and manifests a misplaced confidence in Don Fadrique's military zeal ('el mejor soldado . . .' 2958–9). At the same time, and at previous points in the play, Lope has provided precise historical data: he is very specific about the date (August 1406) and the political context of the events depicted. As Zamora Vicente notes, the opening scene of Act III gives us a versification of the historical context as described in the introductory chapters of the *Crónica de Juan II,* complete with reminders that the King is in Toledo to prepare a punitive expedition against the Moors of Granada. In addition, the King's dynastic status is recalled in scene 22 of Act III, where Enrique and the Queen discuss their son, a toddler who will shortly become King Juan II. Enrique says of the child, ' . . . es un divino espejo,/donde se ven agora retratados,/mejor que los presentes, los pasados' (2937–39). This is an interesting remark because—as Peribáñez carefully explains to his friends in Act I (972–982)— Enrique III is the grandson of Enrique II. Enrique II was an illegitimate son of Alfonso XI, and Enrique II gained the throne, after years of campaigning, by killing the legitimate son, King Pedro I: the royal line shown on the stage is thus descended from a usurper, although it should also be noted that the Queen is the granddaughter of the slain Pedro I, so that little Juan II is half respectable, half not, a feature which fits in with the overall ambiguity suggested by some of the above-mentioned critics.

Such, then, are the two men who come face to face in the very last scene of the play, while the audience waits to see if 'justice' will be done. It is clear that the roles of Peribáñez and the King are mutually dependent: if we regard the King's pardon for Peribáñez as a seal of approval, sympathy for Peribáñez may persuade us to approve of the King. The corollary of this is that, if the King's judgement may be questioned, doubt is cast on Peribáñez' *bona fides*, while the converse of that also holds: if we are not satisfied with Peribáñez' role, we cannot be happy with a King who pardons him. Peribáñez' self-defence (3032–3101) is crucial: it convinces the Queen and, in turn, the King. Punishment is replaced by reward. We must examine Peribáñez' testimony to see how it contributes to his reprieve.

Peribáñez opens with a proclamation of his pure Christian blood, 'jamás/de hebrea o mora manchada', and that of his wife ('también limpia')—a nice touch: the King is organising a campaign against the Moors. During the course of the speech Peribáñez makes it clear that he is a good citizen who has held public office ('truje seis años vara'), and that he was made Captain of 100 men to serve the King in his forthcoming campaign. There is no need to question these claims, but what of his version of the relationship with the Comendador? Fadrique, he says, 'Fingiendo que por servicios,/honró mis humildes casas/de unos reposteros, . . ./' (3048–50); he does not say that he went to request the *reposteros*, enboldened by the *servicios* he had rendered the Comendador on his wedding day; nor does he say how utterly delighted he was at the time to be offered both them and the pair of mules which the Comendador threw in at the suggestion of Luján. Referring to the Comendador's first attempt at seduction of Casilda (Act II), Peribáñez says that Fadrique ' . . . intentó una noche,/que ausente de Ocaña estaba,/forzar mi mujer; . . .' (3056–58), which is a slight exaggeration (Fadrique did not resort to force until later).

Of his return home on the night of the killings, Peribáñez reports that 'hallé mis puertas rompidas' (3082): this can only be true metaphorically since the doors were opened from inside by Inés. The King, though, has to take it as a literal truth, because Peribáñez carefully leaves Inés' role out of his account. The rapid action implied by 'Hallé . . . . llegué . . . . saqué' is slightly at variance with the stealth and caution with which Peribáñez concealed himself in his own house and lay in wait for the Comendador; it also conceals Peribáñez's own hesitation at the 'moment of truth', where the choice of taking some action other than assassination was presented. 'Paséle el pecho' may be true, although Professor Dixon has suggested that Peribáñez stabbed the Comendador in the back: this would be a decision for the producer.[9] Significantly, Peribánez makes no reference whatsoever to Inés and Luján.

Embedded in Peribañez' partial record of events are the invitations to sympathy. He is 'de villana casta', but a worthy citizen, content with his 'humildes casas'. He donned a sword 'para servirte,/no para tan triste hazaña' (3088–89). Standing in front of the King's pennant, which displays the image of the Good Shepherd, he describes how his 'cordera blanca' was saved, 'porque yo, como pastor,/supe del lobo quitarla' (3092–93). To conclude, he wants his wife to collect the reward for his capture. *Argumenta ad misericordiam* are, of course, traditional defences offered by those who cannot deny their 'guilt', and even the impartial spectator will grant that Peribáñez deserves sympathy; anyway, prosecution and defence arguments are, by definition, partial. But can the impartial spectator overlook Peribáñez's distortions, omissions, and—the most disturbing factor of all—his concealment of the killing of Inés and Luján? I have mentioned Peribáñez's gloss on Inés's treachery ('hallé las puertas rompidas'): could it be that this topic is embarrassing for Peribáñez? Would he feel that killing people 'por traidora' and 'por falso segador' would be hard to defend in court?

As part of the case, the appeals to pity are effective: the Queen cries, the King changes his mind. In the sense that the previously-threatened punishment for Peribáñez would have been harsh, we may feel that some sort of 'justice' has been done. But is this an effective *Justiciero* at work? He is surprised that someone so 'humilde' should 'estime tanto su fama' (3106–07). How senior does one have to be to protect one's wife from assault? Peribáñez has barely mentioned *fama*. In the event, the interventions of the Queen are crucial, the evidence on which the royal judgement is based is incomplete, and two of the three killings are not even considered.

This trial is conducted in front of the King's new *pendón*, for which Lope has carefully provided a description. It displays, on one side, the national coat-of-arms (lions and castles) with a hand holding a sword, and the legend 'Enrique Justiciero'; on the other side is a crucified Christ, with the legend 'Juzga tu causa Señor' (an echo of verse 22 of Psalm 73 [Vulgate], as Zamora Vicente notes). We can appreciate that the religious and nationalistic symbolism is appropriate for a crusade against the Moors, but there may be other reasons for Lope's concern with the detail. The banner emphasises—*via* the hand-held sword—the nature of the stage-King's justice, representing the dependence on fear which is brought out by the dialogue (2986–87, 3003–05, etc.): we may reasonably point out that justice involves more than just a 'mano que va castigando', which is, after all, the easy part. Justice also demands wisdom, learning, understanding and—as is established in the *Fuero Juzgo*—mercy.[10] Christ crucified suggests both divine and human realities—infinite love, mercy, sacrifice and forgiveness, contrasted with self-interest, vindictiveness, cruelty and self-exculpation. Christ, we may remember, knew something about *opinión:* one crowd cries 'Hosanna!' five days before another crowd cries 'Crucify him!' Psalm 73 is a cry of desolation, calling on the

God who has deserted his sheep (v. 1); but Israel pre-figures the Church and the promise of Resurrection is always there. The lessons suggested by the pennant, throughout the last four scenes of the play, provide a silent backdrop to the human justice enacted in its presence: pleading his cause before it stands Peribáñez, who has used his sword mercilessly, and eventually finds himself confirmed as Captain of the 100 men of Ocaña.

An interested spectator, watching all this, may feel called upon to respond with something other than polite applause. Our engagement in the play's movement is demanded by (among other elements) the soliloquies of Peribáñez and the Comendador: between the discovery of the portrait and the killing of the Comendador (some 1200 lines), Peribáñez addresses half of his remarks to stage-characters and half to the audience. By the end, the audience will have seen various interlocking elements including 1) a King who, while relatively just by reputation, invites criticism by performance; 2) a court case in which the half-truths and limitations of human justice are exposed; and 3) the inner workings of the antagonists' minds. The audience thus finds itself in the uncomfortable role of onlookers representing the *opinión* which drives an adherent to murder and, simultaneously, in the position of objective witnesses to forces and causes that are rarely fully revealed in real life.

These remarks on the involvement and attitudes of the audience lead to one other point which is worth making, and which develops logically from C. H. Ferguson's perceptive comment on the dangers for Peribáñez and Casilda implicit in the rewards they are given by the monarchs.[11] It also follows from the curiously one-sided presentation of Enrique III, who, while described by historians as grumpy, indiscreet and physically weak, is nevertheless regarded as relatively just and competent.[12] Why Lope has bothered to use this particular monarch may be explicable in terms of the historical moment in which the play is set, which matches the looming anarchy and potential chaos of the events we have witnessed.

The historical Enrique III fell ill during his visit to Toledo, and, according to the historical sources available to Lope, died on Christmas Day, 1406; the crown then passed to the infant Juan II (referred to in the play). Thus, within four months of their appearance before Enrique III, Peribáñez and Casilda, now possessed of some social status, will find themselves caught in the unstable world of political faction and unrest in fifteenth-century Castile: as they owe their new-found status to Enrique III, they will hardly be able to dissociate themselves from the petty allegiances and hostilities accruing therefrom.[13] While it is fair to say that such reflections follow from an awareness of historical realities not mentioned in the play, the fact that Leonardo is still alive ought to provoke similar reflections: will the man who wanted to avenge his master's death regard Peribáñez's social ascent with equanimity? Will he keep quiet about the deaths of Luján and Inés (the latter of whom he was courting, however insincerely)? Will the friends and relatives of Luján and Inés let the matter drop? Will those envious of Peribáñez's promotion begin to gossip about Casilda and the Comendador? Will Peribáñez's well-intentioned defence of Casilda be changed by wagging tongues into a story of 'no smoke without fire'? These are some of the reasonable questions that might disturb an attentive spectator.

The conclusion to be drawn from all these topics—Peribáñez's concern with *opinión*, his confused thought-processes, the unnecessary killings, the inadequate trial before the questionable judge, and the survival of Leonardo—seems to be that we have witnessed the reverse of a proper restoration of order. There are occasional hints of the possibility of order (a wedding mass which *precedes* the action, references to natural and social order, images of divine justice), but, in practice, order is undermined by conflicts that are irreconcilable when cloaked in the language of self-justification (exemplified by the rhetorics of Fadrique's passion and Peribáñez's honour), and it is vitiated by disruptive factors that are far from nullified at the end. Meanwhile, we can discern the limitations of the human justice that purports to sustain order.

In that they remain unresolved, the aforementioned issues should prevent vicarious satisfaction or complacency: they match the author's purpose as soon as we regard the play as the reflection of a *continuing* disorder, of which blood-letting (in the name of *honor*) is a *symptom*—not a cure. The basis for such a view shifts from interpretation to demonstration if the historical circumstances of 1406, with political disorder imminent, are taken into account. Resistance to this argument, on the grounds that Spanish Golden Age plays must show the final triumph of order, presumably rests upon *a priori* critical assumptions rather than upon inductive generalisation.

4. *Aqueste Lance Divino: San Juan's Falconry Images*
JOHN G. CUMMINS

The sources of San Juan de la Cruz's *Tras un amoroso lance* were clarified by Dámaso Alonso, who showed that the poem's first four lines are a slightly modified version of a traditional quatrain which used the commonplace erotic image of the falcon and its prey, and that other lines show echoes of specific traditional poems employing the imagery of the *caza de amor*.[1] Critics have found the meaning of parts of San Juan's poem markedly and perhaps deliberately vague, mainly because of the perplexing mixture of upward and downward movement. My purpose is to re-examine certain aspects of the poem, including San Juan's treatment of his borrowed material, and to suggest that he may have had in mind images and linguistic associations more precise than those so far pointed out. The lines I particularly wish to consider are

> mil buelos pasé de un buelo

and

> Abatíme tanto, tanto,
> que fuy tan alto, tan alto,
> que le di a la caça alcance.[2]

Discussing the same poem elsewhere, Dámaso Alonso reveals himself as no falconer. He writes, for instance, of 'esta canción, basada en la imagen de cetrería: el azor o neblí tras de su caza'.[3] The bird in San Juan's mind is certainly not an *azor*, but one of the long-winged hawks or true falcons, and probably a peregrine, *neblí*. Peregrines were trained as *hawkes of the towre*, to employ a phrase used by Dame Juliana Bernes and John Skelton;[4] their basic tendency to altitude was developed by the falconer to achieve the most admired flight of all, against the heron, in which the two birds were sometimes lost to sight in the clouds.[5] Similarly a merlin

28

might pursue a rising lark upwards until the two were beyond the range of human sight even in a cloudless sky. The goshawk, *azor*, a *hawke of the fist*, was used in a more earthbound, hedge-hopping, hurly-burly kind of chase.[6] The *neblí* provided glory and a dead, and useless, heron; the *azor* gave humbler sport, and rabbit pie for supper. San Juan's bird, then, like that of the traditional quatrain, is almost certainly a *neblí*, a bird celebrated for its speed and dash, but whose characteristics of flight have, I suggest, a more detailed relevance to the interpretation of the poem.

Dámaso Alonso says nothing about the combination of upward and downward flight, reacting only to the upward movement: ¡Qué vértigo de altura! El neblí asciende, como la saeta, tras la garza real . . . ' (*La poesía de San Juan* . . . , p. 236). This also ignores a key aspect of the poem, which is the two-fold nature of the upward movement, not properly described by 'como la saeta'. A heron confronted with a peregrine tries to elude it, not horizontally or in an ascending straight line, but by performing a series of sweeping upward circles. The falcon pursues a similar, and at times apparently unrelated, upward spiral, until it gains an advantage in height which enables it to swoop down on its prey and either kill it with a blow or bind to it and bring it to earth. The merits of a falcon were judged largely on its ability to reduce these upward gyrations to a minimum. Pero López de Ayala's favourite falcon was the peregrine.[7] The gyrfalcon, placed above the peregrine in the rather contrived mediaeval hierarchy of hunting birds because of its size, rarity and beauty,[8] had certain temperamental disadvantages; in Pero López's eyes its only advantage over the peregrine was that its superior strength enabled it to gain height more quickly and to reduce the number of circles necessary to gain ascendancy over its prey: 'E devedes saber que el girifalte que se da a bien mata muy mas ligero e mejor garça o grua e la prision a que fuere lançado que ninguno otro falcon, ca la garça mata muy alta, e al sobir *non faze tantos tornos como el nebli, e va mas derecho en sus buelos*; e como quier que por la su grandeza salga pesado de la mano, pero desque comiença a cavalgar el ayre todavia cobra mayor ligereza' (*Libro de la caza* . . . , fol. 14v). The greater a falcon's ability in this respect, the better: 'Otrosy pon todo [tu] saber e toda tu acuçia en que tu falcon *rebuele y remonte* e en esto afana quanto pudieres ca esto es el caubdal del nebli' (*Libro de la caza* . . . , fol. 48v).

One of San Juan's sources uses the image of these circling *buelos* to express the idea of the laborious, heart-stretching efforts of the lover to win his lady: by *mil vuelos* he approaches her level, from which he hurtles down in a single precipitate fall of ruined hope; two carefully juxtaposed and contrasted aerial movements:

> Sé que por volar tan alto
> las alas se me abrasaron,
> y que *mil vuelos* ganaron
> lo que perdió *un solo salto*.
> Caí de rigor tan alto
> que, pues su bien no se corre,
> mal viento corre. (Dámaso Alonso, *De los siglos*, . . . , p. 255–56)

San Juan, too, combines *mil buelos* (laborious, systematic and, in the context of falconry, realistic) with a different, linear motion, the *ciego y oscuro salto*, which takes over from the conscious and rational aspiring ascent; the peregrine, moved now by a force not in itself, is enabled to surpass even the gyrfalcon in flying 'mas derecho en sus buelos'; to ascend, to repeat Dámaso Alonso's slightly misapplied phrase, 'como la saeta', as no falcon has ever done:

> Por una estraña manera
> *mil buelos* pasé de un buelo.

The nature of the transition between these two types of motion is not clarified at this point; we have to look elsewhere in the poem, where we have a further problem related to the first:

> Quando más cerca llegava
> de este lance tan subido,
> *tanto más baxo y rendido*
> *y abatido me hallava*;
> dixe: No abrá quien lo alcance.
> *Abatíme tanto, tanto,*
> *que fuy tan alto, tan alto,*
> que le di a la caça alcance.

An additional source of San Juan's poem, convincingly cited by

F. López Estrada,[9] includes the following lines:

Vi una garça a par del cielo
y un neblí en su seguimiento,
que bolava;
mas ella es de tanto buelo,
que al más supremo elemento
se acercava . . .
El sacre que la seguía,
si con buelo muy ligero
se encumbrava,
quanto más alto subía
tanto más baxo y rastrero
se quedava.

The verbal echoes and similarity of the paradox are striking. This part of San Juan's poem is the principal cause of the general perplexity about the nature and direction of the flight described: are *abatíme* and *fuy tan alto* a sequence, or coincidental? Margaret Wilson writes of 'uncertainty . . . between upward and downward trajectories . . . Is the bird climbing up to its prey, or swooping down upon it? The violent contradictions of this vertiginous flight suggest the mystic's ecstasies as no logical language could'.[10]

Given the awareness of falconry revealed by the poem as a whole, I think *abatíme* and *fuy tan alto* should be taken as forming a sequence. The question is of course complicated by a new dimension added by San Juan to his source's simple paradox: the dual meaning of *abatirse*. He uses *abatido* as a near-synonym for the source's *baxo y rastrero*; it is passive, almost despairing. *Abatíme*, in contrast, is positive and negative at the same time, with both meanings of the English *stoop*:[11] it describes the forceful, devastating descent of the peregrine, the fastest and most inspiring animate movement perceptible to San Juan's contemporaries,[12] *and* the final abasement of self which enables the poet to attain mystical union. *Fuy tan alto* is therefore subsequent to it, and in both meanings the result of it. Here again the nature of the peregrine's flight is relevant. The falcon's stoop sometimes results not directly in a kill during the downward plunge, but in a subsequent upward movement in which the impetus imparted by the descent enables the bird (*cavalgando el aire*, in Pero López's phrase) to gain fresh advantage: 'A good long-winged hawk, after an unsuccessful stoop, *immediately shoots up to a great height* above the place where the stoop was intended to take effect . . . *In a hard flight that hawk is most successful which after each stoop shoots up farthest, rebounding, as it were, from the unsuccessful stoop,* and so keeping the command of the air . . . The best hawks take great delight in stooping at the lure . . . and, on the lure being twitched aside, *will shoot up in an almost perpendicular line*' (Michell, p. 109, 260). This is San Juan's image. Whereas in the source poem aspiration precedes and accentuates final abasement, in San Juan, after the laborious aspiration, the deliberate abasement/stoop enables and provides the force for the limitless ascent.

I conclude that the pattern of flight in the poem, certainly more complex than is suggested by Dámaso Alonso, and unquestionably vertiginous as described by Margaret Wilson, is nonetheless not as contradictory or as vague as she and others have found it. There is a sequence, though its chronological pattern (obscured by the necessary repetition of the climactic refrain) is not disposed tritely through the poem:[13] the laborious, conscious ascent through the *buelos* of meditation and spiritual preparation; then the positive abandonment of reason and self in the *ciego y obscuro salto = abatíme*; finally a soaring glory and a binding to the prey amid the clouds of oblivion. Given the chance, Pero López de Ayala, with the lofty brilliance of Pedro the Cruel's falcons Pristalejo and Picafigo and his own Pocarropa engraved on his visual memory, would have seen these images crystal clear. For him, and for other prosaic men, there could be few images more inspiring.

5. Lope's *La villana de Getafe* and the Myth of Phaethon; or, the *coche* as Status-Symbol—VICTOR DIXON

Lope de Vega's *El perro del hortelano* and his *La villana de Getafe*[1] seem at first sight very dissimilar plays. The first, set entirely in Naples, centres on a Countess and her unstable passion for a servant; the second, set mainly in Madrid, tells of a singleminded country-girl who is loved and left by an irresponsible gallant, but pursues him to the city and by dint of different disguisings contrives to win his hand.

The two plays, however, have much in common. Both were written, most probably, in 1613 or thereabouts;[2] they are linked, moreover, by the theme of threatened misalliance, and by the manner of its resolution. As J. W. Sage has shown, a significant number of *comedias* of the early seventeenth century are concerned, because of its pressing topicality, with the question of social mobility, and especially with the possibility of love and marriage across traditional divides; opposing attitudes are presented, with no clear favour for one view or the other. The problem-relationships are of two main types: between a servant and a woman very much his superior in rank—the case of *El perro*—or between a peasant, male or female, and a nobleman or noblewoman—the case of *La villana*.[3] As I have argued elsewhere, however, the dramatist hardly ever ventures 'in practice'—that is, in the resolution of his plot—to allow a mismatch; genuine and presumably successful misalliances are extremely rare. Our plays are almost the only examples of each type.[4]

In *El perro*, furthermore, the disparity of rank is repeatedly and even ominously recalled by means of an extended metaphor based on a familiar myth, that of the flight and fall of Icarus;[5] whereas in *La villana*, I shall show here, Lope makes analogous use of the myth of Phaethon.[4]

33

The pervasive influence of both myths on the poetry of Renaissance and Baroque Spain has been amply documented, although their importance in its poetic drama has scarcely been studied.[7] I would wish here only to stress how frequently their obvious similarities were recalled and referred to. They had been mentioned 'in the same breath' by Ovid, Dante, Tansillo and Ronsard, and were associated similarly by Garcilaso, Herrera, Acuña, Aldana, Argensola, Villamediana, Quevedo, Calderón . . . and (at least four times) by Lope de Vega himself.[8] Of course, both were highly 'visual', highly amenable to plastic representation, in the pictorial arts and in illusionistic drama; but remarkably Lope, writing our plays for the minimal scenic resources of the *corral de comedias*, and forced therefore to rely almost entirely on the spoken word, has nevertheless the art and wit to bring them vividly to life in our imaginations and our minds.

In *El perro*, the myth is emblematically evoked at the outset. The first thing the spectator sees is the ambitious scrivener's hat, adorned with lavish plumes; within moments this—because thrown at a lamp, we are told—has been transformed, to all appearance, into a sorry wreck, and the story of Icarus is recalled and 'applied'. Innumerable further references to that story hereafter will imply that the commoner's hopes of marrying his lofty mistress are foredoomed, although we learn in fact that we have been tricked, by a *tropelía*;[9] the sorry wreck was the *gracioso*'s hat, which were shown but no doubt didn't notice. (In the final scene, I suggest, he should produce the plumed one, undamaged, for his 'ennobled' master, with our connivance, to wear again.) In *La villana* the myth of Phaethon is less immediately, and less visually, but no less ingeniously and more playfully evoked. Perhaps indeed *La villana* provides an even better example of how the elaboration of a mythological metaphor can inform the very structure and plot of an apparently 'realistic' play.[10]

In Act I, we see the very Lope-like Don Félix del Carpio[11] taking leave in Madrid of Doña Ana, whom he intends to marry; but in Getafe we also hear the *villana*, Inés, tell how she has previously met and fallen in love with Don Félix in the capital. She cannot forget this 'loco amor' for an 'amor igual' and love the *labrador* Hernando, or any other 'mozo del lugar'; in a sonnet-soliloquy, 'Sube tal vez alguna débil parra', she aspires instead to rise to the rank of Don Félix, 'pues cuanto quiere Amor, todo lo puede' (370–1). When he appears in the village and courts her again, she confesses—though she claims that she is not a *villana* 'en ingenio y condición' (375b)—that she cannot be his equal. Nevertheless he promises to marry her, and in the last scene of the act, in reply to her question 'Pues, dime ¿de qué manera/podré ser yo tu mujer?', he says that when he returns from Seville he will bring her not only 'galas de corte' but a *coche*. When she rides in it, he adds, she shall change her proverbially plebeian name;[12] they gaily review possible alternatives (380–1).

Don Félix, who stopped in Getafe to have a horse re-shod, was urged by his servant Lope to wait at an inn, 'viendo ese coche que encierra/gente de toldo y valor' (371a); and Inés, who by contrast has been seen dancing for a horde of passengers from the 'carros de Toledo' whose drivers had halted their mules in the village, is captivated, not surprisingly, by these unmistakable tokens of a change in her status. Without pressing too far—since after all 'History is bunk'—any analogy with the vogue of the horseless carriage in our twentieth century, we should remember the proliferation of *coches* which coincides in the late sixteenth and early seventeeth with the rapid growth of Madrid, and arouses the impotent ire of moralists, economists and politicians. Whether one owns a coach, and of what quality, becomes a question of obsessive concern; as Pedro Fernández Navarrete complains: 'Es tan fuerte en España la emulación, que confundiéndose las clases y jerarquías, no hay hidalgo particular que porque su mujer no salga en peor coche que sus vecinas, no se anime con vana envidia al gasto a que no es suficiente su patrimonio, arriscando tal vez la reputación.'[13] Thus Mendo, in Lope's *De cosario a cosario*, tries to size up Celia by asking: 'Tu nombre y tu calidad/me muero ya por saber./¿Tienes coche? ¿Eres mujer/de toldo y autoridad?' No city madam, therefore, can be without one, 'aunque venda cuanto tengo', as Prudencia says in *El sembrar en buena tierra*; and Marín in *La llave de la honra* is astonished when Elena declines her husband's offer to buy one: '¿Coche no quieres, señora?/Eres la mujer primera/desde la primer mujer'.[14] We may expect then to hear more of this promise of a 'stylish carriage'. A coach, of course, is unlikely to be seen on the *tablado*, but references to one—as well as to horses and the like—will ring repeatedly in our ears, and Inés, on three different occasions, under three different new names, will be said to ride in it. Like a central character who never appears on

stage, it will come to dominate the play. And increasingly it will be
equated—with ambiguous implications—with that celestial chariot
which Phaethon sought rashly to drive.

In the first scene of Act II, Inés learns from a servant of Don
Félix that she is to be denied her new status and its symbol; he *is*
bringing back a coach, but intends it for the use of Doña Ana:

> Hemos venido en mulas, que traemos
> un coche muy galán para la novia,
> y querría tomar agora postas
> para entrar con más pompa. (382b)

Inés resolves—insanely, it is suggested—to pursue him to Madrid;
Hernando—no less insanely, it is suggested—decides to follow
(382–3). Inés goes to Doña Ana's; affecting rustic simplicity and
engañando con la verdad, she claims at some length to be pursuing an
errant donkey, 'que era destos ojos luz/y el espejo de mi casa', and
contrives to be employed as a maidservant, under the name of
'Gila' (384–5). Hernando, on the other hand, appears at Don
Félix's, costumed *de cochero*, and although he has hitherto driven
only 'un carro enramado/por Santiago el Verde al prado' (370b), is
hired to drive the new coach. Don Félix promises that he shall have
four horses, each equal to 'el que mejor tiró real carroza'—as had,
we may remember, the chariot of the sun, in the most popular
Classical version of the story of Phaethon, Ovid's *Metamorphoses*,
Book II (153–4); Lope mentions two of them, Phlegon and Aethon,
in at least five works. As yet, however, there has been no direct
allusion to the myth, whereas in *El perro*, as mentioned above, the
story of Icarus was recalled by a servant, obliquely and in jest, as
early as lines 125–32. But now that we have a *cochero*, he is soon
exchanging banter with the *gracioso*, who similarly remarks:

> Ya entiendo lo que son gente de azote:
> soberbios, atrevidos y ligeros,
> desde cuando Faetón anduvo al trote. (386–7)

In later works by Lope the allusion will become a jokey synonym;
in *De cosario a cosario* Mendo will ask Celia about "el faetonte de tu
coche", and in a sonnet from the *Rimas* . . . of Tomé de Burguillos
the driver of a 'coche de damas feas' will be a 'Faetón de trasgos'.

After a brief reunion between Don Félix and Doña Ana, the
latter sends 'Gila' and an *escudero* with a present of shirts; Don

Félix, despite more *hablar equívoco* about her 'negro pollino', does not wholly recognise Inés, but insists on sending her back in the coach. His intention in this, of course, is to present it to Doña Ana; but unwittingly he is recognising Inés's prior claim. As she comments aside: 'La palabra habéis cumplido;/ya no tengo que quejarme'. Hernando, moreover, does recognise his passenger, and he it is, perhaps implausibly, who at last both explicitly recalls the story of Phaethon and links it to the symbolism of the coach:

> ¡Qué honroso oficio aprendí,
> pues vino mi coche a ser
> el del Sol, viniendo a ver
> que le llevo todo en ti!
>   Mas ayer oí cantar
> que, despeñado, un mancebo,
> por lo mismo que me atrevo,
> cayó abrasado en el mar.[15]
>   Tú, pues eres sol, mejor
> podrás guiar los caballos,
> que yo podré despeñallos
> con este mi ciego amor.

Of course, one reason for the popularity of the Phaethon myth at this period must have been that control over beasts, especially horses, was habitually seen as symbolic of the capacity to rule oneself and others—hence in part the vogue of the equestrian portrait; whereas loss of control, being thrown or falling, signified the overthrow of reason by emotion and portended disaster, as countless *comedias* bear witness.[16]

The metaphor is clarified and developed in Hernando's sonnet-soliloquy:

> Pidió Faetón al Sol el carro de oro,
> venció al importunado padre el ruego,
> dióle las riendas y, corriendo, luego
> vino a parar sobre el Atlante moro.
>   Allí, vertiendo de uno y otro poro,
> en cambio de sudor, llamas de fuego,
> cayó sobre el Herídano, que, ciego,
> le dio sepulcro en lamentable coro.

> No menos yo, por más ardiente polo
> el carro deste sol a llevar pruebo,
> ingrata más que Dafne con Apolo.[17]
>   Hoy a mayor hazaña el alma atrevo,
> pues si aquél se perdió con un Sol sólo,
> yo con dos soles que en tus ojos llevo. (392a)[18]

Sun-imagery is commonplace in the language of love, and this play has had some more conventional examples; thus Doña Ana seemed initially to be Don Félix's sun, and he hers (367a, 386a; 367a, 383b, 388). What then is the implication of this stress on the equation Inés = Sol? It may be that she alone is worthy of the comparison; on the other hand, she may be a sun only in Hernando's mind. Indeed both he and she may be acting rashly and riding for a fall; so much is perhaps suggested by further references to the metaphor in this act. When Hernando and Inés arrive at Doña Ana's, as she is praising the 'celestial . . . gentileza' of Don Félix, her maid Julia, in an eighteen-line speech, describes the coach (again with its four horses) as one which 'puede al Sol/servir de rica litera'; but Hernando by way of flattery observes that it is worthy of Doña Ana, and Inés declares that she was travel-sick, being more accustomed to riding on a thresher:

> ¿Quién me trajo de las eras
> a pasar de trillo a coche? (392–3)[19]

She has the resourcefulness, however, to subvert Don Félix's plans by convincing Doña Ana and her household, temporarily, that he and Lope are *moriscos*; and the *escudero*, rebuking Lope therefore for having designs on Julia, blusters that he's going for a gun, 'y quisiera por un rayo' (394b). The jest is a strange one, but it conceals, no doubt, another ominous reminder of the fate of Phaethon.

In the first lines of Act III, Hernando again describes his costume and role, to his old friend Bartolomé, as that of a Phaethon to Inés:

>   Mucho me huelgo de verte.
> —¿Y el hábito, no te agrada?
> —En efeto, ¿eres cochero?
> —Faetón soy de aquesta casa,
>   donde llevo al sol de Inés. (396a)

The metaphor is thus reinforced—lest we had forgotten it in the act-interval?—although it might now seem less apt, for Don Félix is putting coach and coachman at the service of another lady, Doña Elena. Inés, however, repossesses her status-symbol; she impersonates Doña Elena's long-awaited cousin and intended from the Indies, Don Juan, and is therefore invited to ride with her to a *feria*. She even indulges on the way, as she later tells Doña Ana, in a little flirtatious footsy:

> Pues en el coche pasaron
>   lindas cosas.
>   —¿De qué modo?
> —Los pies, sin lenguas, hablaron;
>   allá lo imagina todo. (404a)

Don Félix, his best-laid plans agley again, offers the coach to Elena's father, for like a famous horse, that of Gnaius Seius, it seems to bring its owner only evil fortune:

> Sólo os pido una cosa, por mi gusto:
> que os sirváis de aquel coche, que no quiero
> que ande de boda en boda, ya que ha sido
> tan desdichado como fue el romano
> por el caballo que llamó Seyano.[20]

He is half-aware that his misuse of it has been his undoing: 'Quizá que topa en él' (402).

He returns, nevertheless, to his courtship of Doña Ana, and Inés must still fear that she who 'de humildes principios/quise al cielo levantarme/de un caballero que tiene/los suyos tan desiguales' is now being punished by Heaven (404–5). Indeed, when she confronts him he says that he cannot marry her, and offers her instead Hernando, although properly she responds:

> El coche me prometiste.
> ¿Quién dirá que es engañarme
> que, prometiéndome coche,
> con el cochero me pagues? (405b)

They are *desiguales*, and she is poor. On the one hand, however, she now makes him concede (although this is the first we have heard of it) that her father is 'hidalgo, aunque labrador', and that she is 'limpia' (405b, 406a, 408b); and on the other she manages to convince him that 'Don Juan' has brought her a dowry of 4,000 ducats. And so for the third time Lope has her ride in the coach; for Don Félix sends Hernando with it to bring 'Doña Inés' definitively to his side at Doña Elena's. Too late he discovers, when *dos acémilas* arrive with the real Don Juan's parrot and monkey, that the dowry was a deception and that he must value instead 'la virtud/con que he sabido ganarte' (411b).[21]

As in *El perro del hortelano*, a mismatch which is nonetheless a marriage of true minds has been brought about by a kind of parodic anagnorisis; the pretence, in *El perro*, that Teodoro is the long-lost-son of Ludovico, in *La villana* that Inés is the long-awaited-nephew of Fulgencio. But in each case the false revelation is followed by a true one; Teodoro reveals to Diana, his servant and the audience that he is a man of 'nobleza natural', whereas Inés reveals to Don Félix, and to everyone, that she is 'mujer de tan raro ingenio', as well as 'de tal hermosura y talle' (411b). In each play, too, the heroic-tragic implications of the underlying myth are eschewed in favour of a happy (though mildly subversive) ending. In *El perro*, Icarus doesn't fall, although arguably the sun does.[22] In *La villana*, Phaethon suffers no disaster; Hernando has to settle for Julia rather than Inés but he is spared such a fate as that of Silvio, the shepherd who, having loved Lope's Filomena, 'Faetón al sol de su belleza', plunged despairingly into the sea and was turned into a dolphin.[23] And Inés herself, who may have seemed only a false sun, is shown to be a true one—not least because, as Hernando divined, she is shrewder than he at pulling strings.

For a Renaissance writer, the myth of Phaethon, like that of Icarus, was always ambiguous. He might choose to stress either their rash vain-glory, and the 'castigo justo' it occasioned, or alternatively their 'noble osadía' and the eternal glory it won them.[24] And the story of Phaethon, determined to establish his challenged parentage, was whatever else one of self-vindication. Thus his mother Clymene could say, in Sonnet 91 of Lope's *Rimas*, that the earth 'dirá que ciego y ambicioso fuiste,/pero no negará que confirmaste,/muerto en el cielo, que del Sol naciste'; and similarly, in the first scene of *Contra valor no hay desdicha*, Ciro could apostrophise his ambitious love for Filis: 'Con gloria mueres, si atrevido fuiste;/pues ya que no eres Sol, has confirmado,/muerto en el cielo, que del Sol naciste' (BAE XLI, 1). In our play it is as if this aura of triumph, untarnished now by failure, were transferred to a Phoebus more resplendent than ever.

We may feel indeed that in *La villana* Lope's treatment of the myth is not only optimistic but especially playful. The very notion of Phoebus as a female passenger, of his chariot as a *coche*, and of Phaethon dressed as a coachman smacks of Baroque burlesque, recalling Góngora's Leander or Velázquez's Mars; and we may wonder where Lope found inspiration—if it was not 'de propia minerva'—for such strange metamorphoses.

One plausible answer is afforded by emblem literature. The myth was customarily depicted therein, as elsewhere (and as in the case of Icarus, *mutatis mutandis*) by a skyscape, comprising: the sun, a chariot, plunging horses, and a figure falling headlong. 'Optional extras' were: above, Jove, thunderbolt in hand; below, water, land and buildings. Such a *pictura* appeared, for instance, in most editions of the emblems of Alciati—fig. 1 shows that of Frankfurt 1567, fol. 109—between the heading IN TEMERARIOS and eight Latin hexameters about Phaethon.[25] But in the first

Figure 1

Figure 2

edition, published at Augsburg in 1531, the *pictura* in question (fig. 2) showed the hero as a rustic character placidly driving a cart.[26]

A more immediate and more likely source for *La villana*, however, is that work by Sebastián de Covarrubias which may have influenced Lope considerably about this time, his *Emblemas morales* (Madrid 1610). No. 69 of his second *centuria* has a crude picture of a coach (with two passengers, two staid horses and a calm *cochero*), accompanied by the motto: *Nec frena remittit, nec retinere valet* (fig. 3). Below, an *octava real* dwells on the perils of entrusting weighty matters to an inexperienced youth, and this theme is developed in the commentary overleaf, with quotations involving references to *habenas* from the *Adagia* of Erasmus and the *Aeneid* of Virgil. But the relationship of *pictura* and epigram is elucidated only when the motto is identified as a quotation from *Metamorphoses* Book II—it is lines 191–2—and by the comment: 'es buen exemplo el de Phaeton disfraçado en vn cochero'. In fact this whimsical disguising of the incautious young demi-god is the chief originality of the emblem, and may well have been what set Lope's wit working along similarly unconventional lines.[27]

Lope, as we have been noticing, returned to the Phaethon myth many times; but two later cases especially cannot be passed over here. In *Nadie se conoce*, a play he wrote, most probably, a very few

Figure 3

years after *La villana*,[28] it appears prominently but briefly, and not in Acts II and III but in Act I alone. Prince Lisardo of Hungary has incurred the wrath of his father the King by loving Celia, a lady of the court. He therefore sends Celia, disguised as a *villana*, to a nearby village; a courtier, Feliciano, is to accompany her, disguised as a *villano* and her husband. Lisardo calls for a *carroza*; but his servant Fabio insists that they must go in a *carro de mulas*, driven by Feliciano, and in a later scene Fabio describes Celia alighting at the village 'como el sol,/dando al aldea dos albas', whereas 'Feliciano, su Faetonte,/no los caballos guiaba/sino las mulas . . .' In fact when they next appear Celia is 'con hábito de labradora', and known as Diana (!); Feliciano is 'de labrador, fingiéndose su marido' (AcN VII, 683–9). Lope, we realize, has remembered the situation in *La villana* and reproduced it, as if in self-parody, *al revés*. As before, the heroine is driven by the *segundo galán*. She is described as a sun, he as her Phaethon, and each is transformed in appearance. But whereas Inés and Hernando are countryfolk in the capital, Celia and Feliciano are courtiers who live in the country as peasants. They travel, moreover, not in a *carroza*, or even a *coche*, but more absurdly in the sort of *carro de mulas* with which Inés and Hernando were familiar, and which all but appeared in Act I of *La villana*.

There is reason to suspect, moreover, that when Lope published *La villana* in 1620 he remembered it as a witty version of the myth of Phaethon. It was one of the 96 plays, in *Partes XIII—XX*, which he dedicated to particular individuals,[29] and the *dedicatoria* in this case is both emblematic and related to the play. Its kernel is an epigram of mythological subject-matter, which Lope introduces somewhat enigmatically as 'un soneto mío al rayo de aquel generoso caballero, tan desdichado como ilustre, que decía así:

> Venerable a los montes laurel fuera,
> Júpiter servador, tu sacra encina,
> si tu mano feroz la sierpe trina
> en su tronante origen suspendiera.
> Cuando el temor humano considera
> tal vez inmoble la piedad divina,
> teme la majestad, porque imagina
> preciso el orden de la eterna esfera.
> ¿Por qué de un árbol siempre duro hiciste
> defensa al cielo, o tú que su horizonte
> bañado en esplendor trémulo viste?
> ¡Ay, decreto fatal! en todo un monte
> blanco a las flechas de sus iras fuiste;
> y siendo Endimión, mueres Faetonte.'

It proves in fact to be yet another of the dozen or so sonnets in which Lope alludes to Phaethon, the only one indeed in which his name appears in the clinching, closing-with-a-golden-key last line.[30] It is followed too by a commentary, in which, as in some emblem-books,[31] significant phrases are heavily annotated: *Júpiter servador, sacra encina, sierpe trina, Endimión . . .* , the pretext being that they had been criticised in a 'concilio poético', and that Lope wished to defend them before his dedicatee, who was after all Francisco López de Aguilar, his principal defender against the *Spongia* of Torres Rámila. In a typical display of 'encyclopaedic' erudition, Lope adduces a score of authorities, among them emblematists like Alciati and Reusner, and includes another quotation from 'Ovidio, en la muerte de Faetón por el rayo', i.e. from *Metamorphoses* Book II, 325–6. Finally he elucidates the circumstance which produced the poem and the conceit which informs it:

> ... y todo el soneto junto se entiende ansí: D. Miguel de Guzmán era cazador, andaba por los montes, no se hizo hijo

> del Sol, aunque pudiera, siéndolo del Duque de Medina Sidonia; pues ¿cómo le mata Júpiter con su rayo, si fue sólo Endimión por las selvas, y no por el cielo Faetonte?

The point of the epigram is in fact that the *malogrado* Don Miguel, though hunting as if he had been the 'moon-man' Endymion, suffered improperly, by being struck by lightning—he should of course have sheltered under a laurel-tree—the fate of the 'sun-man' Phaethon.[32] Wittily, as in *La villana de Getafe*, mythology is shown to be misleading in its apparent predictions, and Lope, in using the poem as a preface to the play—as an *inductio*[33]—may well have intended to hint at the parallel. At the very least he was alluding implicitly to the importance in *La villana* of the myth of Phaethon.

6. Calderón's Portrait of a Lady in La vida es sueño
PETER W. EVANS

La vida es sueño is, in many respects, a dialectical consideration of the nature of dramatic art.[1] It is a self-conscious play, an instance of 'metatheatre', a work that bears out Shelley's conviction that art possesses a reality 'more real than living man'. Though he may not perhaps have thought of it in these terms Calderón is in fact, through *La vida es sueño*, glancing at the boundaries between realism and artifice, considering the relationships established between spectators and spectacle, interrogating the voyeuristic implications of our desires to see and to know.[2] Astolfo's locket containing Rosaura's portrait, hanging at once like a jewel and a millstone around his neck, is crucially a part of this overall design to chart the bordering territories of art and life.

This is not the only occasion where a Golden Age dramatist uses a *mise en abyme recurso* of this type, and Calderón himself, of course, uses a portrait for similar dramatic and figurative purposes in *El mayor monstruo del mundo*, to draw our attention to the heart of the play's most complex issues. If we are seized by a fit of literal-mindedness we can easily explain away the portrait in *La vida es sueño* as a necessary dramatic prop: without it, Estrella would not have stumbled on the truth of what T. E. May has aptly called Astolfo's 'wandering eye'.[3] There is no denying that the portrait does indeed justify its presence in this way, and the *comedia* is overflowing with portraits, letters and such used precisely in this way. But, of course, there is more to the portrait in *La vida es sueño* than meets the literally-minded eye.

It is another of the play's motifs of representation, and it is fundamentally connected to Calderón's interrelated preoccupations with the spectator's changing relationship with the spectacle and with the thematic interest in family warfare. Rosaura's portrait is to some extent the equivalent of Segismundo's prison tower.

46

In the same essay that includes the remark on Astolfo, T. E. May argues with typical brilliance that Rosaura makes a mess of things by insisting on having her honour avenged and ending up with Astolfo the philanderer. Such a view of Rosaura was overdue; but it may not be sufficient to let things rest there. Calderón may well be saying, as May argues, that the woman who pursues a fickle lover for honour's sake is, to say the least, idiotic, but he is also surely asking us to consider the circumstances which make her so. If we take the portrait seriously, as more than a mere device to complicate matters in Poland, we can see more clearly what Calderón is doing.

Rosaura's misfortune is that she lives at a time when to gain self-approval people realise that they cannot fall foul of a widely accepted code of social conduct: a code of conduct that is not necessarily Calderón's, as many critics have in recent times been at pains to demonstrate, but one which nevertheless held great sway in the society of which he was a part, and which he therefore took some care to represent with due concern for its complexities. The advantages of this code are plain to see: self-assurance, order, security; the constrictions, however, are barbaric customs (revenge and so on), shallowness of thought, ruthlessness of retaliation or ostracism for those who contravene or are victims of the system, and, in many instances, a denial of Christian values and ideals. Living by such a code, and having suffered a humiliation which flouts its prescriptions, Rosaura feels, thinking of herself now perhaps as a pariah, that she is under an obligation, if she chooses to go on living in society, to rectify the situation in the only way available: either to kill or to marry her treacherous wooer. The play makes us feel that the deflowered woman of high rank is a social outcast, however common sexual relationships outside marriage may have been in Calderón's day. All we need to know is that in Rosaura Calderón offers us a view of a woman who through sexual betrayal has lost a sense of her own equilibrium of identity. Rosaura is momentarily stripped of social rank; she must, therefore, seek wholeness by being cast out of her normal social context and by taking on a succession of parts. Like Viola in Illyria, or 'Don Gil' in Madrid, Rosaura tries on a number of disguises, and although each tells us something vital about her constituent selves, none is on its own wholly satisfactory or explanatory, and is merely a stage in her progress towards a desired restoration of her full identity through the resolution of her relationship with Astolfo. Conventional justice is what she seeks in her case against Astolfo, and until she gets it she feels she cannot be restored to her proper place on the social ladder as daughter, and eventually, wife and mother. Rosaura's quest for Astolfo is on one level a search for psychological and social restitution, and her disguises tell us that until she comes to an arrangement with Astolfo she remains an outcast.

Disguise ultimately proves to be, as Viola puts it, a 'wickedness' in this play as well. But not entirely: it quite clearly enables Rosaura to break free of a mould, to become less static or passive in her dealings with men, and to try at least to be a participant in the congested traffic of social life. This is possible precisely because, in common with many other Golden Age heroines, she wears male clothes. Calderón takes advantage of several dramatic and psychological opportunities to comment on the condition of women in seventeenth century Spain as soon as he puts Rosaura in breeches. From a psychological point of view, Rosaura's male disguise at once draws attention to her exhibitionistic tendencies, and releases her inner and perhaps repressed masculinity, which she herself fully recognises in the later stages of the play when she pleads with Segismundo, as a man, to take her side:

> Y así piensa que si hoy
> como a mujer me enamoras,
> como varón te daré
> la muerte en defensa honrosa
> de mi honor; porque he de ser,
> en su conquista amorosa,
> mujer para darte quejas,
> varón para ganar honras. (III, 2914–21)

Here are the self-convessed *varonil* qualities that make of Rosaura an androgyne.[4] In this sense her disguise is therefore not merely a superficial aid that conceals her true nature; it is her true nature, or part of it at least. Far from being a concealment, the disguise is a display of identity.

But beyond the purely sexual and psychological relief that Rosaura temporarily finds in transvestism, there is an equally important and 'metadramatic' function released through her disguise.[5] Rosaura's fancy dress is by its very nature Saturnalian and festive, and as such enables Calderón to link the implications of traditional, ludic rituals with his own obsessive interest in the social, psychological and, above all aesthetic qualities of his own play-acting art. For among the various roles that she is required to play while she is abroad in Poland is that of the spectator/voyeur, and in this role her own unnatural costume perhaps draws the attention of the audience with more firmness to the reality of her status as the spectators' *alter ego*, distanced as she is from her own normal self through disguise. Our own distancing from the realities of our lives as soon as we take our seats in the theatre is aptly symbolised by Rosaura's own remoteness from her usual contexts.

Rosaura, of course, is not the only spectator/voyeur (Clarín and Basilio are other fascinating examples), but that is how she is presented to us when we first see her in the play, as soon as the dust has settled after her accident with her horse, and after we have been familiarised with her victimisation through Calderón's choicest language of excess in the *Hipogrifo violento* speech. She fits quite quickly into her role as our guide to the drama. We naturally see for ourselves that we are in a world of horror, but Rosaura the spectator makes us see more. As an artist figure herself, creating illusions in Poland, she shares with Calderón a capacity for making us look with greater awareness at the complex business of living. This fundamental task that lies in front of the artist has been aptly expressed by Conrad: 'My task which I am trying to achieve is, by the power of the written word to make you hear, to make you feel—it is, before all, to make you *see*'.[6] But Rosaura is spectator as well as artist sharing with the ordinary spectators in the theatre a predilection for seeing life from a narrow angle of vision. Through looking at Rosaura we can see how easily we ourselves as spectators slip into an attitude of mind that reduces the complexity of life to the preferred vision of our own prejudices and experiences. Calderón gives us Rosaura partly in order for us to see ourselves, through her, constructing the framework of our perceptions.

Like some ideal Aristotelian spectator Rosaura feels pity and fear for Segismundo ('Temor y piedad en mí/sus razones han causado' I, 173–4), and, like all *ingenios*, she draws suitable lessons from the spectacle (I, 243–52). But Rosaura's own remarks about response should not blind us into accepting her as an ideal spectator objectively recording the truths of an outer reality. Why should we believe Rosaura's account? What does her painting of the scene tell us beyond the fact that she is a highly disturbed woman seeing life through the spectacles of betrayal? Some of the sights she brings more vividly within our range of vision do contribute to the atmosphere of eeriness that Calderón seems keen to create. We are in the seventeenth-century's equivalent of Gothic horror. But through a slip of language, the reference to births ('La puerta/[mejor diré funesta boca] abierta/está y desde su centro/ nace la noche, pues la engendra dentro.' I, 69–72), Rosaura unwittingly warns us not to take her too seriously as a reliable guide to the truth, here or on any other occasion, in the play. Without wishing to make heavy weather of this significant slip, we might nonetheless want to say that this is the language of a woman still preoccupied by sexuality. The point is that we as spectators are being made to see the action through Rosaura's less than innocent eye, precisely so that we ourselves become conscious of the falsity of the notion of the disinterested spectator. Calderón's own vision is sharp; he sees quite clearly that a character's sight is conditioned by knowledge and experience and, moreover, that visual perception is inseparable from moral acuity.

Two characters who appear to see things in radically different ways from Rosaura, since they both ultimately conspire to deprive her of happiness, are Segismundo and Astolfo. It does not take long for anyone, however, to reach the depressing conclusion that despite her various manifestations of liberation from a multitude of social constrictions, Rosaura is ultimately as myopically attached to the values of her society as the men who plot her destiny.[7]

Segismundo's language is full of eye imagery; meeting Rosaura for the first time, expressing his amazement at waking up in a palace, recollecting that he has once before encountered a person of Rosaura's beauty, turning away from Rosaura near the end of the play when he decides to restore her lost honour: all of these occasions show us Segismundo recording his impressions through an almost obsessive preoccupation with sight. Yet while such language informs us of Segismundo's own fitful process of maturity, it serves to impale Rosaura. Segismundo moves and transfixes Rosaura with his stare. Like a basilisk's, even where he seeks to express his admiration for her, Segismundo's eyes and, by implication, his attitudes, immobilise Rosaura. When in a conventional image he declares that every glance he takes at Rosaura deals him a mortal blow, we cannot help but feel that though they

exalt her his feelings and words of love for her are also instruments
of her own slavery:

> Con cada vez que te veo
> nueva admiración me das,
> y cuando te miro más
> aun más mirarte deseo.
> Ojos hidrópicos creo
> que mis ojos deben ser;
> pues cuando es muerte el beber,
> beben más, y desta suerte,
> viendo que el ver me da muerte,
> estoy muriendo por ver. (I, 223–82)

Like so much else that Segismundo says to Rosaura this speech of
conventional flattery succeeds at best in stripping Rosaura of her
uniqueness. Segismundo's eyes reduce Rosaura's individual stature
to a size not much different, in spite of his eventual preference,
from Estrella's. Why else does Calderón make Segismundo eulogise
Rosaura at the palace in words that are not too dissimilar to those
he uses in praise of Estrella? On both occasions comparisons with
the sun are his starting points (II, 1391–1406, and II, 1593–1617).
What is worse is that these clichés of love are echoes of Astolfo's (I,
475–494). Women are interchangeable in the eyes of such lovers.

But the alternative to narrow-sightedness of a sexual or
ideological kind is not imposed blindness. What Segismundo does
in turning his eyes away from Rosaura is really no different from
what Basilio or Clotaldo do. The king pretends his problems are
not there once he has locked them out of sight; and his toady, a
vain and graceless lackey, lacking restraint in the gratification of
his own naked ambition, but primly avoiding the hug and generous
welcome that any normal father would give his restored son or
daughter, acquiesces in this policy of concealment by ordering the
intruders to be blindfolded at the beginning of Act I. Calderón
surely hopes that Clarín's deflationary remark, '¿Enmascaraditos
hay? (I, 295), articulates the feelings of many in the audience who
find Clotaldo distasteful.

Segismundo, Clotaldo, Basilio, and Astolfo, all living in an
atmosphere of fear, where no one dares say what he or she really
thinks, turn their hearts and minds away from the truth, and

impose their own versions of it on everyone else. Astolfo, in his own mean-minded way is adept at doing just that most particularly in his treatment of women.

Through the dramatization of Astolfo's treatment of Rosaura Calderón takes the opportunity once more of looking not only at the effects of betrayal in love, but also at the vulnerable position of seventeenth-century women who risk themselves in love. From a psychological point of view Rosaura is one of the Golden Age's many portrayals of the woman whose shame is born of a recognition that her trust and devotion breed only contempt. The profoundly ridiculous spectacle that such a woman eventually feels she is making in her pursuit of a forgotten love is partly responsible for the fury of her revenge. Psychological damage of this type might more easily be repaired in a society not quite as rigidly structured as Calderón's, but here its effects are cruel, and it is precisely the stiffness of that society, manufacturing moral and social straitjackets for its women in particular, that he is clearly at pains in this play to highlight. The visual *recurso* of the portrait, and related verbal portrait imagery, provides him with a way of doing so.

Astolfo's contribution to the play is double-edged: firstly, we look through him at fickleness and opportunism (his persecution of Estrella neatly links these twin issues); but secondly, and equally crucial, is his representation of the lover who is happiest in love only when he is protected from coping with the reality of his beloved, only when he is placed at an emotional distance from her, where from a position of fantasy and remoteness he can superimpose on her own authenticity and distinctiveness a distorted image of her created by his own peculiar cravings and securities of mind. The portrait that Astolfo carries around with him is, perhaps, at a figurative level, his vision of Rosaura as fantasy-object, not as she really is, the woman whose reality moved him to abandon her. With a woman's individuality safely arrested, a man fearful of submitting himself to the challenges and instabilities of love can sentimentally and in tranquillity gaze with longing at the image of his beloved, safe in the knowledge that she is immobilised, out of reach, speechless and powerless. But the portrait comes to life in *La vida es sueño*, and Astolfo's fantasies are unmasked.

When accused by Estrella of preferring another woman, whose portrait hangs near his heart, Astolfo replies in a speech which reveals as much through what he unwittingly lets slip as through the direct information he offers us in the *aparte:*

> Yo haré que el retrato salga
> del pecho, para que entre
> la imagen de tu hermosura.
> Donde entra Estrella no tiene
> lugar la sombra, ni estrella
> donde el sol; voy a traerle.
>
> (*aparte*) Perdona, Rosaura hermosa,
> este agravio, porque ausentes,
> no se guardan más fe que ésta
> los hombres y las mujeres. (II, 1768–77)

Speak for yourself, we might be tempted to say; but, in any case the *aparte* is Calderón's dramatization of the fickleness of lovers whose hearts do not grow fonder through absence. Astolfo is an example of a man, common enough in Golden Age drama, untroubled by the consequences of breaking his oath to a woman he has compromised. Moral reprobation for his behaviour would astonish him, and he intends to remain scot-free of any obligations to the woman he leaves behind. These contemptibly immature *aparte* words on the lips of a stereotyped lover emphasise the real sense of the previous six lines, and allow us to see once again Calderón's intricate design in the play's preoccupation with representation. The direct meaning of Astolfo's assurances to Estrella is that as he has now found a far more glittering object of his desire, the more obscure one can be replaced. But although he has not meant to say so, what he actually implies of course is that this process is under no threat of extinction: 'ni estrella/donde el sol' means that Estrella is the sun, Rosaura the star; but Estrella is of course herself only a star, so her place will one day be usurped by another sun. (Astolfo has already prepared us for this inevitability through his comparisons between Estrella and Aurora, Flora and Palas, all figures associated with Rosaura).

Sound complements sight: the words Calderón uses to capture the mood of a man's exploitation of a woman, and in particular of a narcissist who collects women like pin-ups, are matched by his handling of the visual presence of the portrait. Astolfo re-produces Rosaura in the portrait, just as he is now re-producing Estrella in words. The real Estrella is not accessible to his cliché-ridden lover's

view of her. Estrella is Calderón's portrait of a woman who is
capable of offering her lover the possibility of real intimacy and
trust. Here is a woman who is on the verge of entrusting the keys of
her own inner being to a man who has no scruples about using
them merely to unlock her inner self and to leave it open and
vulnerable to theft or assault. As if sensing the danger of such
action she finds instead, as she hopes, a safer guardian for those
keys in 'Astrea':

> . . . tienes
> de mi voluntad las llaves;
> por esto, y por ser quien eres,
> me atrevo a fiar de ti
> lo que aun de mí muchas veces
> recaté. (II, 1786–92)

But Estrella is not to know that in her disguise as Astrea Rosaura
is, like the reduced, re-produced, fantasied and safe representation
of herself in the portrait, yet another inauthentic figure of illusion
in an insubstantial world variously described as a stage-set or a
dream.

The endlessly repetitive cycle of lies, imitations, fakes and
retratos is never broken in the play. All have social as well as more
primitive psychic implications, and Rosaura points us towards
them in an impassioned speech about the specific conditions of
herself and her mother, and, beyond that, to the circumstances in
which women generally find themselves in contemporary society:

> nací yo tan parecida,
> que fuí un retrato, una copia,
> ya que en la hermosura no,
> en la dicha y en las obras;
> y así no habré menester
> decir que, poco dichosa
> heredera de fortunas,
> corrí con ella una propia. (III, 2770–77)

Calderón's interest in portraits and, in particular, the complexities
of meaning which the word *retratar* and its attributes is capable of
creating, is in some ways more memorably displayed in *El pintor de
su deshonra*. In that play he strikes up intriguing relationships, in a
play about a man's dual characteristics of possessiveness in love

and aesthetic sensibility, through the punning associations of *retratar* and *tratar*. Through such processes of interdependence *retrato* and *retratar* in that play come to represent attitudes of oppression that involve husband and wife. In this play the portrait symbol concentrates our mind not only on the vulnerability of the beautiful woman (and that is partly the point of Rosaura's allusion to the beauty of her mother [III, 2732–35]), but also on the processes of reduction and of trivialisation to which through flattery as much as through envy, ignorance or malice, we are all prey. Calderón ensures that we continue to grasp the figurative complexities of the portrait symbol by making Segismundo, in Rosaura's presence, also talk of representation: '¿Tan semejante es la copia/al original que hay duda/en saber si es ella propia? (III, 2947–9). But neither as *copia*, nor as fantasy-object does Rosaura find a way out of the reduced, stylised portrait of herself, which is no more than the representation of a victimised and vulnerable woman. Nor is there any exit from these subtle traps, from Calderón's point of view, in disguise, whether through playing the part of Astrea, or of a man. In this sense is disguise a wickedness, in so far as it leads Rosaura to get what she wants. But who in their right mind, regardless of what has happened, would want to be married to an Astolfo?

Rosaura wants him because she is framed by her society, and Clotaldo's sword, worn by her as a cow carries its owner's brand, is the play's other major visual prop drawing our attention to her framing. The sword offers strength and justice but it also functions, in so far as it is a relic of Clotaldo's, as an emblem at once of virility and of betrayal. Rosaura fails to see that the object she hopes will lead her to justice and the truth is, in fact, since Clotaldo places his own well-being above all else, a symbol that works exclusively in the interests of a selfish man, and, beyond him the social law of the double standard. The sword's magic works. And as poor Rosaura prepares for a life of doom with Astolfo Calderón asks us to look at the predicament of seventeenth century women, framed by their own representation and status in society. This is not to argue anachronistically that Calderón's consciousness of women's subjugation was as sharp as that of dramatists writing now in the more heightened atmosphere of contemporary attitudes to women; it is simply a reminder that Calderón knew what it was like for women to live in the restrictive structures of role and status, as his dramatization of suffering women well shows.

From this point of view the end of the play is terrifyingly bleak and pessimistic. Even if we do not look forward to a cradle of horror of the kind being constructed for Gutierre and Leonor in *El médico de su honra*, we still feel that the four principal characters preparing for matrimony have only relationships conventionally devoid of love in prospect. There is a beautiful, deliberately created tension in the play between, on the one hand the plot's drive towards a satisfactory and symmetrical resolution (Rosaura finds Astolfo, Segismundo and Basilio are reconciled, and so on), and, on the other, beneath this pattern, the dislocations and dissonance created by these very patterns. The marriages created by Segismundo at the end of the play are dramatizations of Calderón's evident horror at the frequency with which seventeenth century families are structured on foundations of treachery, oppression and lovelessness. In setting up structures of this type, at the private level of the family, Segismundo is actually warning us, less by design than by accident, that the system he has in mind for society at large, of which, of course, the family is traditionally a microcosm, is destined to be no different from the masterpiece of confusion, to paraphrase Macduff, that Basilio like Macbeth, though less bloodily, had earlier made.[8]

7. *Machado de Assis between Romance and Satire: A Parasita Azul*—JOHN GLEDSON

'A Parasita Azul' is the opening story of Machado de Assis' second collection, *Histórias da Meia-Noite* (1873): it was first published in the preceding year, in four parts, in the *Jornal das Famílias*.[1] It is not an undiscovered masterpiece, but it is a surprising work which does not merit the almost complete critical neglect which has been its lot.[2] There are fascinating parallels between its plot and those of the great novels published after 1880 — in particular, *Memórias Póstumas de Brás Cubas* (1881) and *Quincas Borba* (1885–91). Most suggestively, the novel whose plot most closely resembles that of 'A Parasita Azul' is Machado's last, the strange and in many ways off-putting *Memorial de Aires* (1906). If this parallel can be established and explained, this long and in some ways uncharacteristic early story may well tell us more of Machado's secrets than its artistic shortcomings would lead one to imagine.

Perhaps the most disconcerting aspect of the story from the point of view of the reader is the discrepancy between the plot and the tone in which the story is told, or to put it another way, between the moral form of the story and its amoral import. The plot is simple and traditional: the most illuminating parallel is perhaps that of the Prodigal Son. In 1849, Camilo Seabra, the son of a rich *comendador* from Goiás in the far interior of Brazil, is sent by his father to study medicine in Paris: his decision, somewhat surprising at such a place and time, is inspired by a French naturalist who had visited the area at the time of Camilo's birth (1828). In Paris, Camilo is at first under the botanist's watchful eye; but after his death, he proceeds to waste his father's allowance in riotous living (though he is careful to get his degree). We first meet him on his unwilling return to Brazil in 1857, his father

57

having finally lost patience with his procrastination. In Rio, he meets a fellow-townsman, Leandro Soares, who has stayed at home all these years. On the long journey home via Santos and São Paulo, this talkative dullard reveals himself to have three passions—hunting, politics and Isabel Matos, who however does not return his affections. Since she does not, he is determined at least that no-one else will have her: 'tinha o sestro aliás comum, de querer ver quebrada ou inútil, a taça que ele não podia levar aos lábios' (II, p. 174).[3] Cutting a long story short (though many of its details and digressions will be returned to), Camilo inevitably falls in love with Isabel, and marries her after it is discovered that he is the lover she has been waiting for for years. She had sworn to marry a boy who, years ago, had fallen and grazed himself while climbing a tree to get a blue parasitical plant—a parasita azul—for her. Leandro is contented with the fulfilment of his political ambition to be a local deputado.

If the Biblical story of the Prodigal Son, along with that of Esau and Jacob, seem closest to the structure of the story as a whole (Leandro is actually referred to as exchanging the 'direito de primogenitura por um prato de lentilhas' (II, p. 191), even though he is no relation of Camilo's), there are other elements in it which recall traditional romance. Naturally, they surround Isabel, who is first seen by Camilo on horseback, like a Scott heroine:

> Vira muitas amazonas elegantes e destras.
> Aquela porém tinha alguma cousa em que se
> avantajava às outras; era talvez o
> desalinho do gesto, talvez a espontaneidade
> dos movimentos, outra cousa talvez, ou todas
> essas juntas que davam à interessante goiana
> incontestável supremacia. (II, p. 173).

The motif of waiting for the promised lover to return is common enough in romance, of course: more than Cinderella, Isabel is perhaps the Sleeping Beauty, bound by her own childhood promise, and guarded by the 'dragon' Leandro, who threatens terrible deaths to anyone else who dares approach her. She is also the lady who imposes tasks on her suitors. Even after Camilo has been revealed as the boy of the parasite incident, she refuses to marry him until he shows his affection for her in some dramatic way. This he does by disappearing, apparently distraught, for some days; Isabel's remorse at being the cause of this near-suicide finally brings her to her senses, though the reader might wonder with the *comendador* why 'uma moça apaixonada por um mancebo, e um mancebo apaixonado por uma moça, em vez de caminharem para o casamento, tratassem de separar um do outro' (II, p. 187). His reasonable suspicion is that his son has run away 'para fugir a um enlace indispensável'.

As this summary cannot avoid indicating, these 'serious' Biblical or romance motifs are continually undermined by the tone of the story, and by its setting, which is not a mythical land, but a 'real' Goiás, where shotgun marriages are more common than suicidal lovers. When Camilo is approached in a crowd by a mysterious old man who turns out to know the secret of Isabel's passion for the parasite, his first impression (and the reader's) might well be that this is one of Leandro's toughs come to warn him off—the first thing he says is 'Veja o que faz'. Nothing of the sort, however; Camilo is right to conclude that he is in a novel:'—Um romance! disse ele; estou em pleno romance' (II, p. 179).

He *is* right, however; none of the realism is allowed to get in the way of the conventional happy ending, in which the young man gets his girl, and even the churlish Leandro is happy with his 'prato de lentilhas'. What is perhaps most surprising is that this takes place without any conversion or repentance that the reader can be sure of. The story is completely without a moral in this sense, for Camilo remains irresponsible and lucky to the end. Admittedly, the stories of Esau and Jacob and the Prodigal Son are not the most conventionally moral in the Bible, but in each there is some final justification for Jacob's trickery and the Prodigal Son's behaviour. Here there is none. Machado goes out of his way to tell us that his disappearance in the final chapter is not caused by suffering, but is simply play-acting:

> O mísero rapaz trazia escrita no rosto a
> dor de haver escapado à morte trágica que
> procurara; pelo menos, assim o disse muitas
> vezes em caminho, ao pai de Isabel. (II, p. 188)

Faced with such incongruences, the reader may well be forced to read the story in a different sense, and to see it as satire rather than romance. This entails largely ignoring the plot with its conventional ending, and concentrating on the characters, who stand condemned as foolish and/or selfish. Many details, which go against the grain of the 'romance', suggest this; even the heroine, Isabel, is described by Padre Maciel as 'uma grande finória', who will not accept Soares 'a ver se pilha algum casamento que lhe abra as portas das grandezas políticas' (II, p. 176). Politics is the consuming passion of the whole community; not only does Leandro regard a place in the provincial parliament as sufficient compensation for the loss of Isabel; we meet the latter's aunt, who is a poor old woman with 'two other defects'—'era surda e gostava de política' (II, p. 183).

At the centre of the story (Chapter IV of the seven into which it is divided) stands the festival of the Espírito Santo, introduced by Machado much as if it were a *flagrante* of traditional Brazilian life, in the style of Manuel Antônio de Almeida's *Memórias de um Sargento de Milícias* for instance:

> Vão rareando os lugares em que de todo se não apagou o gosto dessas festas clássicas, resto de outras eras, que os escritores do século futuro hão de estudar com curiosidade, para pintar aos seus contemporâneos um Brasil que eles já não hão de conhecer. No tempo em que esta história se passa uma das mais genuínas festas do Espírito Santo era a da cidade de Santa Luzia. (II, p. 175)

But the reader should not be deluded; this is not a *costumbrista* sketch, but the centre of Machado's political satire. The festival is presided over by Tenente-Coronel Veiga, whose concern, not unconnected with the desire to outshine his political rivals, is to make the festival as brilliant as possible. By a carefully constructed *crescendo*, Machado builds up to the appearance of the Tenente-Coronel, dressed up as the *Imperador do Divino:*

> Ao peito rutilava uma vasta comenda da Ordem da Rosa, que lhe não ficava mal. Mas o que excedeu a toda a expectação, o que pintou no rosto do nosso Camilo a mais completa expressão de assombro, foi uma brilhante e vistosa coroa de papelão forrado de papel dourado, que o tenente-coronel trazia na cabeça. (II, p. 178)

It is impossible not to see a more generalised political satire here: the repeated references to the connexion between politics and the festival, the crown, and the *Ordem da Rosa* leave us in no doubt that Machado is making fun of the Brazilian Imperial system, of a society mesmerised by a cardboard crown. This long passage, it should be said, is only perfunctorily integrated into the main love story. It is during the festival that the mysterious old man comes up to Camilo, but it is difficult to see that he could not have done so at any other time or place.

One of the objects of 'A Parasita Azul', then, is plainly satirical. It is in this sense the forerunner of *Brás Cubas*, and most strikingly, of *Quincas Borba*. Quincas Borba the character, when he appears in the former novel, is shown to be a direct descendent of Tenente-Coronel Veiga: he too used to play Emperor at the Espírito Santo celebrations;[4] and they are delusions which he passes on to his legatee in the latter novel, above all in the climactic scene in which the mad Rubião places the non-existent crown of Napoleon III on his own head. *Quincas Borba* in fact achieves what can be seen here in embryo—a picture of a totally deluded society with a deluded Emperor-figure at its centre.

At the very least, we have to conclude that this is a romantic story with a considerable element of satire. Of course, there is no literary law against such a mixture—many of Dickens' novels are clear examples. However, I believe that many aspects of the central love-story itself show that Machado was not contented with such a solution; some hints of this (Isabel's ambition, Camilo's feigned 'suicide attempt') have already been mentioned. As we have seen, on the one hand, their affair is a childhood romance which leads to happiness ever after; on the other, it is the convenient marriage of a wastrel and a social climber. These are difficult things to reconcile in a story which is to be artistically or morally satisfying, and it must be said that Machado fails to reconcile them.

What is interesting, however, is that he attempts to do so, at at least three points in the story. The most obvious of these concerns the parasite itself which provides the title. Of course, it is the flower which represents the maiden's purity and honour; so much we can gather from the traditions of romance. But Machado's prose says something else:

> Ama . . . uma parasita. Uma parasita? É verdade, uma
> parasita. Deve ser então uma flor muito linda,—um milagre de
> frescura e de aroma. Não, senhor, é uma parasita muito feia,

um cadáver de flor, seco, mirrado, uma flor que devia ter sido lindíssima há muito tempo, no pé, mas que hoje na cestinha em que ela a traz, nenhum sentimento inspira, a não ser de curiosidade. Sim, porque é realmente curioso que uma moça de vinte anos, em toda a força das paixões, pareça indiferente aos homens que a cercam, e concentre todos os seus afetos nos restos descorados e secos de uma flor. (II, p. 182)

Enough has been said before this for the reader to suspect the truth about Isabel's love—so much, in fact, that 'pergunta vivamente' can only be sarcastic. Camilo, then, *is* the parasite: if he is, of course, he is also 'um cadáver', 'os restos descorados e secos' of what he once was. The obviously symbolic scene which follows, in which the boy wounds himself going up the tree to get the plant, begins to look like a parable of lost innocence, the fall and the wound being symbols of that loss. The choice of the parasite is of course significant enough in itself. They are typical enough flowers of the Brazilian forest, often referred to without ironic intention in more conventionally Romantic descriptions of virgin American nature in the Indianist works of writers like José de Alencar or Machado himself in other moods.[5] Here though, there can be no doubt that the other meaning is also intended, and that Camilo is also a social parasite, a species in whom Machado had already shown some interest.[6] This episode cannot but make us aware of a possible undercurrent in the story, conveyed by symbols, and whose outcome is in many ways opposite to that of the story itself. In connexion with the flower symbol, we should remember that the original decision to send Camilo to Paris is inspired by a botanist. Machado's introduction of this character is perfectly likely historically—such botanists as Auguste de Sainte-Hilaire did journey to the Brazilian interior during the early part of the 19th Century—but the symbolic overtones are fascinating. If Camilo is the parasite, once fresh, now faded and shrivelled, it may be because he has been plucked from the tree by this botanist: the journey to Europe is itself a fall from innocence. The scientific (and, possibly, political)[7] ideals which the naturalist imports are in some sense contrary to Brazil's 'nature'.

Such ideas may seem exceedingly unlikely for a writer like Machado; they posit a type of innocence or original state of nature which it would be very hard to find in the great novels. However, it is difficult to avoid the conclusion that the existence of such an ideal *is* posited, even if it is no more than a working hypothesis. Nor is this as unlikely as one might think, once one has found the appropriate context for the ideal itself. It seems to me that the most likely one, contrary as it may be to some conceptions of Machado's intellectual make-up, is the Romantic idealisation of virgin America, which in Brazil as in other countries became an important element in the search for an independent literature. Machado is well known to have been an opponent of simplistic nationalism—in a famous passage from a critical article written in the same period as 'A Parasita Azul', he is sceptical of an exclusive doctrine which makes the choice of 'national' subjects obligatory:

> O que se deve exigir do escritor antes de tudo, é certo
> sentimento íntimo, que o torne homem do seu tempo e do seu
> país, ainda quando trate de assuntos remotos no tempo e no
> espaço. Um notável crítico da França, analisando há tempos
> um escritor escocês, Masson, com muito acerto dizia que do
> mesmo modo que se podia ser bretão sem falar sempre do tojo,
> assim Masson era bem escocês, sem dizer palavra do cardo, e
> explicava o dito acrescentando que havia nele um *scotticismo*
> interior, diverso e melhor do que se fora apenas superficial.
> (III, p. 804)[8]

The urban setting of Machado's novels, and of the vast majority of his stories, might lead one to suspect that he was completely averse, not only to Indianist but to *sertanejo* settings, or at least regarded them as more suitable for poetry than for prose.[9] 'A Parasita Azul', in fact, could be regarded as proof *for* this argument, for its *sertão* is deliberately unpoetic; by and large, it is simply monotonous, and when it is poetic, the language is conventional to the joint of perfunctoriness:

> Era já noite. A fogueira do jantar alumiava um pequeno
> espaço em roda; mas nem era precisa, porque a lua começava
> a surgir de trás de um morro, pálida e luminosa, brincando
> nas folhas do arvoredo e nas águas tranqüilas do rio que
> serpeava ali ao pé. (II, p. 167).

At this level, there can be no doubt of Machado's scepticism about 'typically Brazilian' subjects; but another plainly symbolic episode reinforces the suspicion that the story depends on the tradition of literary nationalism: more specifically, on the most important novelist within that tradition, Alencar. On the journey from Rio to Goiás, Leandro has a nightmare which he recounts to Camilo the next morning. While out hunting, he catches sight of Isabel on the other side of the river. She announces that she has lost her hat in the stream, and asks him to go down and get it. He hesitates, only to find that Camilo comes up behind him, and goes down to fetch the hat. When he gets down there, however, the river suddenly rises; Isabel rushes down to help him, and the two are about to be swept away when Leandro is awoken by Camilo. The nightmare is, as Camilo says, 'uma porção de tolices', but it is unlikely that any Brazilian reader at the time could fail to be reminded of the novel which made Alencar famous, *O Guarani* (1857).[10] At the end of this very popular work, the Indian hero, Peri, and Ceci, the blonde, blue-eyed maiden whom he has saved from death, are swept over the horizon by suddenly rising floodwaters. The link with *O Guarani* is made even more likely by the idea of going down to the river to fetch Isabel's hat; it is very likely a parody of the scene in the novel in which Peri rescues Ceci's bracelet from the snake-filled abyss surrounding the fort where she lives.[11]

The vital comparison, however, is that involving the end of *O Guarani*. In Machado's story, the rising waters which carry the lovers off seem to cast doubt on the happy ending itself, even though the dream is told five chapters before that ending, and by a jealous fool. It is worth considering the reasons which lay behind the end of Alencar's 'romance histórico', much more romance than historical. From the beginning, the devoted Indian, the noble savage who eventually even turns Christian in order to save his lady, and Ceci, the lady herself, are obviously destined for one another. But when they are finally free from the complications involving the rest of the characters, the tensions underlying the racial differences between them come to the surface and pose delicate problems for the novelist. Where are they to go? They cannot go to Rio, for there Peri will simply be a slave,[12] but neither will Alencar abdicate the values of civilisation as far as to allow him to carry her off to his tribe. So, the storm breaks, and, grasping a palm-tree, they are swept off into a realm where the reader can still exercise his imagination.

It seems likely that, in the dream episode in 'A Parasita Azul',

Machado is expressing his own doubts about the fate of another couple who, in their way, represent Brazil, though his doubts are conscious, and most probably inspired by his own thoughts about Alencar,[13] rather than being, as Alencar's themselves were, the product of his novel's own (contradictory) momentum. The parasite and the social climber may be happy at the end of the story, but on another level they are doomed.

Just as the image of the flower is given an extra twist by the introduction of the botanist, so the image of the river cannot be left here. The old man who comes up to Camilo at the Espírito Santo festival eventually tells him the story of the blue parasite, so proving that Isabel is in love with him. When he does so, Camilo not unnaturally tries to reward him for his pains:

> ... estendeu-lhe a nota. O desconhecido riu-se desdenhosamente sem responder palavra. Depois, estendeu a mão à nota que Camilo lhe oferecia, e, com grande pasmo deste, atirou-a ao riacho. O fio d'água que ia murmurando e saltando por cima das pedras, levou consigo o bilhete, de envolta com una folha que o vento lhe levara também. (II, p. 185)

This is a strange scene, though for readers of Roberto Schwarz's *Ao Vencedor as Batatas*,[14] which places so much emphasis on the importance of favour in Machado's novels, it will seem less outlandish. Primarily, it seems that Machado is again determined to cast doubt on the purity and innocence of the central love-match, which cannot exist (he seems to be saying) without the cooperation of a society which it would nevertheless like to ignore, or fob off with a tip. Admittedly, if Camilo's gesture seems to sully their purity, the old man's maintains it. But that is his affair: other go-betweens—José Dias, the *agregado* in *Dom Casmurro*, and the greatest parasite of all, is the most striking example—will be less upright, and the implications for the lovers correspondingly less edifying.

The most important implications of this story, then, seem to me to lie in the ambiguity with which Machado tries to surround his central pair of lovers. If romance and satire can be mixed with relative ease in the story as a whole, their contradictory impulses issue in something else, most interestingly in a pair of symbols—the flower, fresh and corrupt at the same time, and the river, leading over (Alencar's?) horizon—which maintain a real ambiguity, and partake of both literary worlds.

As was said at the beginning, the interest of this story lies not so much in its own excellence, as on the light it casts on the plots of Machado's major works. Most obviously, *Brás Cubas* returns to the story of the spoilt wastrel of a son who returns from Europe to make his reputation:[15] but in the novel, 'success' is much more obviously failure. Brás remains quite happily a social parasite, but married love becomes adultery, and success the series of negatives with which the novel concludes (v. Ch. 160). Machado has discovered, and embodied in the narrative voice of Brás himself, that the novelist has no need to point up the moral in the plot by punishing his hero with unhappiness, however symbolic. The different world of satire allows him, by taking on Brás's own voice, to assume simple amusement at, and even sympathy for the 'pranks' of his hero.

Quincas Borba, aside from the element of generalised political satire centring on the figure of the Emperor, repeats the basic plot pattern of our story. The provincial boor (Rubião) and the smart operator (Palha) are both in love with the same ambitious woman (Sofia): one has to be contented with delusory compensations (Napoleon III's crown), while the couple live on in morally reprehensible bliss—again, the satirist's perspective removes Machado from any of the awkwardness of tone which afflict 'A Parasita Azul'.

It could be said, then, that the story is an experiment which failed, and that the plainly unresolved tensions between the surface and the symbolic plots had to await Machado's rejection of Romantic plots and acceptance of the healthier premises of satire to reach fruition. This is quite true; I certainly do not wish to quarrel with perfectly sensible conventional accounts of Machado's literary development. However, I do believe that the lessons to be drawn from 'A Parasita Azul' are more interesting than that; in particular, such arguments would inevitably tend to ignore the surface, Romantic plot of the story, on which, after all, it is entirely dependent structurally. Did Machado simply see the folly of his ways, and reject such hangovers from the past?

The most striking evidence that this is not so appears in his last novel, *Memorial de Aires*. If this is not exactly ignored by critics—after all, it is a *novel*—their rejection of it as an artistic failure is unanimous. Augusto Meyer, the best of the modernist critics of Machado, calls is 'um livro bocejado e não escrito'.[16] Again, it seems to me that value-judgements, right or wrong, should not stand in the way of a simple understanding of what Machado was trying to do. If one can dismiss this novel, or excuse it as the product of a tired, sick writer depressed by the death of his wife, one cannot thereby explain its plot.

It is this plot, as I have suggested, which has striking similarities to that of 'A Parasita Azul'. A young man (Tristão) is brought up in Brazil, but goes to Europe (Portugal, in this case), and there forgets the old couple who brought him up (Aguiar and Dona Carmo). He comes back, for reasons which are never made explicit but may well be simply financial, and falls in love with the other adopted child of Aguiar and Dona Carmo, Fidélia, the widowed daughter of a *fazendeiro*. They are married, and in spite of the hopes of the foster parents, leave for Portugal, where Tristão has a political career lined up for him (on his way to Lisbon, in fact, he is elected deputy to the Portugese *cortes*). It is a slender structure on which to build a 150-page novel, and it is true that, in spite of the minor characters, including one Osório, a successor for Leandro Soares, and the interest provided by the narrator, Conselheiro Aires himself, *Memorial de Aires* is not easy to read with pleasure; though that does not mean that it conveys nothing of value to those who persevere. The sense of desolation at the end, when the old couple who have so lovingly cared for Tristão and Fidélia are abandoned by them, hypocritically in Tristão's case at least, has no real parallel in Machado's fiction. At least Bento can still go to the theatre.

Common to 'A Parasita Azul' and *Memorial de Aires*, then, is a plot in which a wastrel comes back from abroad, and marries a girl who plainly in some sense represents Brazil,[17] and for whom he is in some sense destined. There is no question that Leandro or Osório are the rightful suitors, nor that the love between Tristão and Fidélia, like that between Camilo and Isabel, is real. Interestingly, *Memorial de Aires* has something of the same contradiction between plot and moral which infects 'A Parasita Azul': the plot is plainly about betrayal, yet the betrayers, as Aires the narrator insists, are admirable, delightful young people. The Wagnerian connotations of Tristão's name[18] convey something of the same conflict between all-powerful love and treachery.

Machado's return to this plot-form, and re-involvement in its contradictions, seem to imply that it has a certain independent power *as* a plot. It is not too difficult to see why. It clearly has its origins in the same national obsessions mentioned above, and which necessarily haunted Brazilian literature in the 19th Century. These stories, in their common plot, dramatise the contradictions which Brazil's real situation arguably imposed. Of the two suitors for the hand of the (female) essence, one is a provincial idiot, the other a foreign traitor: to idealise one or the other as a noble savage or representative of civilisation is unrealistic. Beyond any moral judgements we might feel inclined to make is the inevitable out-come of the situation itself. The conflict, we should notice, reflects itself not merely in the characters of the suitors, but equally in that of the central female character, who is both ideal and, possibly, self-seeking.

This conflict, whose terms are simple enough, is nevertheless not easily soluble: as with the *civilización/barbarie* opposition familiar in other contexts, and which it resembles in many ways, it is difficult to say which side is in the right. For a novelist as subtle as Machado, this could be an unexpected boon. He turned it into a dialectic whose shifting balances allowed him to explore reality without simplifying it, revealing complexities within a pattern which remains relatively simple in its major terms. If we look at the great novels—at least, *Memórias Póstumas de Brás Cubas, Quincas Borba* and *Dom Casmurro*—we can see that they all have at the centre of their plot a triangle which, with different emphases, falls quite naturally into the pattern outlined above ('foreign' traitor— 'ideal' woman—'national' idiot): Brás Cubas—Virgília—Lobo Neves; Palha—Sofia—Rubião; Escobar—Capitu—Bento. *Memorias Póstumas* follows the pattern of 'A Parasita Azul' most faithfully, by opposing the dilettante to the stupid, cuckolded politician. *Quincas Borba* shows, among other things, how an analysis of the rise of a capitalist can be fitted into the pattern. Palha (who has persuaded the gullible Rubião to buy the foreign knicknacks we encounter in the third chapter of the novel) is above all interested in linking himself to the import business, and so to foreign capital. This story of trickery and exploitation, Machado's greatest satire in the usual sense of that word, is very usefully seen as an opposition between two personalities, 'international' and 'provincial'—certainly, this fits the novel much better than any moral opposition between Palha and Rubião, who is a fool, not a saint. The opposition continues in Machado's greatest novel of all, *Dom Casmurro*. It may be, in fact, that its fascination is partly due to the unexpected weighting of the novel in the direction of the provincial boor, to whom Machado gives the narration, and indeed, to an unprecedented extent, the 'control' of the novel. If it seems inappropriate to describe this civilised, upper-class *carioca* as a provincial boor, that is a measure of what the novel, eventually, allows us to understand. Bento represents a ruling class cocooned in its own world, and mistrustful of what takes place beyond it; the stories it constructs for itself to explain that world are self-destructive as well as destructive of others. Machado's repeatedly-made observation of human envy and resentment, summed up in the description of Leandro Soares quoted earlier ('tinha o sestro aliás comum de querer quebrada ou inútil a taça que ele não podia levar aos lábios') is here taken to its logical conclusion.

This version of the development of Machado's plots is admittedly schematic, but it has the virtue of allowing one to see the structure beneath the irony; Sofia, to give only the most striking example, is not only an ambitious, ignorant and over-sexed egotist: she is also, in the novel's structure, the essence, the 'Southern Cross' which in the novel's last sentence Machado mockingly refers to. In its turn this structure depends, surprisingly enough, on the nationalist tradition which in fact Machado greatly respected in many ways. 'A Parasita Azul' and *Memorial de Aires*, separated by more than thirty years in which Machado wrote all his greatest fiction, witness the real strength of that tradition, even if in their cases the result is partial artistic failure.

8. *Larrea's Poetic Odyssey*—ROBERT GURNEY

Until the publication in 1969 of *Versione Celeste*,[1] followed, in 1970, by the Spanish edition *Versión Celeste*,[2] Juan Larrea's published poetry, for all its possible originality, had been scant. Until 1969 Larrea's poetry had been unavailable apart from those poems published in little magazines, mainly in *Grecia*,[3] *Cervantes*[4] and *Carmen*.[5] Diego's anthologies, containing twenty-five of Larrea's poems, have been the most lasting reminders of his poetry.[6] The publication in Mexico in 1934 of a private limited edition of fifty copies of *Oscuro Dominio* scarcely alleviated the problem of availability.[7]

The major part of Larrea's poetic output is contained within *Versión Celeste*, which begins with 'Evasión', a poem which announces the major themes of his work:

EVASIÓN[8]

Acabo de desorbitar
al cíclope solar

filo en el vellón
de una nube de algodón
a lo rebelde a lo rumoroso   5
a lo luminoso y ultratenebroso

Los vientos contrarios sacuden las velas
de mis carabelas

¿Te quedas atrás Peer Gynt?

Las cuerdas de mi violín   10
se entrelazan como una cabellera
entre los dedos del viento norte

Se ha ahogado la primavera
mi belleza consorte

Finis terre la   15
soledad del abismo

Aún más allá

Aún tengo que huir de mí mismo

The first poem, then, of *Versión Celeste* is 'Evasión' and the final poem, setting aside those placed by Vivanco in Appendix 4, is 'Sans Limites'.[9] Larrea placed these poems at the beginning and end of *Versión Celeste* with a purpose. They represent the limits of what he describes as the 'prelude' to a complex experience:

> 'Claro que este libro (*Versión Celeste*) no es sino un pequeño trozo de una experiencia excepcionalmente compleja, si no me engaño: su preludio.'[10]

In spite of this claim, *Versión Celeste* exists as a separate book of poems and, indeed, Larrea accepts that it may be studied in isolation from his later work and life:

> 'Mas por su carácter se presta a ser considerado en sí mismo, aparte de los que vinieron después.'[11]

The structure of this 'prelude' corresponds, in broad terms, with a period of spiritual change which Larrea underwent betwen 1919 and 1932, the dates of the first and last poems of *Versión Celeste*. This change will be seen to be an evolution from a state of non-being towards a state of being, a movement from a sense of the meaninglessness of existence towards a sense of integration within a meaningful universe, a meaningfulness the poet had never doubted but from which he had felt totally excluded. This evolution is marked by complex systems of images, such as those associated with darkness and light: blindness and sight, mist and sun, night and dawn. It is an inner journey, a fact that is announced by the opening image of 'Evasión':

Lines 1–2

Acabo de desorbitar
al cíclope solar

This image alludes to the myth of Ulysses who, after the battle of Troy, spent long years searching for his native land, Ithaca. One of the trials he underwent on his journey was his battle with Polyphemus, the one-eyed cyclops. Ulysses overcame Polyphemus by gouging out his eye. The verb 'desorbitar' means 'to gouge out the eye', 'la órbita' being the eye-socket. Ulysses eventually escaped from the cyclops' cave by assuming the name 'Nobody', an allusion, it will be seen, that relates to the final line of 'Evasión'.

The myth is introduced to present the dominant theme of *Versión Celeste*, that of the poet's spiritual Odyssey. It announces the beginning of a journey, a pilgrimage or quest for a lost native land, during which many obstacles have to be overcome before reaching the desired goal.

The image of the gouging out of the solar cyclops' eye symbolises a rejection of physical light, the light of the sun, of the senses. Referring to this image, Larrea stated: 'La fábula de Polifemo: la luz solar, la luz de los sentidos'.[12] In place of this light the poet will seek an inner light, a spiritual light. It is a rejection of the world of appearances and the cultivation of the inner landscape of the imagination, perceived in spiritual terms, in which the poet's journey towards a sun other than that which illumines external visible reality will take place. The trajectory will be a spiritual one but the goal is not the one familar to the Christian mystics. Although Larrea used their example as an inspiration and support, his path lay outside their established way to union with God. His destination, in other words, was not clear to him when he set off in the direction indicated in this poem.

It would be wrong to read into the opening image of 'Evasión' too precise a statement of Larrea's spiritual position. Larrea does not accept that at the time of writing the poem he was conscious of searching for God: 'Je cherchais vivre, la Vie dans sons ensemble, complète, totale.'[13] It will be seen, however, that Larrea's definition of Life was an intensely spiritual one.

Meditating upon this image, of the blinding eye, Larrea stated:

'L'âme a deux yeux, l'un qui regarde vers l'intérieur et l'autre qui regarde vers l'extérieur. C'est l'oeil intérieur de l'âme qui regarde dans le sens de Dieu et qui prend son être directement de Dieu. C'est sa véritable fonction. L'oeil extérieur de l'âme se dirige vers la créature et perçoit ses formes extérieures mais lorsqu' une personne se tourne vers le dedans et connaît Dieu, un terme de sa propre connaissance de Lui, et les racines de son être, il est alors libre de toute la création et il est en sureté dans le château de la Vérité.'[14]

This was Larrea's position fifty three years after writing 'Evasión'. At the time of writing 'Evasión' he was not consciously pursuing such an objective. He wrote 'Evasión' 'pour des raisons vitales'.[15] The image of the blinding of the eye was unpremeditated 'une chose spontanée—aller au-delà du réel—une tension surréaliste avant la lettre—au-delà de ce qui se voit, le monde immédiat des sens.'[16]

Larrea explored systematically the mystical concept of Light much later, in Mexico in the 1940s and in the United States in the fifties. In New York he was able to study the German mystic Meister Eckhart, supposed author of *Theologia Germanica*.[17] In Eckhart he found a similar concept to his own of the two eyes, one which sees the exterior world and the other which sees 'un monde intérieur, transcendental'.[18] Larrea's interest in the symbolism of the eye led him to explore the image within the context of an unpublished work on Light entitled *Noche en Cruz*,[19] written in Mexico in the 1940s. The image of the destruction of the eye became a commonplace in Surrealism, a fact noted by Larrea:

'¿Se ha dado cuenta del parentesco poético existente entre el desgarrón del ojo en "El perro andaluz" y las dos primeras líneas de mi poema "Evasión" de mayo de 1919?'[20]

A still of the eye-slitting scene appears in Larrea's *Del surrealismo a Machupicchu* together with a photograph of Victor Brauner's *Self-Portrait*, 1931, in which the painter depicts himself with one eye gouged out, and Picasso's *Dibujo a pluma, 3 de junio de 1938*, which is of a head with a dagger plunged into one eye.[21]

Regarding Larrea's use of the myth of Ulysses in 'Evasión' in 1919, which he employs again in the 1927 poem 'Balade de nos dents en or', (*Versión Celeste*, p. 144), he writes:

'Un dato para el enfoque del 'símbolo del viaje'. No sé si se habrá dado cuenta de que en el poema "Evasión" está presente Ulises tres años antes de que apareciese el libro de Joyce. Asímismo, el Ulises que figura en la 'Balade de nos dents en or' (1927) no tiene que ver ni remotamente con la novela inglesa que en aquella época yacía por completo fuera de mi conocimiento.'[22]

Lines 4–7

> Filo en el vellón
> de una nube de algodón
> a lo rebelde a lo rumoroso
> a lo luminoso y ultratenebroso

'Filo' is a gallicism, derived from 'je file', 'filer', 'to leave'. Given the title of this poem, 'Evasión', the idea of escape is suggested. Conventional Spanish would require 'Huyo' here but, as Larrea stated, *ultraísmo*, within which Larrea was writing in May 1919, demanded unusual words: 'mettre les choses un peu hors du vulgaire'.[23] Explaining this word Larrea commented: 'Filo, je file, je pars' adding that a secondary meaning was also possible: 'filer la laine'.[24] One is reminded of the 1914 poem, 'Yo':

> Hilo mis canciones con rueca de bruja. (unpublished)

'Filo en el vellón' continues the reference to Ulysses. After driving a burning stake into Polyphemus's single eye, Ulysses, and those sailors who had not been devoured by the giant, had to escape from the cave. Although blind, Polyphemus was able to block the entrance to his cave. Ulysses devised the idea of strapping his men beneath the sheep which Polyphemus kept in there. At day-break, when Polyphenus let his sheep out of the cave, the sailors managed to pass Polyphemus who was feeling only the backs of the sheep. Ulysses himself came out of the cave clinging to the fleece of a ram:

> 'A young ram chose I, the best that there was in the flock,
> And, grasping his back with my fingers, curl'd underneath
> His shaggy belly, and there, face upward, I hung
> Clutching his wonderful fleece most resolutely.'[26]

Larrea's association of the sun with the cyclops is not fanciful but has a basis in Greek mythology. Robert Graves, in his *Greek Myths*, writes, having traced the myth back to a Caucasian tale:

> 'Whatever the meaning of the Caucasian tale may have been,
> H. B. Cook in his *Zeus* (pp. 302–23) shows that the Cyclops'
> eye was a Greek solar emblem. Yet when Odysseus blinded
> Polyphemus, to avoid being devoured like his companions, the
> sun itself continued to shine. Only the eye of the god Baal, or
> Molosh, or Tesup, or Polyphemus ('famous') who demanded

human sacrifice, had been put out, and the king triumphantly drove off his stolen rams. Since the pastoral setting of the Caucasian tale was retained in the Odyssey, and its ogre had a single eye, he could be mistaken for one of the pre-Hellenic Cyclopes, famous metal-workers, whose culture had spread to Sicily, and who perhaps had an eye tattoed in the centre of their foreheads as a clan mark.'[27]

Larrea's sensitivity to the significance of the Ulysses/Polyphemus myth, the link between the Cyclops' eye and the sun, the fact that the sun continued to shine after destroying the eye—a symbolic rejection of an alien superstition and religion based on sacrifice, all of which harmonises with the themes of 'Evasión', can be explained by the fact that Larrea was familiar with classical literature. He had studied Greek (as well as Latin and Hebrew) as part of his degree in *Letras* at Deusto.

The image of this stanza describes a flight, in both senses, of flight from the sun, the 'cíclope solar' which has dominated the world of appearances in which the poet has been living, and of flight through clouds where there is resistance, 'lo rebelde', consonant with the poet's rebellion, a loss of peace, 'lo rumoroso', light, 'lo luminoso', which is accompanied by a deep darkness, '(lo) ultratenebroso'. Through the prefix 'ultra', used perhaps as a self-conscious act of identification with *ultraísmo*, there is a link with the 'aún más allá' of the penultimate line. The 'más allá' is characterised by darkness at this stage.

The reference to light, 'lo luminoso', is effectively cancelled out by the juxtaposition of 'ultratenebroso', yet the image of light is absolutely central to *Versión Celeste*. It is to light, 'la luz', 'la lumière', that the 'Tú' and 'elle/ella' of his poems frequently refer, since light is feminine in Spanish and French. Larrea's spiritual aspirations are translated, in *Versión Celeste,* by a constant invocation of light. His poetry reflects an aspiration towards a certain state of being, towards 'la lumière', an image of an essence lacking in the period during which he wrote the *Versión Celeste* poems but glimpses of which, albeit on an imaginative plane, occur in the later poems. In 'Evasión', 'lo luminoso' is negated by the ultra-darkness of which the poet is aware within himself once he closes his eyes to the light of the sun, the light of the physical world. However, it will be within this inner darkness that the poet will pursue the new light. San Juan de la Cruz in *Canciones del alma* ('En una noche obscura') explores this paradox, describing the light within his inner darkness in these terms:

> Aquesta me guiaba
> Más cierto que la luz de mediodía[28]

Defining his concept of light Larrea stated: 'C'est le pouvoir de voir, de voir une autre lumière. Cela se trouve déjà en 'Evasión'—un refus de la réalité physique du monde extérieur— aller au-delà, dans un autre monde, au delà des mondes sensuels. C'est la lumière mystique.'[29]

The full meaning of Larrea's mysticism, as applied to poetry, his 'Mística Lírica',[30] a concept he did not fully develop until after the 1926 manifesto *Presupuesto vital,* published in *Favorables París Poema,*[31] cannot be examined here.[32] The mystical tendency and temperament in Larrea are nevertheless active in 'Evasión'. It will not be until later that Larrea will reflect upon this tendency, after his break with Huidobro in 1926, and develop a poetic theory out of it. 'Evasión' was written upon impulse, without further elaboration (apart from the word 'belleza' q.v. below), and without a preconceived idea: 'Escribí "Evasión" en diez minutos.'[33] Spontaneous as it was, an irruption of subconscious wishes, 'Evasión' is viewed by Larrea as a clear statement of his aims: 'un enunciado de mis propósitos'.[34]

Lines 7–8

> Los vientos contrarios sacuden las velas
> de mis carabelas

The theme of the journey is now translated into sea-imagery. The difficulty of the journey is described in terms of ships being buffeted by unfavourable winds. The caravel was a fast light ship used between the fifteenth and seventeenth centuries. The image recalls the voyages of discovery of that period. Columbus, the Ocean, the New World are recurring themes in Larrea's prose works. He himself was haunted by the temptation of emigration across the seas to the New World or the South Seas. The description Larrea gives of the powerful effect Huidobro's poetry had upon him in

1919 mentions this tendency of his to dream of another world on the other side of the globe:

> 'Gerardo (Diego) acababa de leer 'Poemas Árticos' y traía copiadas a mano tres de sus composiciones: *Luna, Départ,* y una tercera que debió ser *Horizonte*—o si no, *Adiós*—.
> A mí esos poemas, pero sobre todo el primero y más sencillo de los tres, me sumió en una atmósfera enrarecidísima, como de campana psico-neumática, casi de ultra-vida, en acuerdo con la inmensa oquedad mental que había sentido muchas veces en mi adolescencia, haciéndome soñar con los antípodas—por no saber de otra región más apartada.'[35]

Larrea actually succumbed to his dream of the Antipodes in 1929 when he set off for the South Sea Islands with his wife on a journey which terminated, as it turned out, in Peru. This longing for another condition, the desire to escape an unacceptable way of life, which is central to Larrea's psychology, translated itself in 'Evasión' into a variety of images and statements. Explaining his statement that 'Evasión' was 'un enunciado de mis propósitos', Larrea stated, 'La ruta de Colón, en todos los órdenes, a las alturas de América [a reference to Larrea's visit to Peru] para perderse en el infinito'.[36] In 'Evasión' Larrea saw in 1972 a clear statement of his aims and the future direction he was to follow: the route of Columbus, the path of discovery, the search for a New World, on all levels, spiritual, poetic, moral and physical.

Line 9

¿Te quedas atrás Peer Gynt?

Having alluded to Ulysses and Columbus in the context of a rejection of an unacceptable world and the search for a better one, Larrea turns to a figure who represents the search for oneself, for one's salvation: 'Peer Gynt busca a sí mismo, quiere salvar a sí mismo'.[37] The question 'Are you staying behind Peer Gynt?' acquires powerful resonance within 'Evasión'. Ibsen's character, in his search for identity, enters the cave of the Old Man of the Mountain, King of the Trolls. In the second act of the play, the

Trolls attempt to persuade Peer to be like them. The Dovre-Master, for example, says:

> 'I'll scratch your left eye
> A little, to help you see oblique
> But all that you see will be rich and strange.
> Then I'll take the right one out completely.'[38]

Peer Gynt almost falls for the Dovre-Master's logic, quoting the Bible:

> If thine eye offend thee, pluck it out

Peer is tempted to stay in the land of the Trolls but finally escapes from them, in spite of the Troll maidens' cries of 'Tear off his ears, rip out his eyes'. This connects with the opening image of the blinding of Polyphemus. In line 9 Larrea is saying that he will not remain in a grotesque world among people of distorted vision. His identity lies elsewhere.

The allusion to Peer Gynt, however, lingers on. Lines 10–12 of 'Evasión' describe a storm. Peer Gynt had to pass through a storm at sea before regaining his native land. 'Evasión', line 13, describes the drowning of a woman. Peer Gynt rejected Solvejg's love but in the final act is redeemed by that love. *Versión Celeste*, it will be seen, describes a final redemption by a feminine figure, the personification of Light and Life.

The force of this reference to Peer Gynt, on the immediate level, is simply the statement that the poet will not hesitate to pursue his personal salvation by seeking an essence or meaning that will satisfy him. Nevertheless, the drawing of the above parallels between *Versión Celeste* and Peer Gynt's experience is inescapable.

Lines 10–12

> Las cuerdas de mis violín
> se entrelazan como una cabellera
> entre los dedos del viento norte

The fusion of disparate images in startlingly new similes and metaphors, practised by Huidobro, and cultivated by Larrea from 1919 onwards, is an aspect of the technical and imaginative freedom acquired from his contact with *ultraísmo* and Huidobro's poetry in that year. Here the strings of the poet's violin, a metaphor for his poetry, are compared with a head of hair being ruffled and twisted by the north wind, itself an image associated with the 'abismo' of line 16 and the image of flight into an unfamiliar region described in lines 3 to 7. It is an image of disharmony related to the description of his rejection of the *modernista* pursuit of Beauty contained within the following lines:

Lines 13–14

> Se ha ahogado la primavera
> mi belleza consorte

This image expresses the aesthetic change Larrea underwent in May 1919, an abandonment of *modernismo* and the cultivation of *ultraísmo*, an interpretation confirmed by Larrea: "Belleza, Beauté, c'est la femme, ma beauté, c'est à dire que je change ésthetique-ment: les choses qui étaient belles dans les poèmes modernistes, tout ça, c'est noyé".[39] "Evasión", then, is an affirmation of solidarity with the *ultraísmo* of 1919.

When 'Evasión' was first published in *Grecia* (No. xxxi Seville, 30 October 1919, p. 2) line 14 read:

> mi princesa consorte

In a sense, 'princesa' and 'belleza' both refer to *modernismo*, the princess being a *modernista* commonplace. However, Larrea had made the alteration prior to the poem's publication in *Grecia*. Cansinos-Assens, who was handling the poem, failed to make the desired change, which Larrea had made in June 1919, one month after writing the poem and four months before its publication. Regarding the change of 'princesa' to 'belleza' Larrea said: 'C'est assez bien dit, ça, mi belleza consorte se ha ahogado. Il y a une différence. Le changement avait été fait'.[40]

Lines 15–16

> Finis terre la
> soledad del abismo

The 'Camino de Santiago', in all its aspects, was a powerful source of inspiration for Larrea. For example, a pilgrim, having visited the shrine of Saint James in Santiago de Compostela, went on to the sea, where he gathered a scallop shell, 'la venera', the pilgrim's badge.[41] Having completed his pilgrimage within the known world, the pilgrim, curiously, went on to the coast and sat in contemplation of the sea:

> la
> soledad del abismo

It was as if their hymn 'Ultreja, esuseja, más allá, mas arriba'[42] and the spiritual impulse it expressed had remained unsatisfied by their pilgrimage to Saint James's shrine. Using poetic logic, Larrea links this action of the pilgrims with the Spanish monarch's support of Columbus's quest for a New World in 1492.[43] Finisterre, in Larrea's thought, is a 'spiritual concept', 'el concepto espiritual de Finisterre',[44]—symbolising the point beyond which lies the 'más allá'. It symbolises the boundary between known reality and the unknown. On the least metaphysical level, it was indeed, for Spanish consciousness at one time, the most westerly point for the traveller setting out from the Old World in search of the New. Metaphorically, it is an image closely associated with Larrea's profound desire for a fundamental change of his sense of reality and identity. It is the point where existence ends and essence begins. The explorer of this spiritual reality is, like Columbus, going beyond the outer-most limits of the known world. He is alone, 'la/soledad', and without the support of familiar physical reality, as if in an abyss, 'del abismo'. The splitting up of the 'la' from 'soledad del abismo', in lines 15 and 16, conveys the sense of a leap into the dark, a break, the leap of faith into the unknown.

Lines 17–18

> Aún más allá
>
> Aún tengo que huir de mí mismo

The final lines of 'Evasión' are an emphatic assertion of the poet's desire to escape the reality in which he finds himself. They do not say that an escape has been made but that it *must* be made. Like the majority of the *Versión Celeste* poems, this poem expresses an *aspiration* for another reality, not the actual achievement of it. Larrea sees "Evasión" as an expression of a non-physical death wish: 'El suicidio de mí mismo, sui-cidio [sic], mental, moral y espiritual'.[45] This was, of course, quite unrelated to physical suicide. Larrea's belief in life was too strong: 'Yo creía en la Vida, más allá de lo que llamamos 'vida' '.[46] The escape 'even from himself', longed for in the final line of 'Evasión', is an expression of his desire for a total transformation of the self, mentally, morally and spiritually. It calls for the demise of the old self, 'morir para despertar',[47] the awakening of a new self. Before that, in order to reach the Life from which he felt alienated, the poet had to undergo a psychological and spiritual metamorphosis. The road he chose to this greater fullness was poetry: 'la única manera era la poesía'.[48]

9. *Góngora and the Hyrcanian Tigress*—RICHARD HITCHCOCK

The lengthy passage in the *Soledad primera,* in which a *político serrano* traces the feats of sea-faring of the early explorers and inveighs against the despoliation of the Spice Islands, contains some enigmatic elements.[1] The change in subject matter from the preceding description of the calm and peaceful country scene is abrupt. So abrupt, in fact, is the change in direction that it seems as though Góngora is embarking on a new poem. The initial sequence in this new poem astonishes the reader with the vehemence of its sentiments. It is reminiscent, in the impact that it has on the reader, of a passage in the *Dedicatoria,* where the pastime of hunting is held up to ridicule. This sequence depicts, in the words of Jáuregui, a 'tremenda batalla'. The carcases of bears, victims of the hunt, made such cascades of blood that the waters of the River Tormes are stained the colour of coral. This is so exaggerated as to be absurd. Jáuregui considered that such a description did not bring credit to the dedicatee. 'Y assí no devía Vm. hazer tan gran caudal de que este príncipe andaba a caça, sino aplicarle otra ocupación o virtud ilustre i competente a tal senor . . .'[2] Regarded in the most charitable light, this massacre of animals masquerading as a hunt is an unconventional eulogy to a patron. Yet there is no trace of bitterness and no implied criticism in this passage. Góngora seems rather to take delight in the extravagance of his descriptions, revelling in the cries of outrage that will be forthcoming. A note of defiance is struck, here, at the outset of the poem and it is this note that Góngora takes up again in the speech of the *político serrano.* The impact that Góngora seeks to create is, I believe, in both instances, similar. Just as the sequence in the *Dedicatoria* sets the reader wondering why Góngora is apparently taking the noble pastime of hunting to task, so the *político serrano*'s speech is equally ambivalent. This hyperbolic writing is quite intentionally not sustained, so that when it recurs, it loses none of its enigmatic qualities.

In the passage under discussion, the *político serrano*'s speech comes unexpectedly after a quiet descriptive sequence, in which the emphasis is on pleasant nuances, muted emotions, and gentle courtesy. His opening words create, in consequence, a much more startling effect:

> '¿Cuál tigre, la más fiera
> que clima infamó Hircano,
> dió el primer alimento
> al que, ya deste o de aquel mar, primero
> surcó labrador fiero
> el campo undoso en mal nacido pino,
> vaga Clicie del viento,
> en telas hecho antes que en flor el lino?'

The implications of this are enormous, both in the immediate context and in the broader context of the poem as a whole. It is at first sight an unnecessary exaggeration to compare simple sailors with the infamous Hyrcanian tigress. The notion that they could have had anything in common is an arresting one. It is, however, crucial to Góngora's intentions that the two are linked in savagery. Góngora, I think, uses his classical knowledge with care here.

In Dido's speech to Aeneas, the reference is associated with both cruelty and treachery. Dido, despairing at Aeneas's lack of responsiveness, appeals to him as follows:

> 'nec tibi diva parens, generis nec Dardanis auctor, perfide,
> sed duris genuit te cautibus horrens Caucasus Hyrcanaeque
> admorunt ubera tigres.'[3]

The ferocity, cruelty and inhumanity of the Hyrcanian tigers, however this reputation was achieved, were well-known in classical times. Here Góngora evokes not only their traditional qualities, but also the belief that such properties were conferred on their offspring by their mothers. It seems as though Góngora bore the Virgilian context in mind in his use of the phrase 'dió alimento', which reflects Virgil's 'admorunt ubera'. The belief that, in cases where infants are suckled by animals, the foster-mothers pass on thereby their own qualities, was also widespread in the classical period.[4]

Góngora, then, openly following on a Virgilian precedent, is quite unequivocally making a monstrous comparison in which the epitome of ferocity in the classical world is shown to be reincarnated in the Spanish seamen who were engaged in voyages of commerce and discovery in the sixteenth century. The question of '¿Cuál tigre . . .?' requires an answer. Góngora is deliberately employing a rhetorical device here, demanding a response of his reader. The question requires the answer 'No—there never was such a tiger whose properties contaminated the hapless Spanish seamen'. Such a conception is beyond imaginative limits. Yet the emphasis is evidently on inhuman, bestial, cruelty. The reader is asked to believe that such qualities characterized the 'labrador'; this ploughman of the sea is 'fiero', just as the tigress is 'fiera'—the two are inextricably linked. The identification of 'labrador' with 'tigre' is neither simply a Classical echo nor an airy conceit. It serves to emphasise the horrific behaviour of them both, the Hyrcanian tigress responsible for devastation in her lifetime and for passing on her qualities of extreme savagery, and the mariner who has gone through uncharted seas. The clear inference is that these sailors wrought havoc where they landed and this havoc is tabulated in the verses that follow.

Robert Jammes sees the *serrano*'s speech and this introductory sequence, in particular, as written 'sur le mode de l'imprécation',[5] but it is not specifically couched as a curse. The principal effect that these lines have is to provoke the reader into a contemplation of the reasons for such a novel and unexpected comparison.

Quite typically, Góngora makes nothing more of the 'tigre fiera'/'labrador fiero' equation, but the image is exploited in subsequent lines in the verse. The verse concludes as follows:

'Más armas introdujo este marino
monstruo, escamado de robustas hayas,
a las que tanto mar divide playas,
          que confusión y fuego
al Frigio muro el otro leño Griego.'

After the initial hyperbole Góngora introduces his main subject, which is the boat, or the piece of wood that carried the sailors to foreign shores, but an intolerable slur is passed on the reputation of this boat. It is a 'mal nacido pino', thus introducing the note of malediction. The boat thenceforward becomes the villain of the piece. It is converted into a 'marino monstruo', responsible for more damage than the Wooden Horse. So the boat on which the Spanish mariners travelled, charting uncharted seas, or in pursuit of wealth, created as much havoc where they landed as did the Wooden Horse that brought about the fall of the city of Troy. Just as the Greeks inside the Wooden Horse burst out and slaughtered the beleaguered Trojans, so the sailors, by inference, plundered the distant shores. The theme of destruction thus predominates in this verse. A convincing picture of devastation is achieved, devastation through the medium of Nature's fiercest animal, the Hyrcanian tigress, devastation by man endowed with the same rapacious tendencies, devastation by fleets of ships armed to the teeth, and devastation propagated by the Greek assailants of Troy.

There are two interlocking themes linking the imagery in this verse, destruction and deception. The natural savagery of the tigress is bestowed on the sailors, but the destruction wrought by the marine-monsters is more heinous because it involves deception. Simple destruction becomes compound deception. Ships that ply the waters cannot be summarily censured for so doing. This is an evident absurdity, and one that Góngora would expect his readers to recognise, but ships whose crews behaved as deceitfully as did the soldiers inside the Wooden Horse that infiltrated Troy are to be condemned for their treachery.

Góngora is, I believe, suggesting a scale of enormity ranging from primitive ferocity to cruel deception and treachery. The link between the two is provided by the 'mal nacido pino'. These boats were constructed for the express purpose of wreaking havoc and destruction. There is thus a curse upon them.

Superimposed upon this imagery with its thematic links is a structural pattern. The sequence starts in Hyrcania and ends in Phrygia. Hyrcania and Phrygia were both ravaged. They were both the objects of slaughter and destruction, the one by tigresses, the other by bloodthirsty soldiers. These two lands were both in Asia Minor and both provide a framework for the verse, in which havoc is perpetrated by animals on man, and by man on his fellow-men. These lines then, suggestive of much incident, constitute an indictment, not of greed, not yet, but of man's deceitfulness and savagery. There is little more than a fleeting recognition of the age-old belief that there was a curse on the inventor of ships. Comparisons have been sought with Camões here but there are significant differences:

> 'Oh! maldito o primeiro que no mundo
> Nas ondas vela pôs con seco leño!'[6]

The rhetorical question in which Góngora couches a similar sentiment is far removed from the dogmatic utterance of Camões' venerable old man. The emphasis in Góngora's passage is not on the 'mal nacido pino', but on the Hyrcanian tigress. This is what arrests the reader's interest and provides the basis for Góngora's thematic development in the verse. This image, deliberately presented hyperbolically, predominates. The commonplace of the curse is subordinate to the embellishment of the initial image, and any serious intent imputed to Góngora in this verse is relegated with it.

What the reader is presented with in the *serrano*'s speech is not anti-commercial invective, nor a plea for a return to the values of the Golden Age. As Jammes points out, the attitude is an ambivalent one: 'Góngora condamne les navigations, et cependant il ne peut contenir son enthousiasme devant la découverte du Nouveau Monde.'[7] Man's unscrupulous plundering of primitive regions for commercial gain is deserving of censure, but the voyages of discovery are praiseworthy achievements.

Overweening desire may produce unwanted signs of bestiality in man, but Góngora, I am convinced, is not overtly censuring this. Summoning up a double echo of the *Aeneid*, and impregnating the verse with Virgilian resonances and couching these Classical sentiments in extravagant hyperbole, he is striving for the same effect that he achieved in the *Dedicatoria*. Sea-faring is no more attacked in the *serrano*'s speech than hunting is in the *Dedicatoria*. Góngora does, I believe, remind his readers that this speech is not to be taken at its face value in the few lines immediately after its conclusion:

> 'En suspiros con esto,
> y en más anegó lágrimas el resto
> de su discurso el montañés prolijo
> que el viento su caudal, el mar su hijo.'[8]

Here Góngora wryly draws attention to the *serrano*'s long-windedness, in the same breath revealing that the *serrano* had had a son drowned at sea on one of the expeditions. Such a juxtaposition would be unlikely if Góngora had intended to preach a serious message in the *serrano*'s speech.

Furthermore, the phrase 'anegó en lágrimas', is a deliberate, though muted, hyperbole, included, I suggest, to temper any definitive judgement the reader might have made in response to the *serrano*'s speech. Just as the reader has no grounds to read into this entire speech a forthright exposition of the 'ilegitimidad' of the Conquests, neither should his emotions be roused by the 'serrano' as an 'héroe épico que se ha retirado del mundo histórico de la épica'.[9] This phrase and these four lines call to mind Góngora's attitude. The speech has been an exercise in equivocation, an exercise which Góngora has clearly enjoyed. Just as he delighted in magnifying the carnage wrought by the hunt in the *Dedicatoria*, so he has taken pleasure, by employing similar methods and techniques, in constructing a sequence of equal mystification. His motives are characteristically withheld from the reader. The Hyrcanian tigress introduces a speech replete with obliquities. The preaching, such as it is, is couched in terms such that it cannot be taken seriously. Rather, the whole tone of the passage suggests restrained humour; the poet is mocking the reader who believes he sees his own and age-old prejudices mirrored.

10. A Work of John of Wales in Mediaeval Spain*
RUTH LESLIE

In late mediaeval Italy there were in circulation four translations to the vernacular of a moral treatise called the *Breviloquium de virtutibus*, of which twenty manuscripts survive.[1] It is a collection of *auctoritates* made in the second half of the thirteenth century by the Franciscan friar John of Wales (d. ?1285). His Latin works were widely known and used, but of the vernacular *Breviloquium* A. G. Little, who gave an account of his works, said in 1917 that 'there was evidently in Italy a large demand for this sort of thing among educated laymen in the fourteenth and fifteenth centuries—a demand which did not yet exist in other countries'.[2]

It appears that in the Catalan region, however, such a demand did indeed exist, as Little himself later became aware.[3] In 1930 P. Norbert d'Ordal published a Catalan version of the *Breviloquium*, a version which exists in three fifteenth-century manuscripts.[4] By the end of the nineteenth century it was already known that another, later, work by John of Wales, his *Summa Collationum*, had also been translated to a Hispanic vernacular.[5] In fact there were at least two versions in the late Middle Ages: one in Catalan of which four copies are extant, and the other, of which no full version remains, in Aragonese.

Three of the known manuscripts of the Catalan version are in Barcelona and one in Valencia. The first, a late fourteenth- or early fifteenth-century copy, is MS 92 in the Biblioteca Universitaria of Barcelona and came from the library of the Carmen Descalzo. The second, a fifteenth-century copy, is MS 265 of the Biblioteca Central (or Biblioteca de Cataluña) and comes from the Sánchez Muñoz family of Teruel. The third, *lo cual feu escriure Mossen Borra en la ciutat de Valencia, demorant ab lo Senyor Rey de Navarra* in 1438, was mentioned by Villanueva in 1851 after he had seen it in the Archivo del Palacio in Barcelona;[6] it was lost for many years but is now also in the Biblioteca Central, MS 2008. The fourth is in the Archivo del Reino de Valencia, MS Archivo del Real 660, bound under the title *Sequela del libro negro*. This last was made known by Manuel Dualde Serrano in 1947 in the *Anuario de la Historia del Derecho Español* XVIII; at the same time he published the prologue and list of chapters, but without having discovered who was the author. His article contains all that has been published on the Catalan version, which is entitled the *Suma de collacions o ajustaments*.

Manuscripts of the works of John of Wales exist all over Europe, and Spain is no exception: so far I have noted over twenty manuscripts containing one or more of his works in Latin, distributed among the Escorial, Madrid, Barcelona, Tortosa, Valencia and Vich; there is also one in Lisbon, and one in Palermo which apparently originated in Valencia. (None, however, of the twelve printed editions which appeared from 1470 to 1520 was produced in Spain.) The present distribution of the manuscripts does not necessarily reflect accurately their whereabouts in the Middle Ages, but it does suggest that in the late fourteenth and fifteenth centuries the greatest interest in the works of this author was shown in the Kingdom of Aragon. The existence of vernacular versions in this area seems to confirm this.

The Latin *Summa Collationum* or, as it sometimes appears in fuller form, *Summa Collationum ad omne genus hominum* is also known as the *Communiloquium* or the *Summa Collectionum*. Its appeal no doubt arose as much from the arrangement of the material and from the subjects chosen as from the size and range of the compilation. It is divided into seven parts, dealing with (I) the republic, (II) the diverse relations between people, (III) the instruction of people according to their various estates, (IV) the church and the ecclesiastical estates within it, (V) scholars and learning, (VI) those in religious orders, and finally (VII) death and preparation for it. Dualde gives a more detailed summary in his article on the Valencia MS. As can be seen, the work covers the field of moral instruction to all types of people in the various situations in which they may be,—wealth, poverty, sickness, health, in face of death . . . . Within each of the seven parts there are divisions called *distinctiones* which are in their turn subdivided into chapters each of which covers one aspect of the subject. For instance, the first *distinctio* is *De republica et informationes personarum ex quibus constituitur,* and the first chapter is entitled *Quid sit republica,* the second deals with how the republic is constituted, the third with how the laws should be ordered, and so on. Each chapter contains a collection of relevant quotations. The 'authorities' chosen range from the Bible and authors like the Church Fathers—St. Augustine, St. Jerome, St. John Chrysostome and others—to well-known names from the classical world and mediaeval tradition such as Seneca, Cicero, Valerius Maximus's *Dicta et facta memorabiliter* and John of Salisbury's *Policraticus,* which John of Wales appears to know as an author called Policratus.

Among the quotations are, for example, *Ecclesiastes* (X.16) *Vae tibi, terra, cujus rex puer est,* and St. Paul's rebuke to the High Priest as found in *The Acts of the Apostles* (XXIII.3): *Et tu sedens judicas me secundum legem, et contra legem jubes me percuti?* Many stories from Valerius Maximus are reproduced, including the well-known simile which likens the laws to a spider's web which only catches weak creatures, but allows the stronger to escape (VII, chap. ii).

The Latin work is built up from the quotations, with connective elements added by the author. The Catalan version is on the whole faithful to this pattern, but with the degree of licence and the amplification which are normal in mediaeval translation from Latin. A few short examples will give an idea of the translator's methods. (For the Latin I quote from the Augsburg edition of 1475, for the Catalan from the Barcelona University MS.)

In one case the Latin has:

> Certamen festinatum incendit lites. Et sequitur. Si sufflaueris quasi ignis ardebit.

Here the Catalan omits the word *sequitur:*

> baralla cuytada ençen foch e si hy bufes axi com a foch cremara e sy hi scups apagar se ha. (f. 176v.)

In another case the Latin has briefly:

> Apocal. i. Ego pater [=frater] vester & socius in tribulatione. Sunt enim socii multi in prosperitate: pauci in aduersitate.

Here the Catalan translation adds *scriu e diu* and the name John, offers an alternative for *prosperitate,* and amplifies *pauci in adversitate:*

> en lo primer capitol del Apochalipsi scriu e diu axi sent Johan: yo son Iohan frare vostre en tribulacio; car molts son qui volen

esser companyons en les prosperitats e en les consolacions, mes pochs son aquells qui vullen esser persones de tribulacions e companyons daquells qui les sostenen. (f. 173v.)

The Catalan version may add a degree of interpretation to the text. Thus, when the Latin gives

ad Gall. vi. Alter alterius onera portate,

the Catalan translation has

lo apostol ad Galathas vj.º capitol nos amonesta que portem la carregua lo vn del altre

and then adds

vol dir quens supportam los vns als altres. (f. 173v.)

Additions of this type do not appear to be very common in the translation, and one may suspect that such an interpretation as this or the one quoted below incorporates a gloss found in the Latin manuscript used by the translator. However, I have not yet found such a manuscript.

A longer insertion is found where the Latin quotation from *The Song of Solomon* speaks of sixty strong men around the bed of Solomon. The Catalan version adds the following:

Salamo es Ihesu Xrist car aquest es mes que Salamo, lo lit de Salamo es la sgleya de Deu, Car aci jau Jhesu Xrist e segons la humanjtat e segons la diujnitat en lo sant sagrament del altar. (f. 283v.)

To give some idea of the relative qualities of the University MS and MS 265 of the Biblioteca Central, here is the latter's version of the same passage:

Salamo significa Ihesu Xrist, car aquest es mes que Salamo glorios en la sgleya de Deu, car açi jau Jhesu Xrist segons la homanjtat e segons la dignjtat en lo sagrament dell altar. (f. 271v.)

This short passage is reasonably representative, and one can say in general that these two manuscripts differ in orthography and to some extent in wording (*Salamo significa / Salamo es*, etc.), while each also contains different and independent mistakes. In this passage, the reading in the Valencia MS is *car beus que aquest es mes que Salamo, don lo llit aquest glorios de Salamo* . . . ; for the rest, this and MS 2008 of the Biblioteca Central give the version of the University MS with only slight variations.

As a final example of the Catalan version here is the beginning of the prologue, which in Biblioteca Central MS 265 begins:

> Com lo doctor o preycador dell eua [n] geli a sauis e a lechs sia deutor menant lo selvador a el que preych lo euangeli a tota creatura ab curosa diligencia deu be studiar per so que sapia amonestar no ten solament en preycacio comuna e general ans encara en cotlesio familiar e priuada, segons que amonesta lo sauj aclesiastich . . . (f. 1r.)

The other manuscripts give the error *a pechs* for *a lechs*, and the variants *lo saluador a ell manant* for *menant lo selvador a el*, *deu studiar per tal que* for *deu be studiar per so que*, and *collacio* for *cotlesio;* Biblioteca Central MS 2008 also has *preycacio continua* for *preycacio comuna.*

A much deeper study would be needed to establish the relationship between the four manuscripts. However, it looks as though they represent two branches of a single manuscript tradition, one of which is formed by Biblioteca Central MS 265, and the other by the remaining three manuscripts.

As well as the wording, the content of the prologue is interesting. In an age which appreciated collections of material and which made wide use of 'authorities' in sermons and in writing, it is not surprising that this work was found useful; but John of Wales was not merely concerned with sermons: his purpose was rather to arm the teacher for all eventualities in conversation. He emerges as a thoughtful man as well as widely-read, and one who understood teaching as involving far more than simply preaching sermons.

We know that copies of the *Summa Collationum*, in Latin, were indeed possessed by the priests and other learned men for whom it was written. For example, in 1381 we find two copies among the possessions of Ramón de Farrés, Abbot of Ripoll;[7] in 1437 En Joan Calvo, the incumbent at Bordó, bequeathed a copy to Domingo Galindo, a priest who was accompanying the bishop of Tortosa;[8] and in 1461 the work figures among the books of Antonio Bon, canon of Valencia.[9] Nevertheless, the *Summa Collationum* did not belong exclusively to priests and monasteries. It appears in Latin, for instance, in 1468 among books of the nobleman Juan de la Geltrú being sold at auction;[10] in Catalan it figures among the possessions of Mateu Novella, merchant, in 1423,[11] and in 1493 among those of Antoni Jaume Ça-Pila, a citizen of Barcelona.[12] This last came of a family which played an important part in the political life of the city, and his library reflects a particular interest in matters of government.

Although John of Wales was not writing specifically within the tradition of literature directed towards the instruction of princes and governors, it seems that in the Kingdom of Aragon his work was associated with this type of literature. The first part of the work, on the republic and government, probably gave the *Summa Collationum* a wide public in this area and especially in the cities of Barcelona and Valencia, since there was a keen interest in theories of government there in the fourteenth and fifteenth centuries.

We learn of interest in this aspect of the *Summa Collationum* by the early fourteenth century from a letter written by a notary of Zaragoza, Juan de Prohomen, to Jaume II: he tells him that at the request of the prior of Zaragoza he has completed work on a book *quo ha nompne çomuniloquio,* and draws his attention to the similarity of its content to that of the speech he has heard the king make to the Cortes of Zaragoza about *la cosa pública.*[13] The work figures elsewhere in the Aragonese royal correspondence: notably, in 1367 Pere III orders a translation of the *Summa Collationum* for the queen, like the one made for him but in a larger hand and to be completed as soon as possible, and in 1372 and 1373 he asks for the return of the copy which he lent to the Bishop of Valencia *per trelladar* and which he now needs.[14]

In the more literary world, Eiximenis thought highly of John of Wales: among other works which should be in the library of every good citizen he recommends *la summa de collections e diverses altres obretes que feu frater joannes gallensis del orde dels frares menors.*[15] Eiximenis himself made considerable use of John of Wales' work in his *Dotzè del Crestià,* and in the *Regiment de la cosa pública* (1483) which he later incorporated in the *Dotzè*. In fact, the extracts mentioned earlier from *Ecclesiastes, The Acts of the Apostles* and Valerius Maximus all occur also in the *Regiment* (chap. xi), which begins like the *Summa collationum* with a chapter on *Què és cosa pública* and deals with many of the same subjects.

The same extracts mentioned occur in a pre-1396 Aragonese text, the *Rams de flores* (Escorial MS Z-I-2, ff. 105–250), written for the Grand Master of the Order of St. John of Jerusalem, Juan Fernández de Heredia. This text makes no mention of John of Wales, but is in fact largely a selection from and reordering of material from the *Summa Collationum*.[16] It is closely related to the Catalan version, and shows similar variations on and amplifications of the Latin. For example, the passage quoted earlier from *The Song of Solomon* includes the interpretation given by the Catalan text in its fullest form:

> et salamon es ihū xp̄o et guardat que esto es mas que salamon et el lecho de esto salamon es la iglesia de Dios porque Ihesu Xristo aqui iaçe segunt la humanitat et segunt la diuinitat en el santo sagramento del altar. (f. 167v.)

However, the Aragonese is not always an accurate translation or copy, and it contains some curious equivalents for the Catalan: *su fiio como saben* (f. 135v.) corresponds to *su fill Absolon, el vil del adultre* (f. 146v.) to *el vll del adultre, sierpes a los piedes* (f. 154v.) to *serps aspides*, etc.

Finally, it is interesting to note the possibility that Heredia may also have possessed a complete Aragonese version of the *Summa Collationum:* in an inventory of Alfonso el Magnánimo in 1417 there appears an Aragonese *Summa de collacions* (item 25), with three figures in the opening ititial, one of which *te .i. spasa al coll e .i. creu de sent Johan al costat esquerra*.[17] In some of the manuscripts which we know to have been written for Heredia he is portrayed in an opening initial with the cross of his Order on his breast. We may, then, speculate on the possibility that this book was originally one of his.

Much work remains to be done on John of Wales. Here I have merely brought together a few of the widely scattered facts to indicate the place occupied by his writing in fourteenth- and fifteenth-century Spain. He was one of the scholars of the Latin Middle Ages whose work touched vernacular literature at various points, and whose contribution to the cultural climate of the times was not inconsiderable.

11. First-person to Third: an Early Version of Gabriel Miró's Las cerezas del cementerio—IAN R. MACDONALD

Gabriel Miró's *Las cerezas del cementerio* appeared in 1910, after a troubled gestation of at least seven years. He wrote to a friend in September 1910:

> Le confieso que me ha entristecido este libro. Ya sabe V. que *Las cerezas del cementerio* fue concebida hace muchos años. Creí que llegaría a trazar una novela toda trémula de emoción y muy mía. La escribí con grandes dificultades, sin sosiego ni tiempo; y ya, casi al término del segundo tomo, me exigió el editor que los redujese a un volumen de 300 páginas. La mutilación ha sido dolorosísima; y la hice rápidamente, y conturbado por enfermedades de mi mujer y de mis hijas, y por agobios de faltriquera que envilecen el entendimiento.[1]

But before this 'mutilation' there had been another transformation for on 5 August 1907 Miró published in the *Heraldo de Madrid* a 'fragmento de una carta' that is clearly an early version, written in epistolary style, of part of Chapter 18, 'En la cumbrera', of *Las cerezas del cementerio*.[2] Perhaps, one speculates, the bulk of the book previous to the heart-attack and death of the hero Félix, was first written as an epistolary novel. After all, Miró's first novel, *La mujer de Ojeda*, was formally an imitation of Valera's *Pepita Jiménez*, a part-epistolary novel, and much of Miró's earliest writing of any length is either narrated in the first person or from the point of view of a single character of autobiographical derivation. The epistolary style was an obvious, if outmoded, choice.

Internally, too, *Las cerezas del cementerio* suggests epistolary origins. The novel opens with the hero leaving Barcelona, thus allowing for a series of letters to a confidant left behind. From then until his heart-attack Félix is almost constantly on stage.

95

Sometimes we are given the narrator's point of view, mostly we see through Félix's eyes, and only very rarely do we have an inside view of any other character.

But there are several other points of interest to this fragment. Not only does it offer clues to the understanding of *Las cerezas del cementerio*, a much-misunderstood work, and evidence about the development of Miró's narrative methods, but it is also of interest for the theory of the novel in general. Kafka's *The Castle* was initially written in the first person and then rewritten in the third. The manuscript survives and has been studied by Dorrit Cohn.[3] That and the present passage from Miró appear to be the only known cases of a rewriting from first to third person where the original survives. In the case of Jane Austen's *Sense and Sensibility*, for instance, nothing remains of the epistolary version which preceded it.[4]

The *Heraldo de Madrid* text is as follows (I have added the marginal numbers for reference purposes):

LAS CEREZAS DEL CEMENTERIO

Fragmento de una carta
del libro que, con dicho título, se publicará pronto.

De Félix a ****

1   ... Estábamos en un ventisquero, mirando al abismo, cuando toda la inmensidad se estremeció con gritos de desgracia. Los ecos de las montañas los recogían y tornaban pavorosos; parecían baladros y ayes de las almas en pena de las consejas. Latían ferozmente los perros del ganado y nos llegó como una brisa música de esquilas. Nos miramos. El guía se precipitó hacia una barranca; yo corrí hacia un puerto para escrutar otros horizontes; pero allí sólo estaba la calma del crepúsculo. Regresé al paraje de antes; vi lejos la silueta del guía y oí su voz que me gritaba algo en valenciano. Escuché ansiosamente.

2   ¡Una sierpe había matado a una vieja!

—¿Pero está ahí la muerta?—le voceé exaltado.

—Sí, aquí en lo hondo; acaba de morderla y ya se ha hinchado que espanta.

3   Fui con entusiasmo. Avanzaba raudamente, tropezando en las hiendas, rodando algunos trechos por roquedales lisos enormes. ¡Yo, que había pisado, vacilante, bajo la gloria del Sol! ¡Qué comienzo de noche en las Sierras! El deseado día de las cumbres terminaba lúgubre. No es que me regocijase; yo no quise la muerte de la vieja. ¡Claro! Ni se me había ocurrido; pero sucedida, la acogía con avidez de contemplarla.

4   —¿Pero cómo esa vieja podía caminar a estas horas por estos abismos? ¿Qué hacía?

—¿Cuál vieja?—dijo espantado el guía.

—La muerta.

—¿Qué muerta? Si no hay ninguna vieja: es una ovella, una ovella.

5   Y quedé como si entonces supiera el infortunio. ¿Adónde huye la piedad de nuestra alma? Me recorría la sangre heladamente. Me lastimaba de la cordera y odiaba la vieja. He de decirlo: hubiera preferido que la emponzoñada fuese la *vieja*. Una hez abyecta de crueldades habita en nosotros. ¡Qué torcedura tan honda en mis entrañas para mover siquiera el retoñar del remordimiento! Y yo continuaba impasible por lo ajeno y malquiriéndome a mí mismo. Estaba seco y árido como si fuese de cal. ¡Qué me importaba que pudiera resbalar en mi alma una gota de compasión por la víctima fingida si aquélla no era mía, sino exprimida de la voluntad trabajada! Cuando de esta manera logro el bien, creo que alguien fuera de mí es quien lo hace.

6   En la hondonada vimos al viejo pastor, postrado como una ruda talla de la peña. Cerca estaba la oveja; tenía los brazuelos recogidos hacia su pecho, doblados en la suprema sacudida del dolor; las patas, rígidas; el cuerpo, como un cuero inflado, monstruoso, y la testa, fina y estrecha, vuelta y alzada por la angustia; en sus ojos, abiertos, se congelaba luz postrera de la tarde.

7   El viejo no nos habló; ya no gritaba.

Negreaba la cañada; el rebaño posábase esparcido, resignado a no sentir la tibieza olorosa del aprisco.

Nosotros alumbramos las linternas. Dijimos adiós al pastor; él no contestó. Una esquilita quedó tembloreando en la paz.

8   Surgía blandamente de las Sierras como una escintilación sonora, y sobre el rizado canto de los alacranes, la queja de los

autillos y el latidito fino, argentino, de los grillos, se oía siempre
el gañido prolongado de un perro.

En la era de La Olmeda hallé gente que iba en mi busca. Y
apenas pisaba el umbral del casón, mi tía, que estaba en la
salita de las andas del Cristo, exclamó suspirando:

9   —Por fin, por fin! ¡Bendito sea mi Dios que te ha traído!—Y
se me acercó afanosa mirándome—. Vienes mustio o me lo
hacen los ojos; ¡yo no sé qué te veo, Félix!

—¡Pero cómo ha de estar sino rendido!—añadió la criada
Petra.

Esta fámula me dice siempre lo mismo. Estaban sus ropas
lisas, sin la belleza de un pliegue. Yo la odié.

10   Tía Lutgarda volvióse al aposento pronunciando:

—Si subes, avisa a Ricardo que le aguardamos para rezar.

Yo sabía que así me suplicaba lo mismo a mí, y esquivo,
casi mazorral, contesté:

—Yo no puedo.

Tía Lutgarda suspiró; después suspiraron Petra y los
maseros . . .

* * *

11   . . . Me alcé y salí al balcón. Y la noche me amparó
maternalmente; la veía sin ficciones, más grande; olía a árboles
verdes y jugosos, a tierra regada. Por el enjuto cauce de mi
alma entró borbotante el dulce y perdido caudal de lástimas y
amores generosos. Me bañaba un contento bueno y lo amé
todo: Petra tenía razón; yo estaba rendido siempre que ella lo
decía; Mosén Pablo, ¡qué bronco, qué de barro era!; pero acaso
esto fuera llaneza, simplicidad, casi de apóstol primitivo, que yo
no supe comprender; Ricardo, ¡cuán humilde! ¡Oh, la vieja y la
cordera mordidas por la sierpe! Mi viejecita. ¿Y yo anhelé su
muerte? Y me avisaba a mí mismo, oyéndome: 'Si no, si no ha
habido vieja muerta ni viva por aquellos breñales'; pero yo vieja
veía extraviada en la sierra, retorciéndose . . .

12   En el silencio se difundía la musitación de los que oraban.

¿Por qué no habí yo también de bajar y rezar con ellos
todo cuanto quisieran? ¡Sí, sí, hagamos felicidad en las almas;
no desperdiciemos la exquisita ternura de estos momentos tan
sencillos!

Y bajé saltando la escalera, cuyos peldaños de tablas crujieron estrepitosamente en la paz de su ámbito.

13   Tía Lutgarda, Ricardo, Petra, la familia campesina, hasta el abuelo, salieron espantados.

—Es que también vengo a rezar—grité alborozadamente.

Y pasamos a la sala de las andas; me dieron la mejor butaca. Mi tía alzó sus ojos conmovidos al Señor de la Cruz: '¡Oh, mi Dios! Ya reza él también', murmuró como si orase. Los demás me observaban.

14   —Félix, que te oigamos—me dijo dulcemente—. Y prosiguió: 'Mater purísima ... Mater castísima ...' Y contestábamos: 'Ora pro nobis, ora pro nobis ...'; y este susurro subió a las vigas como un homo.

Yo me creía mecido arrullado por una cigarra lejana.

15   Siguió una salve al Corazón de María. Yo veía figuradamente toda la plegaria. Escuchaba los sollozos de hombres y mujeres; sobresalían los gemidos de los niños infortunados; era en un valle angosto, pero sin confines a lo largo, poblado por la Humanidad, que iba vertiendo hebras de llanto; envuelta en el manto infinito del cielo la Virgen volvía a nosotros sus ojos dulces y tristes de hebrea y contemplaba el paisaje inundado. Yo me sentí caer y sumergirme en las aguas de lágrimas. Una mano me contuvo; era la de Petra, porque, efectivamente, me caía de la butaca.

16   —Cene y acuéstese; está usted durmiendo; ¡si es que está usted rendido!

—¡Yo qué he de dormir ni he de estar rendido!—protesté iracundo.

—¡Qué lástima! ¡Qué lástima—decía Ricardo.

Tía Lutgarda, contristada, miraba al Señor de la Cruz ...

Gabriel MIRÓ

This appeared in 1907, the novel itself following in 1910, with further editions in 1916 and 1926, the latter being the basis for modern editions and the text we shall generally use for comparison. There also exists a facsimile of the manuscript of the 1910 edition. The variants from all these stages are given by Pedro Caravia in the *Edición conmemorativa*, and these make it clear that the process of development is almost exclusively a linear one, so that Miró's revisions of his text can be followed step by step.[5]

When we compare the *Heraldo* fragment with the final version the overall improvements are clear. The descriptive diffuseness of 1, for instance, is replaced by something much tauter, while the new 'se sepultaron entre montes' draws together the emotional implications and, linking with 'ánimas en pena', hints at a Dantesque descent of self-exploration, complete with guide. In 5 the whole paragraph, which relates ironically the dialectic of Félix' self-analysis, culminating in his shady use of a Kantian ethical distinction, is reorganised around images of trees and sap that were only hinted at before. In 15 the sequence of Félix nodding off during the *Salve, Regina* is enriched by references to the mountains, scene of the day's excursion, to a miracle of the sort Félix playfully delights in recounting (the servant is appropriately renamed Teresa), and by the imperfects of 'resbalaba', 'caía', 'sumergía' that give an inside view. The whole piece becomes a parody of one of those Ignatian Spiritual Exercises Miró practised at school in Orihuela.

Along with this greater coherence in the final version there is an impulse towards understatement. Narrative redundancies, for instance, disappear, best exemplified in the transition from the hills to the house, where the whole of 8 is removed and obvious details cut. Connective description gives way to definition of the emotion of the moment. But already it is becoming impossible to ignore the influence of the change of narrator. The deletion of narrative redundancies is an improvement in a general way, but it is encouraged by the new mode of narration. Where the epistolary mode demanded an explanatory transition, modern narration thrives on scenic presentation with narrative ellipses that rely on the reader's expectations.

Similarly, when Miró, again moving towards understatement, deletes the overobvious, he both enlivens the text and responds to the change in narrative mode. In 5 these two sentences are removed: 'Y quedé como si entonces supiera el infortunio', and 'y yo continuaba impasible por lo ajeno y malquiriéndome a mí mismo'. Already over-categorical, they become even more so in the new situation, for whereas at first they reveal the letter-writer presenting himself to a friend, seeking, even while being self-critical, for ultimate approval and sympathy, in the later version these sentences would become authoritative. Yet the complexity of the situation is revealed by the fact that the first sentence is modified but retained in the third-person manuscript version, only to be deleted later, while the second sentence is at once replaced by the final '¡Y nada!'. Miró is here struggling to prevent his ironical analysis of Félix succumbing to the authority of the new narrator.

So a simple-seeming matter of altering pronouns and verb-endings turns out to have complicated results. The epistolary novel offers a unique set of relationships. The correspondent has written with a particular reader in mind, he plays to his audience. We, the real readers, are only eavesdroppers on the performance, and have to remember constantly the presumed reader or narratee. Further-more the distance between the recording letter-writer and the experiencing letter-writer, though strictly limited, is always there and measured in time. And the letter-writer's standpoint in time is renewed with each letter. He does not know how the story will develop, while the real reader acquires a constantly renewed relationship with the letter-writer. Félix comments on himself with a particular reader in mind and looking back on events from a day or a few days later. It is this pattern of relationships that is totally altered in the rewriting, for the third-person narrator sets before us a world that is made present to us.[6] We now accompany Félix as the events unfold and our view of him is established by narrative distance and angle. But in the epistolary novel it is time that matters. We are dealing with a 'real' past, that of the letter-writer Félix: the distances between him and the experiencing Félix are established in terms of time. This contrast is one reason why narrative ellipsis can be developed in the third-person version: the epistolary mode is reportorial, the later version presentational.

It is worth at this point briefly mentioning Dorrit Cohn's examination of Kafka's manuscript of *The Castle*, in which the narrative was originally in the first person, but then amended to the third. Cohn finds that 'the "Urschloss" which is hidden under Kafka's corrections is an anomaly: a potential third-person novel miscast in first-person form'.[7] She finds that as a first-person narrative the original 'Schloss' lacks precisely that sense of a span of time between the moment of experience and the moment of narration that is usual in first person narrative and that we find implied in the *Heraldo* fragment. When Kafka saw the incongruity and made the simple grammatical changes that allowed the third person to take over, his narrative breathed more easily. But Miró starts from an orthodox first person who exists in time. He has to struggle to achieve a new narrative coherence and the struggle leaves its marks.

One of the marks is that whereas Kafka's novel has a uniform narrative stance, in *Las cerezas del cementerio* the distance between narrator and hero constantly varies. Often this is effective. The *Salve, Regina* sequence (15), for instance, is in the *Heraldo* version given entirely from Félix' point of view. In the final version it starts with the narrator, moves into an inside view of Félix' dream, and then zooms out to an intermediate position: '¡Es que estaba cayendo de la butaca!' seems to hover between narrator's comment and representation of Felix' thought. With hindsight we can see the origins of this delicately poised situation that allows the joke to be shared by Félix and the reader.[8]

A crucial device in this fluctuating narrative distance is free indirect speech.[9] In his mature work Miró, like most modern writers, used this device frequently and fluently. He would have picked up the technique from earlier writers: Galdós and Alas, for instance, use it often. But there is a curious connection between the first to third-person transition and the use of FIS. The minimum alteration needed to transform a first-person narrative to a third-person one is to adjust the pronouns and the personal verb-endings. The tenses can remain as they are: 'Yo corrí hacia un puerto' becomes 'Félix corrió hacia un puerto'. Here an externally-observable fact is recounted and the conversion is straightforward. But as soon as Félix reports his own consciousness, the minimum morphological changes tend to create FIS: 'No es que me regocijase; yo no quise la muerte de la vieja. ¡Claro! Ni se me había ocurrido; pero sucedida, la acogía con avidez de contemplarla' becomes: 'No es que se regocijara: él no quiso la muerte de la vieja; ¡claro!, ni se le había ocurrido; pero, sucedida la desgracia, la acogía con avidez de contemplarla' (3). Félix' account of his own feelings becomes an account in which the distance between narrator and character fluctuates and in which a new and powerful irony operates because of what Pascal calls the 'dual voice' of FIS: we hear at the same time the voice of Félix and the voice of the narrator mimicking and judging.[10] While the irony of the first-person version was rooted in Félix' unreliability, now it emerges from the gap between the reliable narrator and Félix.

The *Heraldo* fragment already contains elements of FIS (notably '¡Una sierpe había matado a una vieja!') but in the third-person version there are four longer passages involving various degrees of its use: 3, 5, 11/12, and 15. The transformation is usually more complex than in the example above, but the general rule holds: FIS can be created or developed simply by changing person, but keeping the tense, which now serves not to indicate past time, but narrated thought.

I have argued elsewhere that Félix is treated ironically, but this has not been the traditional view.[11] The first consequence of examining how FIS developed in these passages is to confirm that we are indeed dealing with Félix' views, once reported by himself to a friend, but now ironized in a new way by their presentation by a narrator. And if this is the case here it could well be the case throughout the bulk of the novel. The failure of critics to see this must be due to Miró's uncertain grasp of narrative technique, itself largely due to the difficulties of controlling the transformation. This sense of a struggle is confirmed if we look at further details.

In FIS the system of tenses and persons is usually that of indirect speech. What are we to make then of this: '¿Por qué no había él de bajar y rezar todo cuanto les pluguiese? ¡Hagamos felicidad en las almas!' (12). As usual Miró has left the tenses alone and the final result has the air of FIS. But things are not so simple. The first-person version is already in effect FIS. In the first sentence the letter-writer reports his thoughts of a little earlier. In the second he makes a general comment that conveys his mood at that time, a comment which he endorses when he writes the letter. The present tense 'hagamos' is therefore plausible. When the third-person narrator takes over, the 'dual voice' of the first sentence is emphasised and the second sentence—first-person plural, present tense—becomes distinctly odd: a sentence that represents Félix thought (surely it cannot be the narrator's) but without any linguistic indicator (except the exclamation marks) that this is so. By looking at the *Heraldo* fragment we can see how it happened, but it is not surprising that many readers fail to prise Félix and his narrator apart. Miró himself hesitated over the problem: in the manuscript version, the earliest in the third person, the whole paragraph is in quotation marks.

The point would be trivial if it were isolated, but in 5 we find '¡Adónde huye nuestra piedad!' and 'es que duerme siempre en nuestras entrañas.' Logically these seem to be the narrator's words, even though they were originally Félix'. And in 15, even more

confusingly, 'la Virgen(. . .) volvía a nosotros sus ojos.' Even when
we recognise that the 'nosotros' reflects the words of the *Salve,
Regina* ('Turn . . . thine eyes of mercy towards us'), the narrator
appears to be sharing the dream with Félix. Yet Miró revised the
novel fastidiously several times and we are again forced to the
conclusion that the narrator's distance from Félix fluctuates from
moment to moment, reflecting Miró's own ambivalence towards
the self he explored through all his early heroes. The affectionate
irony comes and goes.[12]

But is it right to assume that most of the novel was originally
epistolary? There is certainly no great obstacle. There is some
material that would have had to be added to an epistolary version,
and, since Félix dies, the last three chapters could never have been
his letters. But the bulk of the novel could have been. Proof is
impossible, but there are linguistic suggestions that together make
a strong case:

1. Among the many exclamatory sentences in the novel in
which it is hard to distinguish whose voice we are hearing is this
especially ambivalent one: '¡Oh Señor!, ¿por qué para sentir estas
lástimas y ternezas necesitamos darnos enteramente a la tierra, a la
melancolía de un río y techarnos de cielo y sentirnos amados?'
(*OC*, 380). From the context this looks like FIS but the first-person
plural present-tense verb once again means that there is no
indicator left other than the opening exclamation.[13] An epistolary
origin would be the simplest explanation of how Miró reached such
ambiguous situations.

2. Two apparently straightforward errors of transformation:
'¡Que pensaría, qué sentiría cuando viniese aquí mi tío Guillermo!'
(*OC*, 351), and '¡Nuestra Olmeda!' (*OC*, 339), which can now only
be construed as direct speech with the quotation marks omitted,
but which look like epistolary hangovers.

3. Frequent doubt over the voice we are hearing: 'Y todos estos
menudos soliloquios quizá se los motivase el no hallarse en el
huerto' looks like narrator's comment, but the passage concludes:
'Sí; debía de ser lo romántico y tibio de la sala y la inquietud por la
pérdida del gustoso retiro lo que le inducía fingirse sediento y
atormentado de idealidad . . .' (*OC*, 330). The 'sí', a FIS indicator,
suggests that this is Félix' self-analysis. The confusion is serious as
it matters whether Félix is aware that he is 'fingiendo'. Again the
epistolary hypothesis offers an explanation.

4. Unusual sequences of tenses: 'La compasión acuitaba al viajero. Es que imaginaba que al otro día viviría lo mismo la doncella, y siempre. En invierno, las acacias, desnudas, atormentadas, se doblarán por los vendavales, que hacen temerosos baladros y arrebatan las serojas' (*OC*, 357). The passage continues with presents and futures, clearly representing Félix' thoughts as he looks down on the village he has just left. At the end the reverie is concluded with: 'Todo se lo fingía Félix.' The tenses are effective but unusual: proper FIS would require pasts and conditionals. But the tenses are as they would have been in the letter version: Miró has surely simply transcribed the original, replacing 'me' with 'al viajero'. The example reveals precisely the narrative stance of the letter-writer. He can give us either a report of past events or his present views. Here he would report feeling troubled and then naturally fall into the present tense to give his view of the situation of 'la doncella' Isabel as it continued to be at the time of writing.

5. In the parts of *Las cerezas* that could not have been derived from Félix' letters, there are no cases of unexpected first-person or present-tense verbs. The FIS that is used is quite orthodox.

Taking these points together—they are only examples—it seems likely that the novel was indeed substantially first written as an epistolary novel. In parts it was heavily rewritten and added to, in others it was simply transformed. No overall interpretation of the novel can be adequate unless it allows that where there is room for doubt we are generally following Félix' consciousness in all its twists and turns. That consciousness is treated sympathetically but ironically by a narrator who fluctuates in his distance from or identification with Félix, and that affectionate irony of presentation in turn ties in with the ironic design of the novel which gives us Félix as a parody of Don Quixote.

There is one final area for reflection. Miró used FIS very early: it occurs in *Hilván de escenas* and frequently in *Del vivir*. Yet the possibility suggests itself that the rewriting of a whole novel, *Las cerezas*, from first to third person, served to develop Miró's later more skilful and extensive use of the device. This very tentative notion is perhaps only worth mentioning because of the striking parallels found in Pascal's *The Dual Voice*. Among his three early examples of the use of FIS, Goethe came to *The Elective Affinities* after the epistolary *Werther*, Büchner used diary material for his *Lenz*, and, above, all Jane Austen rewrote *Sense and Sensibility* in the third person from her epistolary *Elinor and Marianne*. The last parallel is remarkable, being the best, and perhaps only (apart from Miró), known example of an epistolary—third person conversion.

One of the delights of Jane Austen's writing is her subtle use of FIS. As Pascal puts it: 'It is astonishing that so rich and sure a use of free indirect speech is to be found in Jane Austen's novels, when she had so slight a tradition to build on.'[14] Others have echoed this sense of wonder allied to the mystery of the sources of the nineteenth-century development of FIS. Is it not possible that one element in Jane Austen's development of FIS was her work on transforming epistolary texts? Mimicry is one foundation of FIS, and the burlesques in Jane Austen's *juvenilia* reveal that she always had a rich sense of mimicry, but we also find that if we follow B. C. Southam's proposed chronology, the first work after the *juvenilia* was *Lady Susan*, an epistolary novel, followed by the lost *Elinor and Marianne*, also in letters, and the likewise lost *First impressions*, the basis for *Pride and Prejudice*, which Southam believes may also have been epistolary.[15] Only after all these would Jane Austen have finally rejected the outworn epistolary form and set about turning *Elinor and Marianne* into *Sense and Sensibility*, her first major third-person narrative.

Since everything between *Lady Susan* and *Sense and Sensibility* is lost only speculation is possible, but it does appear that the *juvenilia* and *Lady Susan* contain almost no clear-cut FIS, while it flourishes in *Sense and Sensibility*. It seems just possible that, beside Jane Austen's talents for mimicry and burlesque, and beside the pressures of the social fabric and the imperatives of her art, we might place the lessons learned in the labour of transforming epistolary novels as sources of her delightful command of FIS. And since Jane Austen stands at the point in the history of fiction where the epistolary novel collapses, to be replaced by the beginnings of modern narrative, Miró's anachronistic conversion job might even suggest a small contributory factor in the largely unexplained nineteenth-century rise of FIS.[16]

12. *The Ode to Francisco Salinas*—TERENCE O'REILLY

When Menéndez y Pelayo wrote about the Ode to Salinas in his *Historia de las ideas estéticas en España*, he described it in the words of Milà y Fontanals as 'bella paráfrasis cristiana de la estética de Platón', and he affirmed that its medieval souices iay in Plotinus, Boethius, the Pseudo-Areopagite and Bonaventure.[1] Since then the patient work of scholars such as Spitzer and Rico has revealed that the classical and Christian notions of harmony which inform it are remarkably diverse and complex.[2] Improved knowledge of the poem's background, however, has not made its interpretation any easier: on the contrary there exist strong differences of opinion about the nature and causes of the ecstasy it describes.

For some, including Dámaso Alonso, the climax of the ode is an experience of union with God described in verses 5 to 8;[3] and Professor Woodward has argued that 'the resonances in this poem . . . are Christian and not pagan'.[4] For others, however, it is about an aesthetic experience; the thought behind it is classical; and it is not mystical in the Christian sense at all. Fr Angel Custodio Vega, the editor of Fray Luis, has defended this view in forthright terms: 'En toda esta poesía no hay el menor asomo del cielo o de cosa espiritual, sino un éxtasis estético, sublime y deleitoso, como toda contemplación de la naturaleza en sus manifestaciones de grandeza y hermosura . . . Todavía es muy pronto para los traspasos místicos'.[5]

Some who hold the latter view also argue that Fray Luis was not a mystic, and quote in evidence a passage from his commentary on the *Canticle* in which he expressed misgivings about writing on mystical experience:

> Est enim magna res, et plane supra hominis vires, et denique ejusmodi, ut vix possit intelligi, nisi ab iis, qui eam non tam

107

doctoris alicujus voce quam ipsa re, et suavi amoris
experimento a Deo didicerunt, de quorum numero non esse
me, et fateor et doleo.[6]

These words, it is true, express an unsatisfied longing for full union
with God, but it would be mistaken to conclude from them that
Fray Luis was not a mystic. In the Middle Ages, and in the
sixteenth century, another term for mystical prayer was contemplation, and as Ruth Burrows, a recent writer on the subject, has
pointed out, contemplation can be bereft of what Fray Luis calls
'the sweet experience of love': a contemplative may be conscious
only of dryness, or of nothing, and may even be unaware that his
prayer is mystical.[7] Furthermore, a longing for union has always
been considered central to contemplative experience. In the
monastic tradition of the Middle Ages contemplation was defined as
a yearning for the life of Heaven, and this eschatological image
certainly informs the great poems of Fray Luis.[8]

However, the interior life of Fray Luis (about which we know
little) is not really pertinent to the interpretation of his writings, for
in a work of the imagination an author is not confined to describing
his personal experience. Fray Luis' own words bear this out:
despite his misgivings he did attempt to describe 'the sweet
experience of love' in his commentary on the *Canticle* and
elsewhere.[9] The appropriate question is not 'Was he a mystic?', but
'Do his poems draw on images and themes associated traditionally
with contemplation?'. In the *Ode to Salinas* there are, I believe, three
motifs which indicate that its subject is mystical prayer. They
concern music, wisdom and friendship.

I

In medieval spirituality a connection was often made between
contemplation and music. It was well expressed by Richard of St
Victor, an Augustinian recommended by Fray Luis as an authority
on union with God.[10] In the *Benjamin Major* he advises the
contemplative who cannot pray to summon a minstrel:

> At this psalmody and spiritual harmony the contemplative
> soul accustomed to spiritual experiences will begin to
> dance . . . and leap up as it were towards spiritual being and
> be raised up above the earth and all earthly things and pass
> over wholly in ecstasy of mind to the contemplation of
> heavenly things.[11]

Emilio Orozco has shown that this tradition was well known in sixteenth century Spain, but he does not believe that it informs the poem, for he does not consider Fray Luis a mystic.[12] However, if we make no assumption about the poet's spiritual life, we find that the poem recalls the tradition clearly.

The ecstasy described in the poem is inspired by two musicians and is described in two stages. The first verse alludes to Salinas playing. Line 5 implies that he is playing a keyboard instrument, and we recall that he was famed as a Cathedral organist. The three verses that follow note the effects on the poet's soul. His memory is restored (verse 2), he comes to know himself (verse 3), and he is caught up into heaven (verse 4). Verse 5 introduces a second musician, God himself, the great artist, who is playing a lyre and whose church is the Universe. The three verses that follow describe the effects: union (verse 6), and rapture (verses 7, 8).

The organ and the lyre were both associated specifically with contemplation. A passage in the *Book of Kings* tells how Elisha, when asked for a prophecy, summomed a minstrel: on hearing the music he began to prophesy (IV Kings 3:15). This text was interpreted to mean that music could dispose a soul for contemplation, and the instrument supposed to have been played was the Old Testament lyre or psaltery. The medieval tradition was summed up by Denis the Carthusian:

> Eliseus videns sibi lumen propheticae gratiae non fulgere, voluit se ad illud per elevationem animi praeparare: ideo fecit psaltem coram se ludere et cantare, quoniam melodia illa cum laude Dei ad elevationem disponit, praesertim in quibusdam, qui ex naturali dispositione ad hoc magis dispositi sunt: quorum nonnulli ex discantu et consonantia melodiae celerrime et intense moventur ad fletum, compunctionem, et contemplationem.[13]

The tradition survived into the period of the Counter Reformation. In a commentary of 1623, for instance, a Jesuit exegete who lectured at Alcalá described Elisha's rapture in terms that resemble the poem:

> Cum caneret psaltes ad musicos numeros, soporati sunt Helisaei sensus, et animus magis a corporeis impedimentis solutus, sicut in somno contingit, seipsum ad coelestium rerum contemplationem afflatumque divinum excitavit.[14]

He also drew a parallel between Elisha and St Francis who, according to legend, was caught up in ecstasy on hearing a lyre.[15]

In the Middle Ages it was the organ, not the lyre, that accompanied the singing of psalms, and after the Council of Trent the organ was the only instrument permitted within a church. Commentators on *Kings* often pointed out that Elisha's experience prefigured that of later contemplatives whose prayer was accompanied by an organ:

> ... non erat aliquis modus quo anima sua ab exterioribus curis
> rediret ad seipsam quam per armoniam: ideo fecit quod
> caneret citharista coram eo. Et ista fuit intentio Ecclesiae
> ordinantis varietatis cantuum in divinis officiis, et organa
> musica, ut variae armoniae diversimode corda hominum ad
> devotionem incitent.[16]

These traditions would have been familiar to Fray Luis and his circle, and it may well be that his poem was intended to call them to mind. In his treatise on the Incarnation he writes that music has a natural power to raise the soul to heavenly things[17] and in the *De Musica* Salinas himself argues that music can dispose a soul for contemplation:

> Religiosiores autem a musica nos reddi manifestum est: valde
> enim erigimur ad rerum caelestium contemplationem
> modulationibus et canticis quae in templis audiuntur, quod in
> sacris solennibus experimur in quibus maiori cum artificio et
> suavitate cantatur.[18]

We do not know when the poem was composed, and we cannot be certain that it alludes to the *De Musica*, or vice-versa, but clearly it draws on a body of ideas quite familiar to the small group of friends among whom it first circulated.

II

One name given to contemplation in the Middle Ages and in the sixteenth century was 'wisdom'. Peter Lombard associated it with the gift of wisdom bestowed by the Holy Spirit, and his teaching was developed by St Bonaventure and St Thomas.[19] In the first Spanish manual for contemplatives, the *Exercitatorio de la vida spiritual* (1500), the reader is urged to pray for the wisdom that 'comes down from above' (Jm. 1:17; 3:15, 17),[20] and the commentaries of St John of the Cross often describe contemplation as 'sabiduría secreta'.[21]

In the *Ode to Salinas* wisdom is an important theme. The first effect of the music, described in verses 2 and 3, is to teach the poet self-knowledge, or wisdom in the Socratic sense. Such knowledge of self is but a prelude to the vision of God, described in verse 5. The image of the divine Musician, which had classical roots, was commonly applied in Patristic writings to the wisdom of God, who brings all the elements of the Universe into harmony:

> Just as a musician, tuning his lyre and skilfully combining the bass and the sharp notes, the middle and the others, produces a single melody, so the wisdom of God, holding the universe like a lyre, draws together the things in the air with those on earth, and those in heaven with those in the air, and combines the whole with the parts, linking them by his command and will, thus producing in beauty and harmony a single world and a single order within it.[22]

The interdependence of these two kinds of wisdom, Socratic and contemplative, was established for the West by St Augustine, whose *Soliloquium* was quoted by St John of the Cross to make the same point:

> de esta noche seca sale conocimiento de sí primeramente, donde, como de fundamento, sale estotro conocimiento de Dios. Que, por eso, decía San Agustín a Dios: 'Conózcame yo, Señor, a mí, y conocerte he a ti'; porque, como dicen los filósofos, un extremo se conoce bien por otro.[23]

In the *Ode* the poet does not merely behold wisdom; he is united with it (verse 6) and called into rapture (verses 7 and 8), and the experience transforms him. His interior senses are awakened to the Divine reality, and mortified to the world, and he is enabled to appreciate the true relation between the worlds of sense and spirit (verses 9 and 10). In a word he becomes wise.

As verse 10 reminds us, the gift of wisdom is imparted to him as he listens to the playing of Salinas, whose keyboard touch is described in line 5 as 'sabio'. This reference to wisdom is one of many parallels and contrasts between verses 1 and 5. In the context of the poem as a whole it implies, I think, that Salinas himself has experienced the close union with God that transforms the poet.[24] His wisdom, moreover, is associated with his playing, an image that helps to explain his effect on Fray Luis, whose ecstasy is inspired not simply by music but by the music of his friend, music that is 'rare' ('extremada' 1.4) and even 'divine' (1.6).

III

The connection between contemplation and friendship was a recurring theme in the writings of St Augustine, for whom the loving union of friends could itself lead to an experience of union with God. It has been argued by Professor Woodward that this tradition informs the poem. His evidence lies in verse 9 interpreted as a eulogy of Salinas who, in line 42, is termed 'gloria del apolíneo sacro coro'. In line 43 'amigos' should read 'amigo' (as it does in some editions) for the friend 'loved above all treasure' is Salinas. These words, it is argued, would be 'exaggerated and almost unpleasant flattery' if it were not for the context of spiritual friendship that links the love of a friend to the love of God.[25]

This reading of verse 9 is, however, open to question. In all the early manuscripts and editions line 43 reads 'amigos' not 'amigo', and the singular form was not introduced until 1761. This modification, moreover, shortened the line from 7 syllables to 6, and as a result it does not scan. Mayáns y Siscar, who made the change, justified it on the grounds that it was appropriate: 'El original dice amigos. Pero debe leerse *amigo*, porque habla con Francisco de Salinas'.[26] However, if Salinas already enjoys the experience the poem describes it makes better sense to suppose that he is not included in the general invitation of verse 9. It is also unlikely that he is being praised in line 42, which probably refers to the angels who stand in the presence of the Lord: they are the choir of Apollo whose glory is the 'aqueste bien' of line 41, union with God. It was indeed conventional to compare the angels in Heaven with contemplatives on earth: the image occurs in the *De Musica* itself.[27]

But although Professor Woodward's interpretation rests on evidence that is unconvincing, it includes a profound insight into the poem that may be justified on other grounds. Salinas is mentioned only twice in the *Ode*, at the start and at the end, but between these two points there are several lines that call him to

mind and that imply a deep spiritual friendship. The substance of
the poet's ecstasy is a transforming vision of the relation that
should exist between the worlds of sense and spirit. To convey this
he constantly alludes to the interplay between the five senses of the
body and the corresponding senses of the soul.[28] On occasion, as in
verse 10, all the senses are mentioned together, but usually the
poem focuses on two. One is the sense of hearing, as might be
expected, the other is the sense of sight, and from the start the two
are closely linked. In verse 1 the striking description of the change
in the air and in the light is a reminder that Salinas was blind: 'he
can hear his music but not see its effects'.[29] Knowing this shapes
one's interpretation of the verses that follow in which the soul's
experience is described as a recovery of spiritual sight. In verse 2 it
is said to recover the memory of its origin and identity, and this
process is described as an illumination: the soul is 'enlightened'
('esclarecida' 1.10). The type of darkness it has left is mentioned in
verse 3: excessive love of passing beauty, a form of spiritual
blindness. This healing of memory and reason leads in verse 5 to
the cleaving of the will to God, described as the opening of the
interior eyes to a vision. When, in verse 9, the poet reflects on his
experience, he remarks that now 'todo lo visible es triste lloro'
(1.45), meaning 'visible' to the physical sense.[30]

These references to sight indicate that the musician, and his
affliction, are never far from the poet's mind. They also convey the
theme that true vision is interior and spiritual; its corollary, that
physical blindness does not really matter, was doubtless a
reassuring message for one who could not see. And this lesson is
mediated to the poet by Salinas himself, a crucial paradox that
takes us to the poem's heart: the musician exemplifies the truths
that his music helps to reveal. By the way in which he plays Salinas
mediates spiritual sight to a dear friend because, though physically
blind, he is spiritually wise, a contemplative like Fray Luis
himself.

13. El concepto de novela cortesana y otras cuestiones taxonómicas—A. PACHECO-RANSANZ

La literatura narrativa española de los siglos XVI y XVII se clasifica y estudia normalmente en función de unas categorías novelescas establecidas ya en aquellos siglos y adoptadas y definidas en el siglo XIX por una crítica de orientación historicista. Se trata de una taxonomía bastante simple en apariencia, pero útil y cómoda, cuya nomenclatura nos es harto familiar: novela pastoril, libros de caballerías, novela morisca, novela picaresca y novela bizantina o de aventuras al estilo de la *Historia Etiópica* son términos corrientes en cualquier manual de historia literaria.

Los sucesivos cambios de orientación en la crítica de los últimos años, y particularmente la importancia que se ha concedido al análisis formal de los textos, han obligado a revisar y a redefinir aquellas mismas categorías segun principios teóricos distintos; esta tarea, sin embargo, se ha llevado a cabo sin alterar substancialmente la nomenclatura tradicional, cuyos términos han adquirido así una ambigüedad y plurivalencia de sentidos que invitan a dudar de su utilidad real para fines taxonómicos.

Piénsese, por ejemplo, en los múltiples valores dados al concepto de novela picaresca y se comprenderá la legitimidad de esas dudas. La serie de definiciones propuestas para despojar al término de sus connotaciones históricas y transformarlo en un signo lingüístico de carácter más universal y de una intención crítica más precisa no han invalidado, teóricamente, su uso específico para la clasificación y definición de los textos españoles; en la práctica, sin embargo, han llevado a conclusiones francamente paradójicas y desconcertantes. Ateniéndose a una u otra de aquellas definiciones, unos críticos han excluído de la clasificación tradicional el *Lazarillo*, otros han negado al *Buscón* la factura propia de las obras con que Quevedo quiso hermanarlo, y finalmente no han faltado quienes, con criterio más liberal, han calificado de picarescas obras que sólo por forzada analogía podrían compararse al *Guzmán*. El *Guzmán de Alfarache* siendo en realidad la única de las tres obras que dieron origen y nombre al género cuya legítima pertenencia al mismo no parece haber sido todavía seriamente disputada.

El caso de la novela picaresca, aunque el más obvio para ilustrar el problema de que tratamos, dista de ser rara excepción. Otros términos de la nomenclatura generalmente aceptada han sido sometidos más o menos rigurosamente a parecida reevaluación crítica, con semejantes resultados. Un caso interesante y singular es el de la llamada novela cortesana, término que sólo indirectamente puede ser asociado a la nomenclatura tradicional, pero que por sus connotaciones críticas y por su creciente popularidad merece particular atención. El concepto de novela cortesana fue inventado hace escasamente medio siglo por González de Amezúa y tardó bastante en ser aceptado e incorporado al contexto taxonómico que estamos estudiando; poco a poco, sin embargo, ha ido cobrando carta de naturaleza y hoy empieza a ser término familiar en los manuales e historias literarias, y blanco seguro del comentario crítico. Yo mismo he expresaso en otro lugar mis dudas sobre su valor taxonómico, pero 'de sabios es el corregirse'.

Influído quizá por la definición tradicional de la novela picaresca, pero partiendo del concepto de novela costumbrista y apoyándose en los criterios histórico-sociológicos de la crítica decimonónica, González de Amezúa definió la novela cortesana en función de la condición social de sus protagonistas, la localización urbana de los relatos y el ambiente erótico de la acción. Estas características le permitieron agrupar sin gran esfuerzo un buen número de textos del siglo XVII difíciles de catalogar en otras categorías, justificando así el acierto inicial y el valor práctico de su invención crítica.

El concepto de novela cortesana posee quizá un valor taxonómico mucho más preciso del que su propio creador le concedío, y del que luego habremos de ocuparnos. De momento, permítaseme simplemente afirmar que el termino 'cortesana' encierra una riqueza de matices literarios y culturales que hacen de él un término particularmente afín a aquellos propios de la nomenclatura tradicional, y la creación de una nueva categoría novelesca así bautizada no sólo proporcionó un adecuado y necesario complemento al sistema taxonómico tradicional, sino que dio además a éste una congruencia y armonía sumamente sugestivas.

El valor potencial del concepto de novela cortesana para fines taxonómicos, sin embargo, corre grave riesgo de ser drásticamente reducido y alterado por algunas de las nuevas definiciones propuestas para el mismo, las cuales, al atender exclusivamente al aspecto formal y estructural de los textos, excluyen de aquella categoría novelesca varias obras que por sus características generales se acomodaban perfectamente a los criterios propuestos por el inventor del término. Dada la heterogeneidad formal que la definición de González de Amezúa permitía en el contexto de dicha categoría, no es de extrañar esa reacción de la crítica contemporánea; pero al mismo tiempo es preciso señalar una cierta incongruencia en esta última al adoptar para sus fines un término ya sobrecargado de connotaciones críticas que, en apariencia al menos, resultan totalmente ajenas a una categorización de carácter formalista.

El uso de una terminología preestablecida sólo se puede justificar, a mi parecer, si para su adopción pueden aducirse razones suficientes que permitan establecer una relación lógica entre los términos adoptados y los criterios taxonómicos que se apliquen para la clasificación de la materia definida por dichos términos. Postulado al que la crítica moderna no parece haber prestado mucha atención cuando libre y gratuitamente se ha adueñado de la nomenclatura tradicional.

Toda nomenclatura aplicada con fines taxonómicos es, en principio, el producto lógico de unos criterios teóricos determinados, y el resultado de un fenómeno histórico-lingüístico en virtud del cual se produce una significativa modificación en el campo semántico de la terminología elegida, que pudo ser inicialmente arbitraria, para convertirla en vehículo apropiado de las ideas implícitas en aquellos criterios. La sutil concordancia que este proceso dialéctico establece entre los signos lingüísticos de que se compone aquella terminología y los principios teóricos a los que dichos signos remiten es, precisamente, lo que hace de una nomenclatura cualquiera instrumento útil para una clasificación realmente significativa. La ausencia de dicha concordancia reduce el sistema taxonómico a proposición arbitraria, y consecuentemente equívoca.

Teóricamente parece posible prescindir de las coordenadas histórico-lingüísticas en que se produjeron los conceptos y terminología propios de una nomenclatura establecida para convertir ésta en instrumento de otros sistemas taxonómicos, que es hasta cierto punto lo que hizo la crítica decimonónica y ha hecho la más reciente con la terminología taxonómica de la novela de los siglos de oro. En la práctica, sin embargo, esta fácil y cómoda solución se paga con la polivalencia y latente ambigüedad necesariamente implícita en los términos así adoptados. Los términos propios de una nomenclatura taxonómica no son signos lingüísticos de carácter convencional y susceptibles por lo tanto a nuevas y variadas definiciones. Las connotaciones semánticas de esos signos lingüísticos, determinadas por el proceso antes aludido, seguirán persistiendo implícitas siempre que los signos se den en un contexto de intención afín a aquél del cual fueron tomados—en nuestro caso el contexto del lenguaje propio de la crítica e historia literarias,—puesto que, quiérase o no, su campo semántico seguirá siendo definido por las mismas coordenadas.

Para ser eficaz, un cambio verdaderamente radical en los criterios taxonómicos aplicados a un sistema de clasificación cualquiera debiera pues ir acompañado o de una ruptura total con cualquier nomenclatura preestablecida, o bien, si es que ello fuera posible, de una reevaluación de dicha nomenclatura que tuviera en cuenta el proceso dialéctico entre la evolucion histórico-lingüística de los términos adoptados y los diversos criterios teóricos que, directa o indirectamente, fueron la causa de dicha evolución.

Ni la crítica decimonónica ni la más reciente pusieron en práctica tales principios para la clasificación de la novela de los siglos XVI y XVII cuando libremente adoptaron la nomenclatura ya establecida por el uso que de ella hicieron aquellos mismos textos. Ahora bien, aún si quisiéramos tildar de gratuita y arbitraria la adopción de dicha nomenclatura sin haberla sometido a la revisión antes prescrita, no por ello podría dejar de sorprendernos el hecho mismo de que tal 'arbitrariedad' se haya podido producir sin resistencia aparente y eficaz por parte de la crítica en general. La incongruencia del fenómeno obliga necesariamente a buscarle una explicación, y puesto que, obviamente, nos resistimos a aceptar como principio que la crítica literaria sea esencialmente gratuita y arbitraria, sólo cabe imaginar que aquella nomenclatura poseía, efectivamente, una riqueza de matices que la hacía susceptible a múltiples y diversas aplicaciones; matices que la crítica moderna habria sabido intuir sin sentir la necesidad de exponer en forma explícita.

Para probar esta hipótesis sería necesaria una cuidadosa reconstrucción del proceso de cambios semánticos a que ha sido sometido cada uno de los términos de aquella nomenclatura para adaptarlos a los diversos sistemas taxonómicos en que ha sido empleada; pero para mostrar su plausibilidad debiera bastar el simple análisis de las connotaciones críticas implícitas en dicha terminología considerada en su contexto original. Dedicaré pues el resto de mis comentarios a señalar los terminos de referencia que, a mi parecer, debieran servir de marco a dicho análisis, y señalaré, como simple hipótesis, algunas observaciones provisionales que del mismo parecen seguirse.

Los términos más característicos de que seguimos sirviéndonos para la clasificación de la narrativa española renacentista y barroca, y que ya fueron adoptados y consagrados por los autores y público de aquella época, son, indudablemente: libros de caballerías—o novela caballeresca,—novela pastoril, novela picaresca y, permítaseme añadir, novela bizantina o de aventuras, si bien esta última no fue designada así, sino aludida siempre por referencia a sus modelos clásicos, Heliodoro y Aquiles Tacio. De estas cuatro categorías conviene subrayar, ante todo, su persistente presencia en todos los sistemas taxonómicos que se han sucedido desde aquella época a nuestros días, y la intención crítica y valor taxonómico con que fueron investidas desde el primer momento, que son mucho más precisos y menos arbitrarios de lo que a primera vista pudiera parecer.

Dejando aparte el caso de la novela bizantina o de aventuras, de la que trataré luego, notemos que el significado corriente y campo semántico normal de los otros tres términos taxonómicos invita, en principio, a suponer que nos hallamos frente a un sistema de clasificación basado en criterios sociológicos, según el cual se habría elegido como término de referencia la condición social de los protagonistas de los relatos: caballero, pastor o pícaro. Aunque lógica, tal suposición podría tildarse fácilmente de anacrónica, pues parece impropio atribuír a la teoría y práctica literaria unos criterios y una intención que no corresponden ni al pensamiento filosófico ni a las circunstancias culturales de aquellos siglos. No conviene, a pesar de ello, descartar esta coincidencia más o menos casual entre aquella terminología y unos criterios familiares a la crítica moderna, puesto que ella, aunque fuera superficialmente, podría explicar ya por qué dichos términos pudieron ser fácilmente asimilados por la crítica decimonónica, la cual, al tomar como punto de partida la novela costumbrista, prestó siempre gran atención a la condición social de los personajes novelescos.

Es necesario señalar, además, que la connotación sociológica, pese a lo que acabamos de indicar, se halla realmente implícita en la nomenclatura que estamos examinando, pero no en el sentido que le dio la crítica decimonónica ni en el que podría darle una crítica de orientación marxista, sino, como luego demostraremos, subordinando lógicamente el elemento sociológico a unos principios críticos de carácter formal que, en la teoría literaria de la época, postulaban una relación causal entre la naturaleza e intención de un texto, la condición social del protagonista y la estructura y estilo del relato. Esta relación implícita entre los términos taxonómicos y el aspecto formal de los textos explicaría, por otra parte, por qué la crítica formalista ha podido también apropiarse sin difficultad de un sistema taxonómico que, aunque por razones diversas, conducía a resultados esencialmente afines a los que dicha crítica persigue.

Dicho de otro modo, es necesario conceder, para entender el fenómeno que analizamos, que la presente ambigüedad y plurivalencia de sentidos de la nomenclatura taxonómica que nos ocupa existía ya, potencialmente, en la terminología original; pero es también necesario subrayar que esa ambigüedad y plurivalencia quedaban allí trascendidas y superadas por la relación lógica y consciente que la teoría literaria de la época estableció entre el significado propio y normal de cada uno de los términos y su valor funcional en el contexto taxonómico a que fueron aplicados; relación que la crítica posterior ha tendido a ignorar o minimizar, y cuya existencia y naturaleza intentaré demostrar a continuación.

Según los principios mismos que antes propuse, para comprender y justificar el alcance y valor taxonómico de la nomenclatura que estamos examinando es preciso partir de la teoría literaria renacentista, puesto que sólo en ella podremos descubrir el campo semántico inicial que se atribuyó a cada uno de los términos, y las connotaciones críticas que pudieron determinar su ulterior evolución.

Para llevar a cabo este examen, y por razones que inmediatamente se comprenderán, conviene precisar en primer lugar el concepto mismo de novela, tal y como en aquel momento se entendía el tipo de narración que hoy bautizamos así, y que en los siglos XVI y XVII, todavía en periodo de gestación, era un género huérfano de definición concreta, y aun de término preciso que lo designara.

Si se estudia atentamente la terminología de la época puede verse que el equivalente más próximo a lo que hoy entendemos por novela fue lo que se llamó entonces poema heroico, concepto tomado de la poética aristotélica, pero modificado en parte por la particular interpretación que la teoría renacentista dio a la idea de verosimilitud, y por la importancia concedida al principio ético-estético del *prodesse et delectare* que domina toda la teoría estética de aquellos siglos.

La calificación del texto narrativo como poema heroico en prosa implica importantes consecuencias para nuestro análisis, pues nos ayuda a comprender la naturaleza y categorización genérica que en aquel momento se atribuyó a la novela. En el contexto de la poética aristotélica el concepto de poema heroico se halla asociado al de poema dramático, pues ambos son considerados ramas del mismo tronco, la poesía, entendida ésta no como forma literaria en verso, sino como contrapunto de la historia. Por analogía, dicha asociación permitía extender la distinción teórica y formal entre comedia y tragedia al poema heroico y al poema cómico y, por extensión, al género o géneros narrativos de ellos derivados o con ellos identificados. Que tal proceso se produjo en el contexto de la poética y de la práctica literaria renacentista es evidente, puesto que en más de una ocasión hallamos calificados de poemas trágicos o poemas cómicos relatos que hoy consideramos esencialmente novelescos.

La categorización de una obra bajo los conceptos de comedia o de tragedia suponía una precisión mucho mayor y más estricta que su simple clasificación en función de los conceptos de poesía e historia, los cuales asumía y matizaba. Siempre según la teoría aristotélica y sus aplicaciones renacentistas, tanto la comedia como la tragedia apuntaban conceptualmente, aunque por caminos distintos, a la verdad universal como objeto propio de la poesía, pero mientras la tragedia supone la expresión suprema de esa aspiración y se mueve preferentemente en el terreno de lo maravilloso y de los arquetipos que mejor poeden sugerirla, la comedia, en cambio, puede descender, y con frecuencia lo hace, casi al terreno mismo de la historia, buscando el apoyo de la verosimilitud por el camino de la realidad espacio-temporal y concreta.

En el contexto de este esquema teórico para la clasificación genérica de los textos narrativos, el concepto de verosimilitud, que jugó un papel sumamente importante en la imperante doctrina del *prodesse et delectare*, fue poco a poco aproximando los conceptos de tragedia y comedia, sin llegar a borrar sus fronteras, pero haciendo posible la creación de un nuevo término, el de tragicomedia, concepto del que quizá habría que partir para descubrir la naturaleza esencial de la novela.

Así pues, antes de que fuera creado el concepto mismo de novela—en el sentido que hoy se da al término—los términos que mejor sirvieron para categorizar genéricamente las obras que hoy consideramos novelas fueron los de comedia y tragedia, o mejor dicho, poema cómico, poema trágico y también, quizá, tragi-comedia.

Este análisis sobre el concepto mismo de novela nos permite regresar a nuestro problema central para enfocarlo desde una más precisa perspectiva. Efectivamente, en un contexto crítico de raíz aristotélica, el uso de los términos genéricos que acabamos de discutir suponía asimismo una categorización formal de los textos, puesto que, como es sabido, en dicho contexto los conceptos mismos de comedia y tragedia implican y determinan el estilo, materia, estructura, y aun la misma condición social de los protagonistas en torno a los cuales gira la acción. Si se tiene en cuenta esta circunstancia, no resultaba pues arbitrario, sino sumamente preciso y significativo, calificar un texto en función de la condición social de su protagonista, puesto que los mismos conceptos de tragedia y comedia como categorías últimas, más el principio del *decorum* renacentista, autorizaban a ver en la figura del héroe o del antihéroe de un texto narrativo el reflejo exacto de los restantes aspectos y características que pudieran contribuir a su clasificación teórica.

Ese valor referencial del protagonista en cuanto al lenguaje crítico de la época podría explicar pues, a mi juicio, el origen de la nomenclatura adoptada para la clasificación de las novelas de aquellos siglos, y también el hecho de que dicha nomenclatura pudiera seguir teniendo un valor crítico en la posteridad.

No pretendo afirmar, por supuesto, que la crítica renacentista y barroca llegó a la solución taxonómica que produjo mediante un razonamiento similar al que acabo de ofrecer. Sugiero simplemente que si críticos y lectores seleccionaron para designar la naturaleza de los textos que leían unos y no otros de los posibles términos que estaban a su alcance, es precisamente porque en esos términos intuyeron un valor referencial y una coherencia como conjunto taxonómico que satisfacía sus postulados críticos, y que sólo a posteriori podemos explicar lógicamente.

Si mi hipótesis es correcta, es posible que en función de la misma pudiera explicarse también el hecho de que no exista en castellano la distinción entre novela y *romance*—en el sentido que da al término particularmente la crítica anglosajona,—distinción que implícita o explícitamente encontramos en otras lenguas europeas. En efecto, dicha distinción quedaría ya expresada en una nomenclatura que si realmente responde a los supuestos críticos que hemos descrito, directa o indirectamente reflejaría también la presencia del elemento cómico o del elemento trágico-heroico en los textos. La presencia de uno u otro elemento, que según nuestra hipótesis quedaría reflejada en la categorización social del protagonista, determinaría asimismo si la verosimilitud del relato se apoyaba en el arquetipo maravilloso o en la realidad histórica y objetiva más o menos falsificada por la intención del narrador; es decir, señalaría exactemente la distinción que separa el *romance* de la novela.

Para comprender el mecanismo de estas distinciones es naturalmente necesario tener en cuenta que en los textos de la época la condición social de los protagonistas no viene expresada simplemente por el término lingüístico que la indica, sino también por el campo semántico del mismo en función de la tradición literaria en que se inserta. Es por eso que el término novela pastoril, por ejemplo, no alude a novelas de pastores reales, sino a aquellas cuyo héroe es el símbolo-arquetipo de un ideal renacentista, expresado por el tan frecuente tópico del menosprecio de corte y alabanza de aldea.

Si aceptáramos estos criterios, podríamos entonces reevaluar y justificar el término de novela cortesana, demostrando que, como antes sugerimos, dicho término posee efectivamente unas connotaciones críticas que permiten incorporarlo de modo coherente y lógico al sistema taxonómico tradicional. En virtud de lo que acabamos de decir, el concepto de novela cortesana se nos ofrecería ahora como contrapunto de la novela pastoril, y en contraste con ella nos orientaía hacia el poema cómico, es decir, hacia la verdad 'histórica' que se opone a la verdad 'poética' del símbolo-arquetipo ensalzado en aquélla. Sin embargo, si se tienen en cuenta los valores ético-estéticos con que Castiglione invistió la figura del cortesano, y que tanto influyeron en el pensamiento y en la literatura de aquellos siglos, el concepto mismo nos llevaría en cambio a considerar los textos de la novela cortesana como auténticos poemas trágico-heroicos, en oposición y contrapunto no respecto a la novela pastoril, sino a la novela picaresca. En este sentido, no dejaría de ser significativo el hecho de que desde 1603 la versión expurgada del *Lazarillo de Tormes* se publicara frecuentemente como curioso y apto complemento de el *Galateo Español,* cuyo parentesco y afinidad con *El Cortesano* no es necesario subrayar.

Concepto en apariencia ambivalente, pero en realidad preciso y rico en matices, el concepto de novela cortesana se podría considerar como un concepto integral, equivalente hasta cierto punto al concepto de tragicomedia, es decir, de auténtica novela o de *verdadera historia,* como en algún momento se llamaron aquellas obras en que verdad poética y verdad histórica se conjugaban en perfecta armonía. Que tal fue el calificativo dado a la obra de Heliodoro, en quien, valga señalarlo, buscaron su modelo los más logrados autores de la novela cortesana, es algo que se debe subrayar, y que dice mucho en favor de la intuición certera con que González de Amezúa supo bautizar la categoría novelesca por él inventada.

Como conclusión, permítaseme un comentario que parecerá intempestivo, pero que no lo es. Había decidido no publicar este trabajo, en el que enterré no pocas horas, 'porque naturalmente soy poltrón y perezoso de andarme buscando autores que digan lo que yo me sé decir sin ellos'. Me atrevo al fin a sacarlo al ruedo público, aunque huérfano todavía de 'acotaciones en los márgenes' y de 'anotaciones al fin del libro,' porque sé y espero que aquél a quien va cariñosamente dedicado comprenderá mi 'suspensión y elevamiento,' y perdonará la osadía, que otros castigarán como merece. Vale.

14. Calderón's Augustinian Auto: El sacro Parnaso–ALAN SOONS

Like many of Calderón's *autos sacramentales* his *El sacro Parnaso* (usually dated 1659) retraces the transformations wrought by the Passion, the event at the basis of the Feast of Corpus Christi, on the progression of human history, from its origins in that order of nature which even the pagans conceived of, through the order of the Written Law, into the order of Grace attainable following the Incarnation. Calderón here dramatizes this movement of transformation in the career and conversion of St. Augustine, the most eminent exponent in so many of his works of the doctrine which substantiates this notion of progression. This *auto* is one more example of that 'architecture of ideas and movements' so admired by Lucien-Paul Thomas, and I should like to demonstrate how Calderón has ingeniously constructed his work on St. Augustine on the very principles of arithmology which never ceased to fascinate the great Bishop of Hippo. One might cite Marrou: 'One is conscious that Augustine finds in arithmology a fertile source of inspiration, to which he attaches a supreme value. Here he is the Neoplatonic philosopher, imbued with Pythagoreanism. None of the other Fathers brought so much passion to the subject as Augustine'[1].

To analyse the textual and scenic progressions of the *auto* one might glance at the scheme which Calderón himself proposes in his *Las órdenes militares:*

> Y pues ya la fantasía
> ha entablado el argumento,
> entable la realidad
> la metáfora . . . .

Fantasía here represents the poet's imagining a contest of poetry on Eucharistic themes between the great Doctors of the Church, which coincides with the historical moment of St. Augustine's conversion. This is the 'fancy' which governs the action of *El sacro Parnaso,* its poetic and scenic elements. Within this, one may distinguish three aspects. First, the series of episodes loosely derived from the relevant books, VII, VIII, IX, of the *Confessions:* the pride Augustine feels in his powers of oratory and abstract reasoning, in the face of the pious pleas of his mother Monica; his sense of abandonment (*con un triste entendido,* 785b[2]) within the *regio dissimilitudinis;* the fateful rest in the shade of the fig-tree, just before the voice of his heart makes itself heard:

> Que a sombra
> de esa higuera discurriendo,
> escuché unas voces
> que llevar pudieron
> tras sí mis sentidos
> donde no sé de ellos.

> (787b)

the bidding of Faith *Tolle, lege,* through the chance cry of a child (*que ella sabe/fiar de los pequeñuelos/lo que a los grandes encubre.* 784a); and the moment of the simultaneous composition of the *Te Deum* with his mentor St. Ambrose.[3] A second aspect of the action of the *auto* is the symbolic prizewinning by the Doctors of the Church, for their exertions on this 'holy Parnassus', when by coincidence Augustine, previously clothed as a *galán*—being an unbaptized rhetor—receives his habiliments of a bishop and a Doctor, and also like the others his eternal symbolic attribute, the pierced heart. The third strand comprised within the action concerns the fates of the characters Judaísmo and Gentilidad after their exclusion from the contest, a result of their neglect to test the efficacy of the stream of Grace, the Hippocrene of this new Parnassus. At all times Gentilidad has sought knowledge, and here competence to enter the contest, through her curiosity alone (*bien que quisiera informarme/ sólo por curiosidad,* . . . , 781b).[4] Judaísmo, on the other hand, merely seeks to compete out of a spirit of contradiction and malice (*sólo saberlos* [*sc.* asuntos de la fe] *quisiera/por rencor, odio y coraje,/para escribir contra ellos, ibid.*) First there is a kind of rehearsal of such a contest, as Gentilidad and Judaísmo envisage it, and which certainly owes more to 'curiosity' than to 'matters of the faith', in the presence of Fe. It resembles the early mediaeval *Theodoli ecloga*

in that it is a series of attempts to bring to light Old Testament
parallels to phenomena of Greek mythology: Noah after the Deluge
as a parallel to Deucalion and Pyrrha after theirs; the Fleece of
Gideon and that of Jason; the Dew of Ahaz and the golden shower
of Danae, etc., with the prize being adjudged to the contestant last
exhausted.[5] Fe closes the contest with an acknowledgment that
both have grasped a shadow of the truth:

> Como cuanto el hebreo sabe
> de la sustancia infalible
> y de la ciencia inefable
> de un solo Dios, es verdad,
> pues fue, antes que me faltase,
> el favorecido pueblo
> de sus divinas piedades.
> Y cuanto tú sabes, dando
> culto a mentidas deidades,
> sólo es viciada noticia
> de las maravillas grandes
> de su poder; porque como
> la luz de la fe te falte
> a quien nunca viste, oyendo
> los prodigios singulares
> de sus misterios, fingiste
> fabulosas vanidades
> a quien los atribuyeses;
> con que, como he dicho, nacen
> las sombras de tus mentiras
> de la luz de sus verdades.

(779a)

However, once contestants appear who have transcended the Law of
Nature and the Written Law, and who have their being within the
Law of Grace, contests are possible in which 'no one need lose',
and in which anyone may win a saint's attribute for all time:

> Aunque aqueste certamen
> da cinco premios,
> premios hay para todos.
> Todos lleguemos
> a este nuevo Parnaso,

pues es constante
que quien llama a todos
no exceptúa a nadie.

(797a–b)

We observe at the end of the *auto* the enraged discomfiture of Judaísmo, and the expulsion of Gentilidad into the waste land.[6] Both are now significantly dressed as *galanes*, that is in the costume which Augustine once wore. Gentilidad is not marked as irrevocably lost, however; she has a permanent ascendancy over Judaísmo (*Feliz, Gentilidad, eres,/pues te da la Fe su asiento*, 796b)[7]. The *gracioso* of Calderón's play is Regocijo, who is intended to arrange the all-important *vejamen* at the contestants' expense, but is prevented by the unpleasantness of Judaísmo from carrying this out.[8] He is, however, the arbiter or *fiscal* of this aspect of the *auto*, its *argumento*.

The *realidad* which governs the metaphor—or complex series of metaphors relating the metamorphosis of the phenomena of the natural world, and that of the Written Law, into those of the world of Grace—was for Augustine one of the highest manifestations of the real, a true *vestigium Dei*, a conduit of spiritual power.[9] This reality is none other than the so to speak non-numerative force of simple numbers, the basis of a comprehensive aesthetic referred usually to the text of *Wisdom* XII, 21: *Omnia in mensura, numero et pondere disposuisti*. In Calderón's age the principal treatise transmitting the arithmological doctrine would be that of the avowed follower of the Saint, Petrus Bongus. *Numerorum mysteria, ex additis plurimarum disciplinarum fontibus hausta. Opus maximarum rerum doctrina et copia repertum*. Bergamo: Cominus Ventura, 1591.[10] I propose to draw upon the explanations of Bongus of the non-numerative powers of the four-number and the five-number, and with immediate reference to *El sacro Parnaso* in the matter of Calderón's successive groupings of his *dramatis personae*.

The decoration of the first cart, according to the instructions left by Calderón (776a), is displayed around the figures of five wooden women—that is, carved out of matter, the *hyle*, and with only two dimensions—and five living women, representing the four Sibyls and the identically dressed Fe. If we were to refer this arrangement to the *metáfora* we might see the women of wood as representative of the law of nature, and the Sibyls, with Fe dissimulated among them, as representative of the Written Law (for after all at least some Sibyls *wrote* their oracles before dispersing the leaves). Fe situates them within the Law as having their prototypes in King David's *timpanistas,* while she herself denotes the Christian Logos moving among them, and among her wooden simulacra, before the Incarnation. Constituting the other section of the *dramatis personae* are the four Doctors of the Church—for Augustine in the first half of the *auto* is represented as a *galán* and is, of course, unbaptized—who represent and sing of the same Logos after the Incarnation, in the Law of Grace. This does, however, present us with the question of chronology, in that St. Thomas Aquinas, so much later in historical time as a Doctor of the Church, has to appear as the fourth baptized contestant. Calderón is quite aware of this when he has Augustine point out:

> De conocerte me huelgo,
> ya que (la objeción salvada)
> es síncopa de los tiempos
> nuestra representación; . . .

$$(783b)^{11}$$

It will be evident that Calderón, in the disposition of his figures, has projected the five-number of the Old Law, with its Pentateuch, and even before that, of unregenerate creation itself, with its five senses especially; and the four-number of the Order of Grace, the four Gospels of its New Testament being the *numerus perfectionis* in all traditions. But it will also be evident that towards the latter end of the *auto* the four Sibyls 'revert to five' as they lead off Gentilidad in their company into the waste land:

> Llevadle al monte vosotras
> y agradezca el que lo entiende
> ver a la Gentilidad,
> en aqueste rasgo breve,
> heredera de la viña
> que el ciego Judaísmo pierde.

$$(795b)$$

There they will dwell in the world of nature, of the senses, until Gentilidad's curiosity, one presumes, will lead her to knowledge of the Incarnation. The four Doctors become five when Augustine joins their number and accepts one of the five prizes awarded after the contest. In this connection we may refer again to the scheme explained by Bongus. The Passion, with the infliction of the Five Wounds, confers a special eucharastic quality—notably in an *auto* celebrating Corpus Christi—on the five-number. For this reason it is used and alluded to at several points in the Mass.[12] The number also came to represent the *Quinque Secreta Christi (incarnatio, passio, resurrectio, ascensio, iudicium)*, and these have their places in the texts sung by the Doctors. We may notice in passing that just as Regocijo was the *fiscal* of the Parnassus-action of the play, so Fe is the *fiscal* of the entire metaphorical projection of the progression between the states of Nature and Grace.

Another principle of Augustinian aesthetics based upon something like the *Wisdom* text is that of *coaptatio* or symmetry.[13] In *El sacro Parnaso* this principle results in binary statements of correspondence between phenomena or personified figures representative first of the unregenerate, then of the regenerate orders of being. As we have seen, Augustine at first enters as a *galán* and logician, later to become the bishop and Doctor of the Church. The pagan nine Muses, five of whom are the female figures merely cut out of wood, become the four Sibyls.[14] This allows for the association of the two orders of mythical female prompters: the Muses are the daughters of Mnemosyne, patroness of memory, and also have a name traditionally etymologized from *moys* (or spring-water) as well as from *Moyses*.[15] Parnassus with its double summit (*biceps*) becomes the mountain of Zion of the City of God:

> . . . componiendo
> un todo de dos mitades
> ese imaginado monte,
> a dos visos, a dos haces
> (ya que Paraíso no
> ni Eliseo como pensasteis)
> es Parnaso, y es Sión, . . .

> (781a)

The Hippocrene of the pagans, the spring of inspiration, becomes the brook of living water which runs from the Temple, and of course symbolizes Grace:

> . . . llegad adonde bebiendo
> los purísimos cristales
> de una fuente, que en el monte

(porque aun de esto no le falte
al sacro Parnaso) tiene
tal virtud que docta añade
al hombre gracia, podréis,
como ella una vez os bañe,
aspirar los dos al premio; ...

$$(781a)^{16}$$

A related application of this same principle of symmetry is
Calderón's placing of the fulcrum of the *auto* at the mathematically
calculated mid-point of the text (786b–787a), at that very moment
when Augustine lets fall from his hands the 'book of his memory',
and is suddenly attentive to a hitherto hidden illuminative process
within his own heart:

¿Qué me asombro? ¿Qué me quejo,
si quizá le ha dado a logro?
Pues en lugar de que pierdo
el libro de la memoria
hallo el de mi entendimiento,
según me ilumina
hoy un rayo bello.

$$(787a)^{17}$$

An occult power has, of course, been working to bring this about,
and this is exteriorised as the voice of his mother Monica. As she is
at all times offstage during her utterances, one might identify her
with the character Fe, who has dissembled herself previously as
tenth Muse and fifth Sibyl, promoting from the remotest times the
general conversion of creation to the Christian order of Grace,
supliendo la fe al sentido.[18] So that Augustine's memory, heavily
implicated in the sensual world as it is, is after the fall of this book
onstage, replaced by the faith he discovers in the book we do not
see, taken up after the instruction (here offstage and outside the
text) of *Tolle, lege*.

In this brief survey of *El sacro Parnaso* it can hardly be said that
many of the complex reticulations of doctrine have been touched
upon. A notable case of this is the threading through the *auto* of
references, now traditional, now paradoxial, now playful, to the
notions of sight and hearing as paths to the perception of matters of
faith, associated respectively with Gentilidad and Judaísmo; here a

glance at the place of *el sentido* has sufficed. It scarcely reveals either any of Calderón's textual and notional derivations from the entire body of St. Augustine's works, which were surely familiar to him, and to many of his audience in that 'Augustinian century'. The special power of this *auto* lies in the tight correlation of its recension of all the Calderonian attitudes to the place of the Eucharist in the history of human becoming, and its perception of the educative process of the *Confessions:* the pilgrimage of one soul out of sensuality and 'memory' into a spiritual mode of being.[19]

15. A Reading of Cortázar's Zipper Sonnet—JOHN H. TURNER

'Con la misma henchida satisfacción de una gallina, de tanto en tanto Lucas pone un soneto.' Thus begins 'Lucas, sus sonetos', one of the series of vignettes that comprise Julio Cortázar's *Un tal Lucas* (1979).[1] The unflattering analogy continues: a sonnet is like an egg 'por lo riguroso, lo acabado, lo terso, lo frágilmente duro.... Efímeros, incalculables, el tiempo y algo como la fatalidad los reiteran, idénticos y monótonos y perfectos' (p. 176). Cortázar's interest in the sonnet (there is evidence here for the complete identity of the author and his persona) goes back as far as his first book of poems.[2] He is evidently fascinated by the extreme rigor of the form and the ingenuity this 'cangrejo de catorce patas' requires. The latest achievement, the Zipper Sonnet, may be read from top to bottom or from bottom to top. On the one hand this sonnet is the result of many nights of hard work ('le llevó un tiempo loco') and the poet feels some pride in this culmination of his personal career and the long tradition, particularly in Spanish, of the trick sonnet. On the other hand, he is ambivalent about the poetic value of the result, wondering 'si un soneto es de por sí una relojería que sólo excepcionalmente alcanza a dar la hora justa de la poesía' (p. 183).

The reader of Cortázar is constantly aware of his knowledge of Golden Age poetry. For example, his cat Teodoro W. Adorno goes, when it dies, to 'el cielo que te tienen prometido'.[3] That he is in the Zipper Sonnet also aware of the Golden Age poetic tradition is clear, not only from the reference at the end of 'Lucas, sus sonetos' to Lope's 'Soneto a Violante', but from several aspects of the poem itself. Aside from the use of a generally classical vocabulary (paroxismo, cataclismo, simulacro, antagonista etc.), it seems to

132

me possible that one might read the word 'obstinado' as implying something of its literal Latin sense—'to stand in the way of'. Besides, there are references to classical literature—the Golden Bough of Aeneas's quest in line 11 and 'amarrándose' which probably evokes Odysseus's encounter with the Sirens. And then again the very ingenuity of using the zipper to suggest something about the capacity for objectivity of the creative consciousness has something of the outrageous boldness of the conceits so admired by Gracián in his *Agudeza o arte de ingenio*.

There is in the prose framework of the Zipper Sonnet a kind of self-effacing modesty tinged with quite evident pride. As Lucas contemplates it, considering how to present it to the world, he is relieved, like Cervantes in the prologue to the first part of the *Quijote,* by the intervention of a friend. A Portuguese version of the sonnet, by the Brazilian Haroldo de Campos (the translation by a real poet of the work of a fictional author?) arrives together with some thoughts on the translation and its differences from the original. 'Nunca se le hubiera ocurrido publicar su soneto con notas,' observes Lucas, slightly ironically since his words do constitute notes of a kind, 'pero en cambio le encantó reproducir las de Haroldo, que de alguna manera parafraseaban sus propias dificultades a la hora de escribirlo.' So we have an oddly diffident introduction by a fictional poet, the poem in Spanish which is, in point of fact, two poems, a translation by a real poet, itself two poems, and some thoughts of Campos and Lucas on sonnets, translations, footnotes etc. By the time we reach the final reference to Lope, 'para una vez más colmar/calmar a Violante' (p. 103), the text seems almost overwhelmed by its highly ironic trappings. But the slightly shocking banality of the central image and the multiple ironies of the context need not prevent us from reading the poem (or poems; there are really two) seriously.

The central image, whichever way one reads the poem, is that of the motion of the zipper, condemned to repeat itself within narrow and predictable limits. This movement which can lead nowhere new comes to symbolize the effort of the creative imagination which tries to see beyond itself and yet finds only itself, to look outward, but sees only inward, to seek otherness while finding only self. Here is the text of the first poem, as printed except for the addition of some minimal punctuation, which Cortázar encourages us to add, albeit 'mental y respiratoriamente':

de arriba abajo o bien de abajo arriba,
este camino lleva hacia sí mismo—
simulacro de cima ante el abismo,
árbol que se levanta o se derriba.

Quien en la alterna imagen lo conciba
será el poeta de este paroxismo,
en un amanecer de cataclismo
náufrago que a la arena al fin arriba,

vanamente eludiendo su reflejo,
antagonista de la simetría
para llegar hasta el dorado gajo,

visionario amarrándose a un espejo
obstinado hacedor de la poesía,
de abajo arriba o bien de arriba abajo (179).

The first image, after the statement of the two possible directions, restated at the end, is of a path that leads, not somewhere else, but to itself (as the first reading of the poem leads to the last line which becomes the first line of another poem and so on). The duplicity of this path suggests two complementary images. The movement which does not move, the path which does not lead anywhere, suggest the mountain which is merely the mirror image of an abyss. What seems to be something is merely an image of its converse, as the image of the falling tree seems to imply the opposite movement. The latter image is probably prompted by the visual impression of the half-open zipper as the trunk and branches of a tree. In the second quatrain, by far the most obscure lines of the poem(s), we are introduced to a hypothetical protagonist. The suggestion seems to be that whoever can envision the opposite direction implicit in motion, rising tree in falling, mountain in abyss, path outward in path leading back, will be able to imagine this 'fit', or sudden bursting forth of movement or emotion (this poem or poetry in general?). In yet another paradox, in an awakening to the possibility of disaster at sea, he will arrive safely on land. This person (how to avoid the image of the pilgrim at the beginning of the *Soledades*?) eludes in vain his reflection, opposing himself to symmetry in order to reach the golden bough, symbol of possible kingship for a runaway slave. He is a person gifted with insight who, again paradoxically, lashes himself (to avoid being

distracted like Odysseus?) to a mirror. The suggestion seems to be
that the poet is condemned to struggle to see the world around him
but to see always and only himself. The self-contemplation
(reflection in the sense of meditation) required of the maker of
poetry prevents him from seeing things except on his own terms. It
is even possible that the word 'reflejo' which refers here to
reflection in both common senses, of mirror image as well as of
contemplation, may even here have some of the connotations of the
English 'reflex', which would certainly accord with Cortázar's
continual criticism of automatic, conventional thinking. Is there an
implication here that the reflection required of the poet may
become automatic and lead only to seeing himself? Perhaps this is
made more likely by a possible literal reading of the word
'obstinado' in the sense of 'standing in his own way'.

Here is the text of the other poem, with a suggested
punctuation:

De abajo arriba o bien de arriba abajo,
obstinado hacedor de la poesía,
visionario amarrándose a un espejo

para llegar hasta el dorado gajo,
antagonista de la simetría
vanamente eludiendo su reflejo,

náufrago que a la arena al fin arriba
en un amanecer de cataclismo,
será el poeta de este paroxismo
quien en la alterna imagen lo conciba.

Árbol que se levanta o se derriba,
simulacro de cima ante el abismo,
este camino lleva hacia sí mismo,
de arriba abajo o bien de abajo arriba

A poet friend to whom I showed a translation of this poem said
he thought it worked better from bottom to top. He had, of course,
the advantage of already having read it the other way, as most
readers will have. It seems to me that the leap from line 1 to line 2
in this second poem, requiring an association of the movement of
the zipper with the maker of poetry demands a great deal of the
imagination, although the succession of images which follows is as

easy to follow as in the first poem. The persistent (and perhaps self-confounding) poet is a seer who insists on self knowledge in order to reach the goal of his quest, the symbol of authority. He rejects symmetry but it is in vain that he seeks to avoid his own reflection. Like a pilgrim saved from shipwreck on a morning that had promised disaster, he who sees the possibility for safe arrival in the act of setting out in tragedy will be the one who can turn this act into poetry, the one who can see the rising tree in the falling, the mountain in the valley, like a path that leads nowhere but to itself.

There is a complex of interlocking analogies in the poem(s). As the first sonnet contains within itself the shadow of the other, as the downward movement of the zipper or downward reading of the poem reflects and implies the opposite motion, as arriving is the same as starting out, as looking out is a way of looking in, so the reader of the poem is forced, not merely to think about the paradoxes, but actually to enact them. We go through the motions of starting from point A and arriving at point B only to discover that we are still at point A. The essential paradox, that of a search that leads back home in the end, is that of all quests, and is expressed in this poem by a startlingly new metaphor, that of the zipper. Of course this image is made all the more vivid in that, as readers, we are forced to re-enact the pointless activity of the poet. And, to complicate everything still further, the central image of the zipper (as prelude or finale of an act of love?) is the key to the erotic connotations of the whole poem. The reader of Cortázar is already used to associating eroticism and metaphysics in his work, and there is a long and very close association between the sonnet form and amorous themes, an association of which Cortázar reminds us early in the introduction to the Zipper Sonnet by his reference to 'estro (en primera y tambien en segunda aceptación)' (p. 176). And then what are we to make of these paroxysms, rising and falling trees, the search for the other? It seems to me impossible to read a sonnet in which the movement of a zipper suggests creativity, without these erotic implications, The poet is here, as so often in the sonnet tradition, also the lover, the searcher after transcendent experience, the finder of self in attachment to other.

The key to the multiple levels of the poem appears to be the word 'paroxismo'. This 'fit' is, on the one hand, simply the movement of the zipper. As Haroldo de Campos decides in his

Portuguese version of the poem, the 'poeta' of the text would be the creator of this sonnet seeing text B inherent in text A. It may also be a sudden movement toward truth and it may also be, if there is a possibility of reading the sonnet on an erotic level, the act of love. At all events, we are dealing with a quest, a movement outward looking for something, a movement which is condemned to lead only inward. The suggestion seems to be that there is no knowledge but self knowledge, no insight but into one's self. Creative activity is seen to be as closely circumscribed as the closed movement of the zipper.

One of the themes of modern literature—as well as of modern science—is precisely this question of the limits of objectivity. The extent to which the eye of the beholder can record what it sees without interpreting or even influencing the phenomena according to its own point of view is a central concern in Cortázar's work. It is the focus of the story 'Las babas del diablo' in which the narrator worries over the attempt to tell his story and the photographer agonizes over what may have happened and what his involvement might or should have been. In 'El perseguidor', perhaps Cortázar's finest piece of fiction, Bruno struggles to separate his personal feelings about Johnny and his desire for fame and money, from his true artistic task, the attempt to convey in writing the particular brilliance of the jazz musician. The point is made even more explicitly in 'Los pasos en las huellas' where Jorge Fraga confronts directly and constantly the dilemma of trying to write about someone else, while haunted by the fear that he is always writing about himself, a fear that in one dramatic moment seems to crystallize into certainty:

> Clara y sencillamente sintió Fraga que cualquiera como él sería siempre Claudio Romero, que los Romero de ayer y de mañana serían siempre Jorge Fraga. Tal como lo había temido una lejana noche de septiembre, había escrito su autobiografía disimulada.[4]

In *Rayuela,* too, a search for 'the other side' leads first to Paris and then ultimately back to Buenos Aires where Horacio seems to come nearer to finding what he was looking for. This is one of Cortázar's major themes and it is expressed in the Zipper Sonnet in an extraordinarily compact and striking way. As so often in Cortázar, the trivial takes on transcendental significance.

16. Lírica femenina in the Early Manuscript Cancioneros
JANE WHETNALL

There is a small number of poems *en boca femenina* in the manuscript *cancioneros* that collect the lyric output of the first half of the fifteenth century.[1] They are so few and so unobtrusive that they have attracted little attention to date but I think they are worth examining as a group, for several reasons. In the first place, they purport to be the lyric expression of women, and women's songs have a particular importance in the history of Peninsular lyric. Secondly, although they are undeniably courtly in style and content, and most probably all written by men, they differ in a significant way from typical *cancionero* lyrics with a male subject. And, thirdly, they also differ from the few examples of popular verse *en boca femenina* that is found in the early *cancioneros*. In fact these poems constitute something of an enigma, being of a tradition and yet apparently outside it. The purpose of this article is to give an account of the feminine courtly lyric that will satisfactorily reconcile these various aspects of the phenomenon.

Women's songs, in the form of *kharjas, cantigas de amigo,* or *villancicos,* are regarded as landmarks in the fragmented lyric tradition of Spain and Portugal. They are assumed to derive ultimately from popular oral tradition but the survival of all three kinds of lyric is, in different ways, due to the patronage of the lettered. These fifteenth-century poems too may draw on a tradition that is older than the *cancioneros.* They may even provide a link with the Galician-Portugese tradition, occurring as they do after a substantial lacuna in textual evidence of lyric activity in Castile or Portugal. Alan Deyermond saw the need for such a link when he regretted 'the absence from *Baena* of any counterpart to the *cantigas de amigo*' as an obstacle to our acceptance of complete continuity between the Galician-Portuguese and Castilian lyric traditions.[2] Our knowledge of fourteenth-century lyric in Castile

138

derives largely from the selection made of it by Juan Alfonso de
Baena. But he included disproportionately few love poems in his
cancionero which, according to Brian Dutton, reflects 'the rather
pompous taste of bourgeois clerks, scribes and officials' and is not
therefore a representative selection of courtly taste and poetic
activity for the period it covers.[3] Later *cancioneros* supply a
corrective to the distorted picture *Baena* gives of poetry during the
minority and reign of John II but none of them has *Baena's*
retrospective sweep, so we must build on what other scraps of
evidence we have in support of the idea that there was possibly a
flourishing lyric in the earlier period as well.[4] The poems I wish to
discuss certainly bear no obvious resemblance to the *cantigas de
amigo*. However, their mere existence implies a line of tradition that
may go far back into the fourteenth century, lost to us through the
same accident of history that may have deprived us of other genres
of lyric, written in either of the two literary dialects vying for
preeminence at the time.[5]

   These feminine lyrics do not sit uneasily alongside the
numerous male complaints at suffering endured for the sake of a
heartless, oblivious, or merely absent lady. They offer an
equivalent portrait of a grieving, possibly wronged, woman, whose
laments mirror rather than complement the protests of the courtly
lover.[6] On whole they belong stylistically to the mainstream of
cancioneril verse of the appropriate period. The difference, where it
exists, is one of tone: the ladies speak their distress with a
directness that, as far as one is able to generalize about such a vast
quantity of verse, seems to be absent from corresponding poems
from the man's point of view.

   The interplay between learned and popular strains in *cancionero*
verse is fundamental to an assessment of its contribution to the
history of the Castilian lyric tradition. There is enough evidence to
show that traditional songs formed part of the cultural background
of *cancionero* poets from the earliest times; that, in effect, our first
glimpse of Castilian popular lyric is contemporaneous with the first
manifestation of cultured lyric in Castile, Aragon and Navarre. The
evidence is patchy and consists mostly of quoted *villancico* and
ballad fragments, *contrafacta*, or courtly treatments of popular
themes, some of which found their way only incidentally into
collections intended primarily as literary records.[7] To the extent
that popular song is preserved in the manuscripts women's songs

are represented by a fair proportion of these fragments. The *Cancionero de Herberay*, which for a non-musical compilation shows a marked bias in favour of popular and courtly songs, contains two complete *cantigas femeninas*, both anonymous and unequivocally traditional in style: 'Soy garridilla e pierdo sazón', a *mal maridada* according to the rubric, and 'Siempre m'avéis querido', a frank offer of love in *zéjel* form.[8] The tone of these two early *villancicos*, one defiant, the other compliant and provocative, puts them on another plane from the learned poems *en boca femenina* which seem always to be the mouthpiece of women as helpless victims of circumstance.

However, the courtly poems must be seen to take precedence over the popular ones both chronologically, if we regard them strictly as datable texts, and quantitatively, in terms of the number and length of relevant compositions. For although the outright *cantigas femeninas*—that is, *canciones* or *decires* written in their entirety from a woman's point of view—are few (I have found only five), large sections of other compositions contain the views of a woman expressed either as interior monologue or as part of a dialogue. The poems I am going to discuss are, in chronological order: 'Triste soy por la partida', 'Catiua muy triste, desaventurada', 'Grant sonsiego e mansedumbre', the *Comiat entre'l Rey e la Reyna en el biaje de Napols*, 'Forçada soy de maldezir', 'Mi mal celar m'es la muerte', the *Planto de Pantasilea* and 'Retraída estava la reina'. A surprising range of other compositions is eligible for consideration as partial feminine lyric, like debate poems in which the poet converses with his lady. These seem to constitute a recognised subgenre that includes the dialogue between the Archpriest and Doña Endrina in the *Libro de buen amor*, 657–86, and I do not wish to discuss them in the present context.[9] Nor is there much to be gained from including the scabrous *respuestas en boca femenina* composed by male poets on behalf of individual women.[10] However, they do provide evidence of a practice, reflected in *Baena* at least, whereby court ladies could enlist the help of professional spokesmen when the need arose. It is easy to imagine that some of the feminine lyrics we have were written in response to a formal request from ladies who wished to make a public, although anonymous, declaration of their feelings. This may have been some compensation for the fact, observed by Deyermond, that there are hardly any women poets known to us from the *cancioneros*.[11]

As no *cancionero* rubrics survive which indicate that a more decorous use was made of the covention it is only a possibility to be borne in mind. A more likely one, perhaps, is that a poet might feel spontaneously drawn to expressing the poignancy inherent in a public event or state occasion from the point of view of the female participant. One such poem is *Baena* 26, written by Villasandino in 1375: 'esta cantiga fiso el dicho Alfonso Aluares quando desposaron la Rreyna de Navarra con Don Carlos, porque sse yva':

> Tryste soy por la partida
> que se ora de aquí parte
> meu señor, que muy syn arte
> del su amor soy conquerida.

The *estribillo* is followed by three *octavas* in the mixture of forms characteristic of literary Castilian-Galician:

> Ora vay longe de aquí
> quen meu coraçón deseia,
> por miña coyta sobeia
> tenpo ha que tenpo perdí.
> Señor Deus, ¿qué meresçy,
> ben obrando a meu poder,
> que por vn solo plazer
> he pessar toda mi vyda?

It is a restrained and mournful lyric, presumably well matched to the occasion of its composition. But the *estribillo* seems to have had a further life of its own. A Castilian version of it occurs in a quoting poem by the Count of Mayorga (d. 1437), introduced as:

> . . . esta canción dolorida
> diré los jueves aparte:
> 'Triste soy por la partida
> pues mi persona se parte
> de la qual beldad sin arte
> me vence sin ser vencida.'[12]

Only the first line and the rhymes are the same in the two quatrains but the differences in the later version are evidently designed to accommodate the change of gender in the speaker and the elimination of the archaic (or Galician) form 'conquerida'.[13] It is possible that Suero de Ribera (fl. 1430s) is quoting the same *estribillo* when he writes:

> . . . el mi triste coraçón
> se vos despide cantando,
> no 'Senyora'n qui fianza',
> mas 'Triste per la partida'.[14]

These two quotations appear to testify to the enduring popularity of Villasandino's poem, still regarded as a standard *despedida* as much as sixty years after it was written although it was recorded in only one manuscript collection.

The earliest example of a Castilian *mal maridada* may have been composed in 1403, if we accept Dorothy Clotelle Clarke's attribution of it to Imperial and the historical circumstance which she suggests inspired it.[15] 'Catiua muy triste, desaventurada', *Baena* 237, occurs without a rubric in the section of *Baena* allotted to Imperial, but between *preguntas* and *respuestas* that he shares with other poets. In five *octavas* of rather uneven *arte mayor* a woman laments her undeserved misfortune in marriage:

> Mouiosse ventura por mal me faser
> e tróxome a tienpo que fuese cassada
> por mi peccado, ventura menguada,
> con quien non sabe el bien conosçer . . .
>
> . . . mesquina por mengua de buen casamiento
> so e sseré jamás en tristura.

Its clumsy rhythm and repetitive phrasing are barely redeemed by the convincing pathos of its tone, reinforced by the dogged but vague enumeration of injuries and woes. Clarke has high praise for the sensitiveness of its emotional content and seeks to excuse its formal defects as experimental: 'one of the earliest successful attempts to use the *decir* framework for strictly lyric expression' (p. 29). The discrepancy between the strong emotional appeal of the poem and its formal weakness results from a failure to solve the technical problem of fitting a lyric theme to a non-lyric metre. This view is challenged by Colbert I. Nepaulsingh's favourable assessment of the poem's artistry.[16] His penetrating analysis of 'Catiua muy triste, desaventurada' uncovers theological complexities that go beyond the literal portrayal of distress and relate to his account of Imperial's pessimistic life-view: 'le interesa más al poeta demostrar que la protagonista es un testimonio vivo e irrefutable de su filosofía que expresar su simpatía por la aflicción que ella está sufriendo' (p. 42). This does not alter the fact that it is a woman in a peculiarly female predicament that Imperial has chosen to exemplify the plight of injured innocence. The passages that Nepaulsingh cites as literary parallels for the complaint are all taken from the speech of women.

The improvement in style which a different metre brings can perhaps best be illustrated from *Baena* 240, which is possibly also by Imperial and more certainly about Angelina of Greece. The second half of 'Grant sonsiego e mansedumbre' is given up to two *octavas* of internal monologue by the captive foreign princess.

> Paresçía su senblante
> desir: '¡Ay de mí, catiua!
> Conviene de aquí avante
> que en servidunbre biua.
> ¡O ventura muy esquiua!
> ¡Ay de mí por que nasçí!
> Dime ¿qué te meresçí
> porque me fazes que syrua?

The language is the same, the terms of reproach as indeterminate as those of 'Catiua muy triste, desaventurada', but the expression is altogether more accomplished.

Twenty years on, in 1420 or soon after, the *despedida* theme receives still more confident treatment in a poem by Santa Fe. Like 'Triste soy por la partida' it is a royal valediction, but this time in the form of a dialogue between Alfonso V of Aragon and Queen María: *Comiat entre'l Rey e la Reyna en el biaje de Napols* (Palacio 269).[16] The queen speaks the four-line opening verse and four of the eight *octavas* that follow, including the dramatic highpoint of the encounter:

> Senyor ¿qué vos oyré
> que res no me viene bien?
> ¿Quál será aquel o quien
> con qui me conssolaré?
> ¿Qué faré
> donde conssolaçión sienta?
> Gran deseio me turmenta
> y amor.

These few short lines recreate the urgency of direct speech, the three interrogatives conveying the panic and desperation of the anxious queen, the last sentence signalling a relief from tension as she allows resignation to take over and the crisis is passed.

Pedro de Santa Fe is probably also the author of the only full-scale feminine lyrics of the period 1420–35. 'Forçada soy de maldezir' begins a fresh folio in *Palacio* following a truncated poem by Santa Fe.[17] It may have lost one or two earlier stanzas as well as its rubric, but what remains is a lyric of considerable emotive impact:

> Forçada soy de maldezir
> mi esperança ya d'oy más . . .
> Cuytada, dónde fallaré
> quien sia mi defendedor?
> La mi bondat, la mi honor,
> ¿si los veré?
> Car vienen me miedo e temor
> e me dizen que yo morré.

The explanation for the speaker's distress is reserved until the last few lines of the poem: 'que el qui m'a de emparar/ se a mudado', and the *tornada:*

> Mi bien veo olvidado
> e siento mayor pesar
> quando la veo otra amar
> por qui m'a desemparado.

This poem, too, reaches its climax in repeated claims on our compassion that effectively emphasize the isolation of the betrayed girl.

> Mesquina, ¿quién m'avrá mercé?
> ne ¿quí's querrá de mí doler?
> ¡Qué crueldat tan desegual
> beyer que sufra tanto mal
> sin merecer!

'Mi mal celar m'es la muerte' appears among the works of Santa Fe in *Herberay* and *Modena* under the rubric 'El mesmo'.[18] It sets itself apart from the feminine lyrics discussed so far in that it more closely resembles a typical courtly love poem whose subject happens to be a woman. Aubrun calls it a 'maumariée entièrement courtoise' (p. 239), but in fact the principle of discretion is maintained and we can conclude only that a forbidden and perhaps unrequited love is being thwarted by a jealous guardian or husband—'Yo en estranyo poder'. For the rest it deals in typical *cancioneril* dilemmas:

Mi mal celar m'es la muerte
y el fablar sepultura . . .

Seso me manda que calle
e mi passión no consiente . . .

In this it conforms to the pattern of most *cancionero* lyric, revealing little of the true-life situation that may (or may not) be the cause of the poet's misery. We are permitted one hint of domesticity that fixes it as a woman's poem, and there is one rhetorical question, but it is framed in such a way as to present a clear contrast to the frank desperation of the other feminine plaints:

Comportar de cada día
l'enemigo familiar,
¿qué más pena ser podría?
discretos, queret pensar.

Here Santa Fe shows perfect control of the reticence, melancholy and ambivalence that enabled *cancionero* verse to serve as a vehicle for the expression of other men's lovesickness.

The *Planto que fiso Pantasilea*, 'Yo sola membrança sea', is the only fifteenth-century *cantiga femenina* that we can be sure was at all widely known, since copies of it survive in seven different manuscripts.[19] From the earliest of these we know that it must have been written by 1442–45, probably within the previous ten years, by Juan Rodríguez del Padrón.[20] A long *dezir* lamenting the death of Hector, spoken by the Amazon queen who had loved him from afar and never saw him alive, it is something of an anomaly among *cancionero* lyrics. The combination of classical theme with narrative and lyrical elements (in about equal proportions) was traditionally associated with the ballad format. In spite of its heroic subject and setting 'Yo sola membrança sea' contains a number of standard *cancionero* clichés, familiar from love poems, that fall reassuringly on the ear:

¡O triste, mejor me fuera
que nunca fuera nasçida!

> a lo menos non oviera
> la muerte tan conosçida . . .
>
> . . . Sé que me puedo llamar
> la más triste apassionada
> de quantas saben amar.[21]

If any modern sensibility is capable of feeling sympathy for Penthesilea's fate, lines such as these seems unlikely to arouse it. In comparison with the subtle rhythms and spontaneity of Santa Fe this reads very much like a rhetorical exercise. On the other hand, a comparison with its prose equivalents in Rodríguez del Padrón's *Bursario* and with appropriate passages in the *Historia troyana polimétrica* would undoubtedly yield some interesting conclusions about stylistic variation in the handling of classical material.

The Aragonese court in Naples supplies the last instance of partial feminine lyric for this period in 'Retraída estava la reina', one of the earliest *romances cultos*. Although it appears without attribution in the manuscripts it is generally assumed to be the work of Carvajales and I follow the text given in Emma Scoles's edition of his poems.[22] The sorrows of María of Aragon's grass widowhood were anticipated by Santa Fe's *Comiat* on Alfonso's departure for Italy. Now, in the late 1450s, quite possibly after the queen's actual death,[23] her side of the story is told in thirty-seven lines of monologue containing intermittent exclamations of self-pity:

> Maldigo la mi fortuna que tanto me perseguía.
> ¡Para ser tan malfadada muriera quando nascía!
> ¡E muriera una vegada e non tantas cada día! . . .
>
> . . . ¿Quién sufrió nunca dolor qual entonces yo sufría?

A further rhetorical question is supplied by the fictional prose letter (*epístola*) from María to Alfonso that accompanies the ballad in all three manuscripts: '. . . ¿de quién me quexaré o a quién me querellaré de ti, si non a ti solo, en cuyo poder toda mi esperança bive?'.[24] As well as the presumed thematic debt to Santa Fe some of the lines of this ballad show a clear formulaic affinity with the *Planto de Pantasilea*, with which there is reason to connect it as the two compositions belong to the same manuscript tradition.

These few poems constitute the main examples of feminine love lyric in the manuscript *cancioneros* of the first half of the fifteenth century.[25] What have they got in common, what can we deduce about their presence in the *cancioneros*, and what can they tell us about the tradition of the feminine lyric in Spain? Thematically they seem to fall into three interrelated categories: the *despedida* ('Triste soy por la partida' and the *Comiat*), the *mal maridada* ('Catiua muy triste, desaventurada', 'Retraída estava la reina' and, possibly, 'Mi mal celar m'es la muerte') and, forming an intermediate group between the two, the less specific complaints of forsaken women ('Grant sonsiego e mansedumbre', 'Forçada soy de maldezir') and the lament of Penthesilea. The theme of abandonment and isolation could be said to characterize the *cantiga femenina* as a genre.

What unites them even more than their themes is their diction, the readiness with which they break into the exclamations and interrogatives of direct speech, often piling these up in a series of apostrophes with marked dramatic effect. Although amorous *quejas* of this sort are not exclusive to feminine lyrics, there are good reasons for believing that there was a deeply felt traditional association between heightened colloquial diction and the female predicament. Striking parallels can be found in a wide range of prose sources, from the *quejas* of Doña Urraca in the *Crónica de veinte reyes* to the bitter outcry of a young wife in the *Corbacho*.[26] It could be that the traditional stereotype this pattern of monologue evokes is a figure of fun, the railing shrew of folktale. But I think it unlikely: the dignity of the royal *despedidas* and the melodic grace of some of Santa Fe's verses betoken a more distinguished ancestry.

We have to proceed more cautiously in the search for poetic analogues that could be regarded as historical antecedents for these *queja* motifs. They are not exclusive to feminine lyric as individual phrases but when we find them together in a series there is a strong resemblance that suggests some connection. One of the earliest *cancionero* poems, if its attribution to Macías is correct, includes the lines:

> Senyores, non sé qué diga,
> nin sé a quién me querelle,
> nin sé [carrera] que siga,
> nin sé bien que me consuele,
> cuytado, ya ¿qué faré . . . ?[27]

The anaphora of this passage suggests that it is a weary, set response to a formulaic but variable sequence of questions: ¿qué diré?, ¿a quién me querellaré?, ¿adónde iré?, ¿con qué me consolaré? In the last quarter of the fifteenth century Diego de San Pedro twice deploys such a sequence, in the *Siete angustias* and at greater length in the *Passión trobada:*

> ¿Adónde iré, qué haré,
> hijo, bien de los mortales?
> ¿A quién me querellaré?
> ¿Con quién me consolaré?
> ¿A quién quexaré mis males?[28]

Diego de San Pedro's vernacular sources are for the most part unidentifiable. His model for this *planctus* of the Virgin at the foot of the Cross could well have been a sequence of vernacular *quejas* belonging to the lost tradition of Castilian liturgical drama.[29] What he reproduced quite faithfully would have long since become fragmented, received a secular application and, like many passages of Biblical verse, been absorbed into the common stock of received lyric formulae, for sacred or profane use. Broken down into its component phrases, 'ay, ¿qué faré?', '¿a quién contaré mis quejas?', a complete register of amorous complaints can be found in the later *cancioneros*. It is not impossible that they should trace their origins back to a dramatic enactment of an apocryphal version of the Passion.

This is not the place to take the argument further into the realms of the origins of romance lyric with reference to formulaic diction in the relevant *kharjas*.[30] Dámaso Alonso's address on 'Tradition or Polygenesis' includes a salutary reminder of the danger of underestimating the universality of human experience.[31] The colloquial phrases in these poems are used every day, many times a day, in all languages, by people in moments of crisis or indecision. But because such passages occur most often and most consistently in women's poems, and because this is what gives them a lyric intensity that raises them, in my view, above the measured, calculated, anodyne majority of *cancionero* love poems, I think I am justified in speculating that there was a perceived link, maybe amounting to a literary convention, between this form of expression and the plight of a woman in distress, and that it was available for poets to draw on when they wished to compose a lyrical complaint *en boca femenina*. Diego de San Pedro's use of the sequence of *quejas* suggests one plausible archetype of bereaved womanhood, distracted by grief, which could have served as a source of poetic inspiration from the beginning of the Christian era.

Still two questions remain. First, why was there so little feminine lyric in the *cancioneros*? The possibility that it might have been written and not recorded is hard to reconcile with the enormous and varied quantity of verse collected in different kinds of *cancionero* in the course of the fifteenth century. But in order to understand why it might not have been written we would need to know a great deal more about the aesthetic and ideological preoccupations of poets and about the social function of love poetry in the court life of the period. Secondly, if there were cultural factors inhibiting the composition of love poems from a woman's point of view in the first half of the fifteenth century, how we account for the few examples we have? Do they represent the tail-end of a genre of learned lyric that was currently in decline?

I have argued that consistent colloquial diction seems positive evidence for some sort of pre *cancionero* feminine lyric tradition. Evidence of a different kind may be provided by a remarkable early fifteenth-century composition that was not collected in any *cancionero*. It is preserved in a manuscript in Paris, Bibliothèque Nationale anc. fonds esp. 216, described by Dutton *et al.* as a 'miscelánea histórica con 5 poemas' (PN2).[32] The first of these poems, 'Ay mar braba, esquiba' (f. 73), appears to have been written by a woman, Mayor Arias, for her husband, Ruy González de Clavijo, when he set out on Henry III's embassy to Tamburlaine in 1403.[33] In thirteen stanzas the lady alternately entreats, cajoles and bargains with the sea for the safe return of her husband, who is named in the last stanza. His leavetaking of her, 'Poys me boy sin falimento' (f. 74), is more conventional, shorter, and has a different metre and rhyme scheme.

The *estribillo* that begins and ends 'Ay mar braba, esquiba' identifies the poem as a *contrafactum* of an old *villancico*, 'Alta mar esquiva', which survives in at least two sixteenth-century versions:[34]

> ¡Ay mar braba, esquiba,
> de ti doy querella,
> fazes me que viua
> con tan grant manselai

If not itself the original, this earliest-known version strongly suggests that the original song was a *cantiga femenina*. The later *contrafactum* by Lope de Stúñiga (fl. 1435), 'Gentil dama esquiva', could therefore be construed as appropriating a feminine lyric for male use, like the Count of Mayorga's translation of 'Triste soy por la partida'.[35] 'Ay mar braba, esquiba' is an intriguing composition on several counts and awaits a more detailed study than can be attempted here. The integrity of tone, style and content evinces a natural affinity between its traditional lyric format and its aristocratic frame of reference; its maritime setting evokes a whole series of *cantigas de amigo*, the *barcarolas*. How is it related to the feminine lyric of male authorship in the *cancioneros*? It seems to me that the only real common ground between the two is one of circumstance: this is another *despedida* composed for a public occasion. But what are we to make of the fact that Mayor Arias's poem is written in Castilian, whereas Ruy González's reply is, in intention at least, written in the hybrid dialect that passed for Galician in Castilian literary circles?[36] I am inclined to take this symbolic discrepancy at face value and conclude that while noblemen and courtiers followed the dictates of poetic fashion, their wives and daughters remained true to Castilian; that ladies, no less than peasant girls, were guardians of the vernacular and of a lyric tradition that enshrined the culture of their own sex, unaffected by changing linguistic trends at court.

For the sake of argument let us suppose that the few learned poems we have been looking at are the relics of an older tradition that was only sporadically acknowledged by *cancionero* poets and compilers. For some reason the genre of feminine complaint poems happened to run counter to the prevailing masculine ethos of fifteenth-century court lyric. It seems that no lyric genres were held in high enough regard in the fourteenth century to warrant preservation in permanent collections like *cancioneros*. But we must be prepared to entertain the hypothesis that love lyric was none the less cultivated in the Castilian dialect by fourteenth-century court poets, and that a representative proportion of this verse will have been feminine lyric.[37]

Notes

Publications of L. J. Woodward

'*La vida retirada* of Fray Luis de León', *BHS* 31 (1954), 17–26.

'Les images et leur fonction dans *Nuestro Padre San Daniel de G. Miro*', *BHi* 56 (1954), 110–132.

'*El casamiento engañoso y el coloquio de los perros*', *BHS* 36 (1959), 80–87.

The life of St. Peter Claver, Burns Oates (London 1961)—Trans.

'Two Images in the *Soledades* of Góngora', *MLN* 76 (1961), 773–785.

'Fray Luis de León's *Oda a Francisco Salinas*', *BHS* 39 (1962), 69–77.

'Author–Reader Relationship in the *Lazarillo de Tormes*', *FMLS* I (1965), 43–53.

'El sueño de Clarín', *Hacia Calderón* 3 (1976), 123–128.

'Le *Lazarillo*—oeuvre d'imagination ou document social', *Théorie et pratique politiques à la Renaissance* (Paris 1977), 333–347.

'La dramatización del tiempo en el auto *Los alimentos del hombre*', *Hacia Calderón* 4 (1979), 123–128.

'*Recta ratio* and Cervantes' *La gitanilla*', *Actas del I Congreso Internacional sobre Cervantes* (Madrid 1981), 1890–96.

'Logic and Rhetoric: the term *Suposición* in Calderón's *No hay más fortuna que Dios*', *Tercentenary Studies in Calderón* (Toronto 1982), 178–197.

'Hebrew Mysticism and Luis de Léon', forthcoming in *BHS* 61, part 3 (1984).

Essay 1

1. It is difficult to ascertain how complete this 'conversion' is. Pamela Waley, 'The Unity of the *Casamiento engañoso* and the *Coloquio de los perros*', *BHS* 34 (1957), 201–212, points out that Campuzano's 'promise of reformation'—'Dicen que quedaré sano si me guardo; espada tengo; lo demás Dios lo remedie' (201)—is "somewhat tepid" (p. 206). On the other hand Ruth El Saffar, *Novel to Romance: A Study of Cervantes's 'Novelas ejemplares'* (Baltimore 1974), sees Campuzano's confession to Peralta as evidence of self-transcendence: 'It is this resurrection of the spirit that makes possible the Ensign's full confession of his faults in his narration to Peralta' (p. 70).

2. These and all subsequent italics mine. Page references are to the *Novelas ejemplares*, ed. F. Rodríguez-Marín, seventh edition, 2 vols (Madrid 1975), II, p. 175–340.

3. L. J. Woodward, 'El casamiento engañoso y el coloquio de los perros', *BHS* 36 (1959), 80–87, justly refers to this as, 'a lesson as banal to Cervantes as it may be to the reader' (p. 80).

4. Fray Luis de León expounds the virtues of the pastoral life in the chapter of *Los*

151

nombres de Cristo entitled *Pastor:* '...que, aunque es oficio de gobernar y regir, pero es muy diferente de los otros gobiernos. Porque lo uno, su gobierno no consiste en dar leyes ni en poner mandamientos, sino en apacentar y alimentar a los que gobiernan.' See *Obras Completas Castellanas,* ed. Felix García, O.S.A., 2 vols. (Madrid 1967) I, p. 468.

5. See Ludwig Wittgenstein, *Philosophical Investigations,* translated by G. E. M. Anscombe (Oxford 1963), p. 223.

6. Waley, art. cit., p. 211.

7. See John 10:34, 'Respondit eis Iesus: Nonne scriptum est in lege vestra quia ego dixi: Dii estis?' The reference is to Psalm 81:6–7, 'Ego dixi: Dii estis, Et filii Excelsi omnes. Vos autem sicut homines moriemini...'

8. Woodward, art. cit., p. 83.

9. See the Epistle of James 3:10, 'Ex ipso ore procedit benedictio et maledictio.' This epistle contains much that is relevant to the *Coloquio* in its treatment of the relationship between faith and works, wisdom, humility and control of the tongue. The difficulties of self-knowledge are touched on in 1:23–24, 'Quia si quis auditor est verbi, et non factor, hic comparabitur viro consideranti vultum nativitatis suae in speculo: consideravit enim se, et abiit, et statim oblitus est qualis fuerit.'

10. In his *Exposición del Libro de Job* Luís de León, commenting on 4:12–13, remarks that the dead of night is a particularly propitious time for the human mind to receive Divine revelations in dreams: 'Y como es su origen el cielo, avecínase a las cosas dél y júntase con los que en él moran; ...y súbese al cielo que entonces se le abre resplandeciente y clarísimo, y mete todos sus pensamientos en Dios y en medio de la escuridad de la noche le amanece la luz.' See ed. cit., II, p. 96–97.

Essay 2

1. John H. Turner, *The Myth of Icarus in Spanish Renaissance Poetry* (London 1976). 'Qué de invidiosos montes levantados' is referred to very briefly on page 90.

2. Robert Jammes, *Etudes sur l'oeuvre poétique de don Luis de Góngora y Argote* (Bordeaux 1967), p. 425.

3. The text used is the Millé edition, *Obras completas,* ed. J. and I. Millé y Giménez, 6th edition (Madrid 1972), p. 574–75.

4. As will be seen from my analysis, I cannot agree with Dámaso Alonso that the poem is in fact an epithalamium, an elaborate compliment to a pair of lovers. The intensity of the emotions expressed and their remarkable resolution suggest something far more serious than 'un mero fingimiento literario'. *Góngora y el Polifemo,* II, 6th edition (Madrid 1974), p. 201–04.

5. Referring to the probable influence of Tasso's 'Già il notturno sereno' on 'Qué de invidiosos montes levantados', Alonso implies that Góngora's apparent reticence here could well have been due to the 'clima moral hispánico', ibid., p. 202–04. I would contend that this detail is of paramount importance in any attempt to understand the poem, and is quite deliberate.

6. "*Lidiar.* Folgar, jugar el marido con la mujer; o en el lenguaje de Góngora, reñir batallas de amor." B. Alemany y Selfa, *Vocabulario de las obras de don Luis de Góngora y Argote* (Madrid 1930), p. 584.

7. This is a clear anticipation of the famous concluding lines of the *Soledad primera:* "bien previno la hija de la espuma/a batallas de amor campo de pluma."

8. L. J. Woodward, "Two images in the *Soledades* of Góngora", *MLN* 76 (1961), 773–785.

9. Salcedo Coronel refers to an express imitation of Petrarch's 'Si è debile il filo a cui s'attene' in Góngora's poem, but Dámaso Alonso is correct in stating that the resemblance is entirely superficial (op. cit., p. 202). For his part, Alonso believes the 'italianismo' of the poem is due to the strong influence of several poems of Torquato Tasso. I believe that this is no more important to the essential qualities of Góngora's poem than is the use of images from Petrarch in the opening lines of the Spanish work.

10. My analysis of the poem is in part an attempt to explain the entire thematic and emotional coherence of Góngora's composition, which has been described elsewhere in quite different terms. Robert Jammes, for example, writes that the poem 'développe deux thèmes opposés, dont la contradiction lui donne un accent particulièrement poignant.' '. . . la *canción* s'achève, paradoxalement, sur une série d'images tendres et voluptueuses et sur un hymne fervent à l'amour heureux.' (op. cit., p. 425–26).

Essay 3

1. The edition to which line-numbers, Acts and scenes refer is that of Alonso Zamora Vicente (Clásicos Castellanos 159). The recent critical analyses include the following: Charles H. Ferguson, 'Personaje, imagen y tema en *Peribáñez*', *Revista de la Facultad de Humanidades de San Luis Potosí* 2 (1968), 313–332; Mary G. Randel, 'The portrait and the creation of Peribáñez', *RF* 85 (1973), 145–158; J. E. Varey, 'The essential ambiguity in Lope de Vega's *Peribáñez:* theme and staging', *Theatre Research International*, n. s.1 (1976), 157–178; John Bryans, 'Providence and discretion in *Peribáñez*', *J Hisp P* 2 (1977–78), 121–133; L. L. Zeller, 'The dramatic function of comic relief in Lope de Vega's tragicomedia *Peribáñez*', *PQ* 57 (1979), 337–352; Alix Sara Zuckerman, 'Honor re-considered: Lope de Vega's treatment of honor in his conjugal honor plays' (Ph.D. dissertation for the City University of New York, 1979). Incidentally, the present article offers no analysis of the comendador, Don Fadrique, whose character and language have been fully explored by other critics.

2. John Bryans is—to my knowledge—the only critic to be seriously disturbed by Peribáñez's slaying of Inés and Luján. I share his reservations about that, as well as about Peribáñez's honour, discretion, and justification; in comparison with Bryans, however, my own reading of the play leads me towards different, and, I confess, more mundane conclusions. Other critics are generally inclined to regard the murders of Inés and Luján as, somehow, justifiable.

3. This awareness is evident in the very terms with which Peribáñez rejects the idea: 'Porque plumas de señor/podrán darnos por favor/a tí viento y a mí peso' (783–785): the literal meaning cannot be taken seriously, so we are forced to reflect on the metaphorical allusions—*viento* as 'gossip', *peso* as

'care' or 'coin', *dar el viento* as a hunting term ('to give the scent'), *plumas* as a mark of wealth, and so on.

4. The complexities of the concept are apparent in *Las siete partidas*, with its three-fold definition of *honra* as 'adelantamiento señalado con loor, que gana ome por razon del logar que tiene, o por hazer fecho conoscido que faze, o por bondad que en el ha' (*Pda.* II, *tít.* 13, *ley* iv), supplemented by the examples it gives of *deshonra*, which include sending too much smoke upstairs and throwing too much water downstairs (seriously!—see VII-9-vi). For a recent account of Golden Age honour that is both succinct and comprehensive, see Alix Zuckerman's Ph.D. dissertation, 'Honor Reconsidered'. D. R. Larson demonstrates the variations in Lope's own treatment of the issue in *The Honor Plays of Lope de Vega* (Cambridge, Mass. 1977).

5. Comments from a variety of 'non-poetic' contemporary texts suggest that there is nothing unusual about a sceptical attitude towards the *honor* = *opinión* relationship; see, e.g., Castillo de Bovadilla: 'ay muchos hombres de tan poco valor, que les parece que honrando à otros, diminuyen su pundonor, y quieren acrecentar la autoridad propia con el menosprecio de la calidad agena...' (*Política para Corregidores* [1597], V-1-51), or Juan de Zabaleta: 'no se engañe el mundo: lo que llaman honra comúnmente es la estimación, y ésta no toda, sino la que hacen de un hombre los mozos sin prudencia y los viejos sin juicio; por cumplir con éstos, se hacen las venganzas, que para con los varones cuerdos, sólo el que obra sin culpa es honrado' (*El día de fiesta por la mañana* [1654], *Cap.* 1). Of particular interest, as always, are the views of Saavedra Fajardo as expressed in *Idea de un príncipe político Christiano representada en cien empresas* [1640]: in *Empresa* 14 he writes that 'está constituído el honor en la opinión agena para que la temamos', but goes on to explain at some length that it can be quite disadvantageous to have a good reputation because it makes people envious and spiteful towards you; and he reveals a suitably sceptical attitude towards the whole business in *Empresa* 58 where he encourages the Prince to dangle *honor* before his minions like a carrot as this is one of the cheapest ways known of getting your subjects to spill their blood and cough up their property: 'si no fuera hijo de lo honesto y glorioso, le tuviera por invención política'. Fajardo, characteristically, forestalls charges of cynicism by warning that 'es muy dañosa en los súbditos aquella estimación ligera o gloria vana fundada en la ligereza de la opinión...' Notwithstanding the quarter-century time-lapse, it does not seem unreasonable to suppose that Lope's reflections on the subject could have approximated to Fajardo's.

6. Vázquez de Menchaca, for example, describes the problem as 'difficult' and makes reference to a wide selection of authorities. See *Controversias fundamentales* (1564), *Lib.* I, *Cap.* XI and *Cap.* XVIII.

7. *Recopilación de las leyes destos Reynos* (Alcalá de Henares 1598), *Libro* 8°, *Título* 23, 'De los homicidios', *ley* 4. This law was drafted for the *Fuero Real* of Alfonso XI, and was retained for at least four centuries, still surviving intact in the *Novísima Recopilación* of the late 18th century.

8. For L. L. Zeller, this is part of the comic relief essential to a *tragicomedia*, Alix Zuckerman sees it as part of Lope's irony, while Charles Ferguson notes that 'el monarca que ha adoptado tal apodo [Enrique Justiciero] se

distingue pronto ordenando una ejecución sin juicio previo' (art. cit., p. 329).

9. Victor Dixon, 'The symbolism of *Peribáñez'*, *BHS* 43 (1966), 11–24, p. 12 n. 2.

10. 'Mas todavia les [los iueces] mandamos, que contra los omnes viles, que son pobres, que atiemplen la pena de las leyes en alguna cosa a los pobres. Ca si lo quisieren todo afincar, cuemo manda el derecho, en ningun tiempo non ferien nenguna merced.' (*Fuero Juzgo, Libro* XII, *Titol.* 1, *ley* 1).

11. 'La posibilidad de felicidad en su nueva categoría no excluye la posibilidad de ruina.' (art. cit., p. 330).

12. Lope must have known this from Fernán Pérez de Guzmán's character sketch in *Generaciones y semblanzas*, which tells us that Enrique chose good advisers, 'con cuyo consejo ordenaba sus rentas e justicias . . . . E ansi con tales maneras tenia su hazienda bien ordenada, y el Reyno pacifico e sosegado'. Lope has made little attempt to present these positive aspects of Enrique III: even the 'Justiciero' tag is introduced as Enrique's own invention ('en lugar del Tercero/quiero que este nombre asombre', 2994–95). Furthermore, the Queen, who is described by Pérez de Guzmán as 'muy sometida a privados, e regida dellos', is changed by Lope into the person who influences the King.

13. Cf. Angus Mackay: 'The later medieval political history of the Iberian peninsula was bedevilled by dynastic crises and civil wars. In Castile, for example, not one of the nine reigns from 1296 to 1504 remained unaffected by either the serious problems posed by a minority or the dangers of a disputed succession', *Spain in the Middle Ages* (London 1977), p. 121.

Essay 4

1. 'La caza de amor es de altanería (Sobre los precedentes de una poesía de San Juan de la Cruz)', *BRAE* 26 (1947), 63–79 (reprinted in Dámaso Alonso, *De los siglos oscuros al de oro* [Madrid 1958], p. 254–275). See also Dámaso Alonso, *Poesía española. Ensayo de métodos y límites estilísticos* (Madrid 1950), p. 253–56.

2. I have used the text published in San Juan de la Cruz, *Cántico espiritual. Poesías*, edited by C. Cuevas García (Madrid 1979), p. 342–43.

3. Dámaso Alonso, *La poesía de San Juan de la Cruz (desde esta ladera)* (Madrid 1942), p. 234.

4. 'Ther is a Gerfawken . . . Ther is a fawken peregryne . . . And these be hawkes of the towre' (facsimile edition of *The Boke of St. Albans*, published in R. Hands, *English Hunting and Hawking in the Boke of St. Albans* (Oxford 1975), p. 54–55; 'Mirry Margaret,/As mydsomer flowre,/Jentill as fawcoun/Or hawke of the towre' (John Skelton, *Poems*, edited by R. S. Kinsman [Oxford 1969], p. 131–32).

5. Pero López de Ayala's *Libro de la caza de las aves* tells us that 'tovieron por bien aquellos que esta arte fallaron . . . non solamente tomar con ellas aquellas aves e prisiones e en aquella manera que la natura les otorga de tomar mas con el trabajo e sotileza del caçador tomassen otras aves e prisiones, e por

mas estrañias guisas que las que solian tomar, asy como *el falcon tomar la garça alta en las nuves perdida de vista, otrossy tomar la grua yendo alto por el ayre* (Compare San Juan's lines 'tanto bolar me convino/que de vista me perdiesse'). Quotations from the *Libro de la caza* are from the fifteenth-century British Museum manuscript (Add. 16392). The mediaeval popularity of the work persisted into the Golden Age; a number of the surviving manuscripts are from the sixteenth century or later.

6. 'And yit there be moo kyndis of hawkes. Ther is a Goshawke. and that hauke is for a yeman. Ther is a Tercell. And that is for a powere man. Ther is a Spare Hawke. and he is an hawke for a prest . . . And theis be of an oder maner kynde. for thay flie to Querre and to fer Jutty and to Jutty fferry' (*Boke of St. Albans*, p. 55).

7. '. . . en sus talles sson mas gentiles, que han las cabeças mas primas e las alas puntas mejor sacadas, e las colas mas cortas, e mas derribadas en las espaldas, e mas aperçebidos e mas ardidos, e de mayor esfuerço, e en sus governamientos son mas delicados delos otros que dicho avemos, e quieren ser governados de mejores viandas, e ser siempre traydos muy bien en la mano por el gran orgullo que han'. 'Ca en verdat este es el Señyor e principe de las aves de la caça, e quien bien supiere regir e governar el nebly todo el regimiento delas otras aves puede mas ligeramente saber' (*Libro de la caza*, fols. 9v, 19r).

8. 'Ther is a Gerfawken, a Tercell of a gerfawken. And theys belong to a Kyng . . . Ther is a fawken peregryne. And that is for an Erle' (*Boke of St. Albans*, p. 54). Fifteenth-century *cancionero* poets such as Villasandino use a similar, though less systematized, hierarchy in addressing royalty and noblemen.

9. 'Una posible fuente de San Juan de la Cruz', *RFE* 28 (1944), 473–77.

10. *San Juan de la Cruz. Poems* (*Critical Guides to Spanish Texts*, 13) (London 1975), p. 42.

11. The *Diccionario de Autoridades* gives both meanings of *abatirse:* '. . . descender, baxar, o baxarse: como . . . abatirse el ave de rapiña quando baxa a hacer alguna presa . . . Vale también humillarse, envilecerse, perder el ánimo, o las fuerzas'.

12. Even an essentially practical Victorian falconer conveys some of its brilliance: 'No one knows how the speed and force of a falcon's stoop are gained. All we can say is that it is the fastest movement made by any living thing in the world. It is not flying, and it is not falling, but a combination of the two, with some other impulse which we do not understand. Mere weight must be at least a most important element, for a heavy hawk seems always to come down quicker as well as far more forcibly than one of the same species which is lighter. But weight is only one factor in the agglomeration of influences which make the stoop of the peregrine and the ger so swift. It must be seen to be believed. There is no conceivable way of measuring its speed' (E. B. Michell, *The Art and Practice of Hawking* (London 1900), p. 122–23).

13. The manuscripts differ as to the stanza order. My interpretation suggests that the version which ends with the stanza beginning 'Por una estraña manera' is logically more acceptable.

Essay 5

1. References throughout are to the edition by F. Ruiz Morcuende in Vol. X of *Obras de Lope de Vega publicadas por la Real Academia Española* (*Nueva edición*) (= AcN), Madrid 1930. This was based on the editions of Lope's *Parte XIV* of Madrid 1620 and 1621; I have checked my quotations against both, but supplied my own punctuation.

2. See AcN X, p. xxx; my edition of *El perro* (London 1981), p. 18; and S. G. Morley and C. Bruerton, *Cronología de las comedias de Lope de Vega* (Madrid 1968), p. 91 & 374–5.

3. J. W. Sage, 'The Context of Comedy: Lope de Vega's *El perro del hortelano* and related plays', *Studies in Spanish Literature of the Golden Age presented to Edward M. Wilson*, edited by R. O. Jones (London 1973), p. 247–66.

4. See *El perro*, p. 49–52. The most familiar 'exception' is *El villano en su rincón*, which is nevertheless fundamentally conservative in outlook.

5. As first noted by J. G. Fucilla, 'Etapas en el desarrollo del mito de Icaro en el Renacimiento y en el Siglo de Oro', *Hispanófila* No. 8 (1960), 1–34; but see also Louis C. Pérez, 'La fábula de Icaro y *El perro del hortelano*', *Estudios literarios de hispanistas norteamericanos dedicados a Helmut Hatzfeld*, edited by J. M. Sola-Solé and others (Barcelona 1974), p. 287–96; Javier Herrero, 'Lope de Vega y el Barroco: la degradación por el honor', *Sistema* 6 (1974), 49–71; *El perro*, p. 34 ff.

6. As first noted by Sibylle Scheid, *Petrarkismus in Lope de Vegas Sonetten* (Wiesbaden 1966), p. 104–7.

7. On Icarus, see especially John H. Turner, *The Myth of Icarus in Spanish Renaissance Poetry* (London 1977); on Phaethon, A. Gallego Morell, *El mito de Faetón en la literatura española* (Madrid 1961); J. M. Rozas, 'Dos notas sobre el mito de Faetón en el siglo de oro', *Boletín Cultural de la Embajada Argentina* (*Madrid*) I, No. 2 (1963), 3–14; idem, edition of the *Obras* of Juan de Tarsis, Conde de Villamediana (Madrid 1969).

8. See the studies of J. H. Turner and A. Gallego Morell, and *El perro*, p. 39–40.

9. 'A fake transformation, a conjurer's trick'; see L. J. Woodward (article mentioned below, note 33), p. 84; also B. W. Wardropper, 'La eutrapelia en las *Novelas ejemplares* de Cervantes', *Actas del Séptimo Congreso Internacional de Hispanistas*, ed. G. Bellini (Rome 1982), p. 153–69.

10. Cf. E. M. Wilson, 'Images et structure dans *Peribáñez*', *BHi* 51 (1949), 125–59; B. W. Wardropper, 'The Implicit Craft of the Spanish Comedia', *Studies . . . . Edward M. Wilson*, p. 339–56; David M. Gitlitz, *La estructura lírica de la comedia de Lope de Vega* (Valencia 1980).

11. See esp. Marcel Bataillon, '*La desdicha por la honra*: génesis y sentido de una novela de Lope', *Varia lección de clásicos españoles* (Madrid 1964), p. 373–418, esp. 389–93.

12. See Lope de Vega, *El marqués de las Navas*, edited by J. Fernández Montesinos (Madrid 1925), lines 429–31 & note; Miguel Herrero, *Oficios populares en la sociedad de Lope de Vega* (Madrid 1977), p. 85.

13. *Conservación de monarquías*, Discurso 37, *BAE* 25, p. 528b.

14. Each of the scenes quoted includes a comic enumeration of various kinds of *coche;* see AcN XI, p. 642; the edition by W. L. Fichter (New York 1944), p.

60–1; AcN XII, p. 458–9. On the proliferation of coaches and allusions thereto, see R. L. Kennedy, 'Certain phases of the sumptuary decrees of 1623 and their relation to Tirso's theatre', *HR* 10 (1942), 91–115; W. L. Fichter, ed. cit., p. 184–5; and the bibliography in both.

15. 'En el mar' might suggest confusion with Icarus; note however that Lope often mentions the Eridanus or Po, but also has Phaethon fall into the sea in his *Andrómeda*, lines 461–4, and *La prueba de los ingenios*, *BAE* 246, p. 284.

16. See for instance J. E. Varey, 'La campagne dans le théâtre espagnol au XVIIe siècle', *Dramaturgie et société*, ed. Jean Jacquot (Paris 1968), p. 47–76, esp. p. 52 & 60.

17. In this confusing 'variation', Hernando compares Inés with Daphne, *himself* with the sun-god; the two myths are also combined, but more coherently, in *La prueba de los ingenios*, loc. cit.

18. A ms. of *La villana* in what remains of Lord Holland's collection (see *El perro*, p. 65) contains a curious text. Its dramatic and metrical structure are similar to those of Lope's play, but it has very few identical lines. At this point, for instance, although Hernando has spoken at similar length to Inés with no reference to mythology, he has a sonnet-soliloquy which mentions both Phaethon and Icarus:

> El Icaro soberbio y atrevido
> levanta para el cielo el débil vuelo,
> y para la soberbia es desconsuelo
> quedar a la calor del Sol rendido.
>
> Faetón pide a Febo enternecido
> le deje el coche con que alumbra el suelo,
> y cae en el Erídano, que el cielo
> siempre de los soberbios se ha ofendido.
>
> Yo, loco agora con mirar tus ojos,
> a tal extremo de desdicha vengo
> que hacen en los míos tornasoles.
>
> ¿Que has de triunfar, Inés, de mis despojos?
> Mas en la mano la disculpa tengo:
> que a ellos ciega un Sol y a mí dos soles.

A comparable ms. in the same collection is described in an article by J. M. Ruano de la Haza, 'An early rehash of Lope's *Peribáñez*', *B Com* 35 (1983), 6–29.

19. Such contrasting of different worlds, *corte* and *aldea*, patrician and peasant, by reference to representative objects, is totally characteristic of Lope, most notoriously in *Peribáñez*. Note that according to Marín in *La llave de la honra* (AcN XII, p. 459): 'El primer coche del mundo/fue el trillo, para que sepas,/que de andar encima dél/le añadieron las dos ruedas.'

20. See esp. Aulus Gellius, *Noctae Atticae* III.9. Lope saw himself, like Don Félix, as the victim of a *caballo seyano*, in his case the Pegasus of poetic talent; the title-page of his *El peregrino en su patria*, Sevilla 1604, is topped by an emblematic winged horse, with the motto: SEJANVS MICHI PEGASVS, and a similar image, with the inscription 'Pegaso siempre para mí seyano' is

described in *El jardín de Lope (BAE* 38, p. 425–7). See also *La Dorotea* V, 11 & *El peregrino* . . . , IV.

21. *La villana* ('Representóla Valdés') was presumably written, like *La dama boba* (1613) for Jerónima de Burgos; so was Tirso's *Don Gil de las calzas verdes* (1615). In this play the heroine pursues her errant lover to Madrid, adopts (as well as a female name and persona) the false name and role he has affected, reducing him to despair and eventual submission. Though the general idea becomes commonplace, the 'desatinada comedia del Merçenario' may in some respects have been modelled on *La villana*.

22. See *El perro*, p. 42–7.

23. Other Lope characters who are compared to Phaethon and destined for a tragic fate are Federico in *El castigo sin venganza*, lines 567 & 1458–9, and Carlos in *El piadoso aragonés, BAE* 213, p. 326b.

24. See *Rimas*, sonnet 90, and *La mañana de San Juan en Madrid*, lines 45–6.

25. See for instance Nicolaus Reusner, *Emblemata* (Frankfurt 1581), III, Nos. 28 (Icarus) & 32 (Phaethon). Icarus and Phaethon were depicted *together* in Florentius Schoonhovius, *Emblemata* (Gouda 1618), No. 3.

26. Note also, however, that Alciati's second volume (Venice 1546), included another emblem, headed TEMERITAS, which concerned the unidentified rider of a horse out of control, and that in later collections this appeared in close proximity to IN TEMERARIOS and depicted a charioteer.

27. It is hard to agree with Lorelei Robbins, 'The Role of Commentary in Emblem Books', in *The European Emblem: towards an Index Emblematicus*, edited by Peter M. Daly (Waterloo, Ontario 1980), that we find in Covarrubias 'no instances of commentary changing the meaning of an emblem, or elucidating it for the first time'; compare No. 108, to which she herself refers, and which proves unexpectedly to relate to the friend of Phaethon, Cygnus, also from *Metamorphoses* II [378–80]. On Covarrubias and Lope, see D. W. Moir, 'Lope de Vega's *Fuente Ovejuna* and the *Emblemas morales* of Sebastián de Covarrubias Horozco (with a few remarks on *El villano en su rincón*)', *Homenaje a W. L. Fichter* (Madrid 1971), p. 537–46; and Victor Dixon, '*Beatus . . . nemo: El villano en su rincón*, las "polianteas" y la literatura de emblemas', *Cuadernos de Filología* III, 1–2 (1981), 279–300.

   Note also that in Bernardino Daza's *Los emblemas de Alciato traducidos en rhimas españolas* (Lyons 1549), fol. 88v., Phaethon is conventionally depicted, but that the verses below begin: 'Ves a Phaeton como hecho carretero . . .'

28. Morley & Bruerton, p. 366–7, date it '1615–21 (probablemente h. 1618)'.

29. See Thomas E. Case, *Las Dedicatorias de Partes XIII–XX de Lope de Vega* (Chapel Hill 1975), esp. p. 91–3.

30. See esp. G. J. Brown, 'Lope's Epigrammatic Poetic for the Sonnet', *MLN* 93 (1978), 218–32.

31. E.g. Diego López, *Declaración magistral sobre los emblemas de Andrés Alciato* (Nájera 1615), or *Andreae Alciati Emblemata cum Commentariis Claudii Minois I. C. Francisci Sanctii Brocensis, & Notis Laurentii Pignorii Patavini . . . opera et vigiliis Ioannis Thuilii . . .* (Padua 1621).

32. Natale Conti, whom Lope quotes, had explained euhemeristically the myth of Endymion and Diana by arguing that Endymion habitually hunted by the light of the moon, or that he was the first astronomer carefully to observe its

motions, whereas Phaethon was the first to study the sun (as Lucian suggested in his *Astrology:* 'So Endymion established the motions of the moon, so Phaethon inferred the course of the sun'); see his *Mythologiae...libri decem* (Frankfurt 1588), Bk. 4, Ch. 8, p. 336–8; Bk. 6, Ch. 1, p. 552–7. Note that Don Miguel's death was recorded in a letter drafted by Lope himself which seems to date from September 1619, a mere month before the *aprobación* of *Parte XIV*.

33. Cf. L. J. Woodward's characteristically illuminating interpretation of '*El casamiento engañoso y el coloquio de los perros*', *BHS* 36 (1959), 80–7.

Essay 6

1. All references are to Don Pedro Calderón de la Barca, *La vida es sueño*, edited by Albert E. Sloman (Manchester 1961).

2. A glance at Freudian theory helps to elucidate some of the implications of the interdependence of intellectual, visual and sexual drives:

'At about the same time as the sexual life of children reaches its first peak, between the ages of three and five, they also begin to show signs of the activity which may be ascribed to the instinct for knowledge or research . . . Its activity corresponds on the one hand to a sublimated manner of obtaining mastery, while on the other hand it makes use of the energy of scopophilia. Its relations to sexual life, however, are of particular importance, since we have learnt from psychoanalysis that the instinct for knowledge in children is attracted unexpectedly early and intensively to sexual problems and is in fact possibly first aroused by them.'

See *The Standard Edition of the Complete Psychological Works of Sigmund Freud*, edited by James Strachey (London 1953), VII, p. 194.

3. See *Rosaura*, in *Hispanic Studies in Honour of Frank Pierce*, edited by John England (Sheffield 1980), p. 124. Though my conclusions on Rosaura's function in the play differ, I am also indebted to seminal work on the play by E. M. Wilson, in '*La vida es sueño*', *Revista de la Universidad de Buenos Aires*, 4 (1946), 61–78, and, W. M. Whitby, in 'Rosaura's Role in the Structure of *La vida es sueño*', *MLR* 48 (1953), 293–300.

4. On the *varonil* type, see Melveena McKendrick, *Woman and Society in the Spanish Drama of the Golden Age* (London 1974).

5. See Lionel Abel, *Metatheatre: A New View of Dramatic Form* (New York 1963).

6. See Joseph Conrad in the preface to *The Nigger of the 'Narcissus'* (1897).

7. In '*El casamiento engañoso y el coloquio de los perros*', *BHS* 36 (1959), 80–7, L. J. Woodward's analysis of shifts in point of view may be seen at its best.

8. On the significance of Rosaura's 'retrieval of her portrait', and, more generally, on the play's wider issues see the valuable chapter on *La vida es sueño* in Edwin Honig, *Calderón and the Seizures of Honour* (Cambridge, Mass. 1972). I cannot accept James E. Maraniss' view in an otherwise useful book, that Calderón's 'unbending fidelity to the inseparable values of honour and order . . . prohibit the union of the play's two main characters and thus suppress the author's intuition of the heart so that a reason of state can be held'. See *On Calderón* (Columbia and London 1978), p. 29. For a recent

challenging view of Calderón, see Gwynne Edwards, *The Prison and the Labyrinth. Studies in Calderón's Tragedy* (Cardiff 1978).

Essay 7

1. José Galante de Sousa, *Bibliografia de Machado de Assis* (Rio de Janeiro 1955), p. 463.
2. The only article on the story of which I am aware is Brito Broca's 'Um conto romântico', in *Machado de Assis e a Política e Outros Estudos* (Rio de Janeiro 1957), p. 93–97. It deals principally with the political theme, and with the character of Leandro.
3. All references to Machado's works are to the *Obra Completa* (Rio de Janeiro 1962), 3 Vols.
4. See *Memórias Póstumas de Brás Cubas*, Ch. 13 (I, p. 530).
5. See, e.g. III, p. 104, in 'Potira', the first poem of *Americanas:* 'Parasitas, esposas do arvoredo,/mais fiéis não, mais venturosas que ela'.
6. Especially in an article written as early as 1859 (when Machado was only 20) entitled 'O Parasita', published as one of a series of 'Aquarelas'. See III, p. 951–53.
7. The naturalist had also been an ardent Republican, judging by his poetic life of Furius Camillus, one of the heroes of the Roman Republic, and which is the origin of Camilo's name (II, p. 162). It is difficult to be sure of Machado's meaning here, though such details are almost never gratuitous. It is hard to believe that he regards Republics in general as in some sense foreign to Brazil's nature, and that this can thus be seen as a covert statement of support for the Empire, which he mocks more overtly in this very piece. It is more likely to be satire on idealistic, Romantic politics in general.
8. From 'Notícia da Atual Literatura Brasileira: Instinto de Nacionalidade', published, like *Histórias da Meia-Noite*, in 1873.
9. *Americanas*, Machado's most substantial contribution to Indianism, was published in 1875.
10. See José de Alencar, *Obra completa* (Rio de Janeiro 1964), II, p. 25–280.
11. Ibid., p. 123–27.
12. 'Numa cidade, no meio da civilização, o que seria um selvagem, senão um cativo, tratado por todos com desprezo?' Ibid., p. 266.
13. At the end of a preface to *O Guarani*, written in 1887, Machado refers to the final moments of the novel as an unconscious allegory, though (flatteringly) of Alencar's own glory: III, p. 926.
14. São Paulo 1977.
15. One detail in particular recalls 'A Parasita Azul'. Marcela, whose peasant origins contrast with more romantic stories told about her, has a predecessor in the 'Russian princess' who captivates Camilo, and of course turns out to be of less exalted lineage.
16. *Machado de Assis* (Rio de Janeiro 1958), p. 50.
17. Fidélia, her name, while its operatic connexions cannot be forgotten, represents a (failed) hope for Brazil's future after the critical years in which the novel

is set, 1888 and 1889. The daughter of a slave-owning *fazendeiro*, she nevertheless tries to dispose of the *fazenda* (which she inherits at her father's death) in the best interests of the slaves.
18. Machado himself makes this connexion quite plain. See I, p. 1132, 1142.

Essay 8

1. J. Larrea, *Versione Celeste* (Turin 1969). Introduzione e traduzioni di Vittorio Bodini.
2. J. Larrea, *Versión Celeste* (Barcelona 1970). Edited by Luis Felipe Vivanco.
3. *Grecia, Revista de Literatura* (Seville, then Madrid 1918–1920). Editor Isaac del Vando-Villar.
4. *Cervantes, Revista Hispanoamericana* (Madrid 1916). From 1919 ed. R. Cansinos-Assens, the *ultraísta* phase. Larrea's poetry appears in it in 1919.
5. *Carmen. Revista chica de poesía* (Santander/Gijón 1928–29), Ed. Gerardo Diego.
6. E.g. G. Diego, *Poesía española contemporánea, antología* (Madrid 1968), fourth edition.
7. J. Larrea, *Oscuro dominio* (México 1934) ('Lo hicieron Justino Fernández y Edmundo O'Gorman, Alcancía').
8. *Versión Celeste*, p. 49. First published in *Grecia* (Sevilla, octubre 1919).
9. *Versión Celeste*, p. 300.
10. Letter to the writer of this article, Córdoba, 16 August 1969.
11. Same letter.
12. Interview 2, Córdoba, 8 July 1972. The interviews referred to here are a series conducted with Larrea by the author of this article in 1972. Thirty five formal interviews were held (as well as various less formal contacts) mainly at Larrea's home in Córdoba, Argentina, from 8 July until 6 August 1972. Larrea spoke in Spanish, French and some English.
13. Interview 31, Córdoba, 1 August 1972.
14. Same interview.
15. Same interview.
16. Same interview.
17. Larrea attributes *Theologia Germanica* to Eckhart but there is some uncertainty about the identity of the author. F. C. Happold in his *Mysticism* (Harmondsworth 1963), (Revised edition 1970, reprinted 1971) p. 294, argues in favour of an anonymous author.
18. Same interview. Eckhart (approx. 1260–1327) was condemned by the Church for his mystical and pantheistic theories. He fell foul of the official Church with statements such as 'The eye with which I see God is the same as that with which he sees me'. F. C. Happold, *Mysticism* (Harmondsworth 1963), p. 72 of 1971 reprint. Larrea also found in Eckhart a similar position to his own regarding the image of the statue to be found at the centre of the soul: see 'En costume de feuilles mortes', *Versión Celeste*, p. 142.
19. *Noche en Cruz* also contains essays on nineteenth and twentieth century poets.
20. Letter to C. B. Morris, Córdoba, 11 February 1971. Reference to Luis Buñuel and Salvador Dalí's film *Le Chien andalou*, 1929.

21. J. Larrea, *Del Surrealismo a Machupicchu* (Mexico 1967), between p. 48–49.
22. Letter to the writer of this article, Córdoba, 14 June 1972. (Correspondence relating to the Symbol of the Journey.)
23. Interview 4, Córdoba, 9 July 1972.
24. Same interview.
25. Same interview.
26. Homer, *The Odyssey*, Book 9, Everyman's Library, (London) p. 116. Ulysses' adventure with Polyphemus is described in *The Odyssey*, IX, 105–542.
27. R. Graves, *Greek Myths* fourth edition, second impression (London 1962), p. 717–719.
28. San Juan de la Cruz, *Cántico espiritual y otros poemas* (Buenos Aires 1969), *Subida del Monte Carmel, Canciones* ('En una noche obscura') p. 7.
29. Interview 10, Córdoba, 12 July 1972.
30. The title of a section of the unpublished *Orbe* (1926–1934), no pagination.
31. *Favorables París Poema*, no. 2, Paris (October 1926), p. 1–5.
32. See R. E. Gurney, 'A Current of Basque Mysticism in the Spanish Vanguard', *Modern Languages Journal*, (Middlesex Polytechnic, no. 1 1983). See also R. E. Gurney, *The Poetry of Juan Larrea*, (University of London Ph.D. Thesis, 1975), Chapter 6.
33. Interview 2, Córdoba, 8 July 1972.
34. Same interview.
35. Letter to the writer of this article, Córdoba, 7 December 1973.
36. Interview 2, Córdoba, 8 July 1972.
37. Same interview.
38. H. Ibsen, *Brand, Peer Gynt* (Vol. III of *The Oxford Ibsen*), ed. J. W. McFarlane (London 1972), p. 298.
39. Interview 4, Córdoba, 9 July 1972.
40. Interview 4, Córdoba, 9 July 1972.
41. A passage from Larrea's *Rendición de espíritu*, Vol. II, *Cuadernos Americanos*, (Mexico 1943), offers an insight into Larrea's latter visionary thought, and describes the pilgrim's continuation to the sea: 'Tierra nueva, cielo nuevo. En él parpadea Venus, la estrella matinal compostelana, la diosa del amor—más allá de Roma—cuyo símbolo, la venera en que cuajó como una perla, recogían los peregrinos compostelanos en el mar del Finisterre para con ellas caracterizarse. A estas conchas se las llama 'conchas de Santiago'. (p. 147.)
42. J. Larrea, *La religión del lenguage español* (Lima 1951), p. 38. Larrea is quoting from *Liber de Sancti Jacobi, Codex Calistinus. Estudios e índices* (Santiago 1944), p. lxi and lxii. Between 1949 and 1956, Larrea was awarded a series of scholarships, first by the Guggenheim Foundation and then by the Bollingen Foundation to study the myth of Saint James.
43. J. Larrea, *Teleología de la cultura* (Mexico 1965), p. 11–14.
44. J. Larrea, *La religión del lenguage español*, p. 38.
45. Interview 2, Córdoba, 8 July 1972.
46. Same interview.
47. The title of the final chapter of *Rendición de espíritu*, vol. 1., p. 233.
48. Interview, 2, Córdoba, 8 July 1972.

Essay 9

1. Góngora, *Soledad primera*, 366–502. The references throughout are to the edition of John Beverley (Madrid 1980). Aspects of this speech have been discussed by Robert Jammes in his *Études sur l'oeuvre poétique de Don Luis de Góngora* (Bordeaux 1967), p. 140–144 and 602–605. In so far as it has a bearing on Góngora's attitude to the New World, it attracts the comments of Dámaso Alonso in 'Góngora y América', originally published in 1927 and reproduced in *Estudios y ensayos gongorinos* (Madrid 1955), and in *Obras completas* V (Madrid 1978), p. 602–612.

2. Juan de Jáuregui, *El Antídoto contra la pestilente poesía de Las Soledades aplicado a su autor para defenderle de sí mismo* (1614), edited by Eunice Joiner Gates, (Colegio de México 1960), p. 89. M. J. Woods, *The Poet and the Natural World in the Age of Góngora* (Oxford University Press 1978), claimed that the Duke of Bejar is pictured as a triumphant huntsman and states that 'it would have been difficult, of course, for Góngora to attack an activity which his noble patron enjoyed as an example of cruelty and a violation of natural harmony' (p. 162). Such a reading is to ignore the tone of the passage. It is not possible, either, on the evidence of this passage to sustain the argument that 'Góngora positively approved of hunting as one of the proofs of man's resourcefulness'. The additional evidence, adduced by J. F. G. Gornall in 'Góngora's *Soledades:* 'alabanza de aldea' without 'menosprecio de corte'?', *BHS* 59 (1982), 21–25, does not lend conviction to this argument. Both critics, to my mind, seem to take for granted a serious attitude on Góngora's part.

3. *Publi Vergili Maronis, Aeneidos: Liber Quartus*, edited by Arthur Stanley Pease (Harvard U.P. 1935), p. 314–319. 'The region about the Caspian, including Hyrcania at its southeast end, was considered particularly barbarous, and its jungles and forests were full of dangerous beasts', supra p. 317. For other Classical antecedents, see José Pellicer de Salas y Tovar, *Lecciones solemnes a las obras de Don Luis de Góngora y Argote* (1630), reprinted by Georg Olms (Hildesheim 1971), p. 431–2.

4. Pease, op. cit. p. 318–319.

5. Jammes, op cit. p. 602. He adds: 'Cette malédiction initiale peut paraître, en effect, quelque peu livresque . . . .'

6. Luis de Camões, *Os Lusiadas*, edited by Frank Pierce (Oxford 1981), Canto IV, verse 102. More apposite, perhaps, would be the neutral comment in Ovid, at the beginning of his *Metamorphoses*, Book 1, 94–96, where in the Golden Age:

> "nondum caesa suis, peregrinum ut viseret orbem,
> montibus in liquidas pinus descenderat undas,
> nullaque mortales praeter sua litora norant."

'Never yet had any pine tree, cut down from its home on the mountain, been launched on the ocean's waves to visit foreign lands: men only knew their own shores', *The Metamorphoses of Ovid*, translated by Mary M. Innes, (Penguin Books 1971), p. 31. There was no shortage of sixteenth-century Spanish versions of the *Metamorphoses*. See Rudolph Schevill, *Ovid and the*

Renascence in Spain (1913), reprinted by Georg Olms (Hildesheim 1971), p. 245–249.

7. Jammes, op. cit. p. 602. See also the comments of Juergen Hahn, *The Origins of the Baroque Concept of Peregrinatio* (Chapel Hill 1973), p. 58–60.

8. Ed. cit. lines 503–506. Woods, op. cit. p. 78, sees this passage as an example of the sensitivity of the peasants in the *Soledades,* and implies that the old man is deserving of the reader's sympathy. This interpretation clearly suggests an unequivocal seriousness of intent on Góngora's part, which, to my mind, is an unwarranted assumption.

9. Beverley, ed. cit. p. 34.

Essay 10

* This was originally presented as a paper to the Fourth International Conference of Hispanists in Salamanca in 1971 under the title 'Algunos aspectos de Juan de Gales'.

1. M. Barbi, *La leggenda di Traiano nei volgarizzamenti del* Breviloquium de virtutibus di Fra Giovanni Gallese (Florence 1895).

2. *Studies in English Franciscan History* (Manchester 1917).

3. *Franciscan Papers, Lists and Documents* (Manchester 1943).

4. Joan de Gal.les, *Breviloqui,* ed. P. Norbert d'Ordal, O. M. Cap. (Barcelona 1930).

5. E.g. Morel-Fatio mentioned it in *Grundriss der romanischen Philologie de Gröber,* II (Strasbourg 1897).

6. J. Villanueva, *Viage literario a las iglesias de España,* XVIII (Madrid 1851).

7. A. Rubió y Lluch, *Documents per l'historia de la cultura catalana mig-eval,* II (Barcelona 1921), no. 248.

8. 'Documents', *Butlletí de la Biblioteca de Catalunya* 3 (1916).

9. J. Sanchis Sivera, 'Bibliología valenciana medieval', *Anales del Centro de Cultura Valenciana* 3 (1930).

10. J. M. Madurell Marimón, 'Manuscritos trecentistas y cuatrocentistas', *Hispania Sacra* 4 (1951) no. 61, item 5.

11. 'Documents', *Butlletí de la Biblioteca de Catalunya* 4 (1917).

12. J. M. Madurell Marimón and J. Rubió y Balaguer, *Documentos para la historia de la imprenta y librería en Barcelona (1475–1553)* (Barcelona 1955).

13. A. Rubió y Lluch, op. cit., I (Barcelona 1908), no. 67.

14. Ibid. nos. 221, 253 and 257.

15. *Dotzè del Crestià* (Valencia 1484), cap. 192.

16. Cf. Ruth Leslie, 'A Source for Juan Fernández de Heredia's *Rams de flores*', *SN* 45 (1973).

17. Ramón d'Alós, 'Documenti per la storia della biblioteca d'Alfonso il Magnánimo', *Miscellanea Francesco Ehrle, Scritti di storia e paleografía* 5 (Rome 1924).

Essay 11

1. Vicente Ramos, *Gabriel Miró* (Alicante 1979), p. 180.

2. *Obras completas* (Madrid 1961), p. 415–17. Henceforth abbreviated *OC.*

3. 'K. enters *The Castle.* On the Change of Person in Kafka's Manuscript', *Euphorion* 62 (1968), 28–45.

4. I am indebted to Prof. Franz Stanzel for drawing my attention to Kafka and Austen in this respect during a lecture he gave at Aberdeen University and in a personal letter. He also pointed out Joyce Cary's remarks on converting part of *Prisoner of Grace* from first to third person: 'So the whole content, the meaning of the chapter was altered without the alteration of a single word in it' (Cary is referring to a passage in dialogue). See Cary, *Art and Reality* (Cambridge 1957), p. 98.

5. Details of all the texts and variants compiled by Pedro Caravia in G. Miró, *Obras completas, Edición conmemorativa*, 12 vols (Barcelona 1932–49), II, p. 247–83.

6. Käte Hamburger's concept of the 'epic preterite' is relevant here, a narrative tense that is grammatically past but in fiction introduces the reader into the present world of the characters: *The Logic of Literature* (Bloomington 1973), p. 64 ff.

7. 'K. enters *The Castle*', p. 30.

8. Miró's hesitations here can be seen in the fact, not mentioned by Pedro Caravia, that in the 1916 edition '¡Oh, milagro de Nuestra Señora!' is placed in quotation marks.

9. I use the term and its abbreviation employed by Roy Pascal in his *The Dual Voice* (Manchester 1977).

10. See for instance, *The Dual Voice*, p. 137. Seymour Chatman, *Story and Discourse* (Ithaca 1978), p. 206–8, gives a somewhat different emphasis, distinguishing helpfully between ironical and sympathetic effects of FIS. However the 'covert narrator' remains present in his analysis even when narrator and character are unified.

11. *Gabriel Miró: His Private Library and his Literary Background* (London 1975), p. 89–91, 95–6, and 100–4.

12. Dorrit Cohn ('Narrated Monologue: Definition of a Fictional Style', *CL* 18 [1966], 97–112), makes, like Seymour Chatman, a distinction between identification and distance in the use of FIS: lyric and ironic uses of the device. Clearly Miró's narrator alternates, blends, and confuses the two uses, though they are not strict alternatives since the presence of the ironic undermines the lyric. But the distinction is illuminating and Cohn's term 'lyric' again helps understand all the criticism that has seen *Cerezas* as a 'lyrical' novel without perceiving the irony.

13. All commentators from Bally onwards point out that exclamation is an indicator of FIS. See Pascal, p. 20, and Chatman, p. 202.

14. *The Dual Voice*, p. 59.

15. *Jane Austen's Literary Manuscripts* (Oxford 1964), p. 52–4.

16. I wish to thank Doña Olympia Luengo Miró for allowing me to study the facsimile of the manuscript of *Las cerezas del cementerio*, and to thank the British Academy and the Carnegie Trust for the Universities of Scotland for their financial help.

Essay 12

1. Menéndez y Pelayo, *Historia de las ideas estéticas en España* in *Obras completas*, ed. Miguel Artigas, vol. 2 (Santander 1940), p. 75–6.

2. Leo Spitzer, *Classical and Christian Ideas of World Harmony* (Baltimore 1963), p. 112–5; Francisco Rico, *El pequeño mundo del hombre* (Madrid 1970), p. 170–89. See too Théodore Gérold, *Les Pères de l'église et la musique* (Paris 1931); John Hollander, *The Unturning of the Sky. Ideas of Music in English Poetry 1500–1700* (Princeton 1961).

3. Dámaso Alonso, *Poesía española* (Madrid 1962), p. 184–5, 191–2; Rico, p. 184. All references to the text are to the critical edition by Angel C. Vega (Madrid 1955).

4. L. J. Woodward, 'Fray Luis de León's *Oda a Francisco Salinas*', BHS 39 (1962), p. 77.

5. Fray Luis de León, *Poesías*, edited by Angel Custodio Vega (Barcelona 1975), p. 16 no. 4; M. Durán, *Luis de León* (New York 1971), p. 78; Fray Luis de León, *The Original Poems*, edited by Edward Sarmiento (Manchester 1953), p. 73–4.

6. Luis de León, *Opera* vol. 2 (Salamanca 1891–5), p. 39. I am grateful to Bernard and Janet Hamilton for their help in interpreting this passage and its context.

7. Ruth Burrows, *Guidelines to Mystical Prayer* (London 1976), p. 45–56; *Interior Castle Explored* (London 1981).

8. Jean Leclercq, O.S.B., *The Love of Learning and the Desire for God* (London 1978), p. 65–86.

9. E.g. in the section on 'Exposo' in *Los nombres de Cristo*, in *Obras completas castellanas*, edited by F. García O.S.A. (Madrid 1957) 1, p. 663–8; and in his defence of the writings of Santa Teresa, ibid., p. 915–917.

10. Ibid., p. 917.

11. Richard of St. Victor, *Selected Writings on Contemplation*, translated by Clare Kirchberger (London 1957), p. 211; *PL* 196, col. 191–2.

12. Emilio Orozco, *Poesía y mística. Introducción a la lírica de San Juan de la Cruz* (Madrid 1959), p. 83–109, especially p. 99–101.

13. Denis the Carthusian, *Opera omnia* (Montreuil-sur-mer 1896–1935), vol. 4, p. 15.

14. G. Sanctius S.J., *In quatuor libros Regum* (Lyons 1623), col. 1379–1380. I am indebted to Dr. Nigel Griffin for identifying this writer as Gaspar Sánchez S.J. (1554–1628): see C. Sommervogel S.J., *Bibliothèque de la Compagnie de Jésus* (Brussels 1890–1900), vol. 7, cols. 524–526.

15. Ibid. 'S. Franciscus ad lyricinis cantum ad coelestium rerum contemplationem exitabatur'.

16. Alphonsi Tostati Hispani, *Commentaria in lib. III Regum* (Venice 1596), 26v–27r.

17. '... Ultimus et praecipuus finis caeremoniarum est incrementum interioris pietatis ... aliae caeremoniae ... id efficiunt naturali quadam efficacia, ut cantus et res musicae, cui naturaliter inest vis ad excitandum animum ad coelestia': *Opera*, vol. 4, p. 234.

18. *De Musica* (Salamanca 1577): the passage quoted occurs on the second of eight unnumbered pages which constitute the Preface.

19. See the article on 'Contemplation' in *Dictionnaire de spiritualité* vol. 2, part 2, cols. 1979–81, 1984–8; William Johnston, *The Mysticism of The Cloud of Unknowing* (Wheathampstead 1978), p. 135.

20. García Jiménez de Cisneros, *Obras completas*, edited by Cipriano Baraut (Montserrat 1965), vol. 2, p. 256, 274, 280.

21. See the many references in *Vida y obras de San Juan de la Cruz*, edited by Lucinio Ruano O.C.D. (Madrid 1973), p. 1059. On the influence of this notion of wisdom on Renaissance Neo-Platonism see Eugene F. Rice, *The Renaissance Idea of Wisdom* (Cambridge, Mass. 1958).

22. Athanasius, *PG* 25, col. 83–6 (I am grateful to Dr. Carolyn Lee for drawing my attention to this passage); Eusebius of Caesarea, *PG* 20, col. 1583–6; Augustine, *Epistola* 166, p. 13 in *Obras* (BAC, Madrid 1962), p. 313–4, quoted in Spitzer, p. 31.

23. *Noche oscura*, Book 1, chapter 12:5 in *Vida y obras de San Juan de la Cruz*, p. 639.

24. Cf. Rico, p. 181–2, 187.

25. Woodward, p. 71.

26. Quoted in the edition of Sarmiento, p. 63.

27. 'Nec alia de causa choros monachorum, aut cauonicorum, in terris institutos fuisse credibile est nisi ut quemadmodum caelestibus in choris angeli Deo semper assistunt, pulcherrimis eius laudes melodiis ac rythmis celebrantes' *De Musica, loc cit.*

28. On the senses of the soul see Wolfgang Riehle, *The Middle English Mystics* (London 1981), p. 104.

29. Woodward, p. 73.

30. Two readings of this line exist, both well authenticated (the other is 'todo lo demás es triste lloro'): see the notes in the edition of Vega, p. 452.

   An earlier version of this essay was read at a seminar on Fray Luis on the occasion of Professor Woodward's visit to University College Cork in November 1981. It accompanied another paper on the *Ode to Salinas* by Professor Patrick Gallagher. Both papers were later read at a meeting of the Association of Hispanists at Newcastle in March 1982. I am grateful to Professor Gallagher for his collaboration on these two occasions.

Essay 14

1. Henri-Irénée Marrou. *Saint Augustin et la fin de la culture antique* (Paris 1958), p. 451.

2. Quotations are from the Aguilar edition of the *Autos sacramentales* by A. Valbuena Prat, with certain references to the very indifferent Pando edition.

3. C. H. Flack, *Te Deum Laudamus* (Cambridge 1935) gives the hymn's Ninth Century title *Hymnus quem S. Ambrosius et S. Augustinus invicem condiderunt* (7) and comments (9) 'The story that the two saints, at (Augustine's) baptism, were inspired to utter, verse by verse, this supreme confession of faith and hymn of praise, is doubtless a picturesque one, but has little foundation in fact'.

4. St. Augustine sees *curiositas* as daemonic, cf. '. . . in ipsa religione Deus tentatur, cum signa et prodigia flagitantur, non ad aliquam salutem, sed ad solam experientiam desiderata' *Conf.*, X, p. 35.

5. Another form it might take was that of establishing parallels between Old Testament and New Testament phenomena, as in the *Synodicus* of Wernerius of Basel.

6. The waste land is at the same time the historical last refuge of pagan cults (cf. *Sicut haec barbaricis gentilia pagis*, Prudentius, 'Contra Symmachum', I, p. 449) and on the metaphysical level the abode of those not predestined to the

Civitas Dei (cf. Orosius: 'Praeceperas mihi, ut adversus vaniloquam pravitatem eorum, qui alieni a civitate Dei ex locorum conpitis et pagis pagani vocantur, sive gentiles, quia terrena sapiunt . . .' Prologue to *Historiae*).

7. Augustine based his version of this ascendancy on the test of *Genesis* XXV, v. 23. The elder shall serve the younger, who becomes the *verus Israel*.

8. Regocijo as *fiscal* probably has his origins in *Confessions* IX: 'Est gaudium, quod non datur impiis, sed eis qui te gratis colunt, quorum gaudium tu ipse es; et ipsa est beata vita gaudere de te propter te, ipsa est et non altera'. The apprehension of the two *impii* Judaísmo and Gentilidad translates their inability to experience joy:

> JUDAÍSMO: Si el verte me asusta, qué
> hará oírte? Baste, baste.
> Y pues que te perdí (*sc.* la fe) dices,
> no me aflijas, no me mates.
> GENTILIDAD: Yo, pues que nunca te vi,
> no es bien que al verte me espante,
> de tu razón el dudar
> el primer discurso enlace.

(778h)

9. Augustine asserts the aesthetic value of numbers in *De musica:* 'Nos tantum meminerimus, quod ad susceptam praesentem disputationem maxime pertinet, id agi per providentiam Dei, per quem cuncta creavit et regit, ut etiam peccatrix et aerumnosa anima numeris agatur, et numeros agat usque ad infimam carnis corruptionem: qui certe numeri minus minusque pulchri esse possunt, penitus vere carere pulchritudine non possunt?' VI, 56 (Maurist edition, Paris, I, p. 880).

10. Cf. Bongus's declaration at the outset of his treatise (p. 7): '. . . sed mihi nunc sit instar omnium auctoritas sancti et magni viri Augustini . . . : "Numeri ratio contemnenda nequaquam est, quae in multis sacratarum Scripturarum locis (8) quam magni sit aestimanda elucet diligenter intuentibus . . ." [*De civitate Dei*] . . . "Numerorum imperitia multa facit non intelligi translate et mystice posita in Scripturis" [*De doctrina Christiana*]'.

11. This 'syncope' of time is perhaps also based on a locus in the *Confessions* (XI, p. 14–28), explained by W. Callahan, 'Basil. A New Source for Augustine's Theory of Time', *Harvard Studies in Classical Philology*, 63 (1958): 'Augustine, looking from the beginning at the way we measure time, wonders how we can measure past and future time, which do not exist, or present time, which strictly speaking has no extension. Since a thing must exist in order to be measured, Augustine comes eventually to the conclusion that all time *must now exist in the mind*, and that time, in fact, is nothing else than a *distentio animi*, this extension or distention having three phases, in that past time is identified with the mind's memory, future time with its anticipation, and present time with its persisting attention.' (p. 437, italics Callahan's.)

Calderón allows Gentilidad (781b) to allude to the contest on the new sacred Parnassus as occurring outside measurable time: '. . . las gentes, que ya/acudiendo por instantes,/siglos y naciones pueblan/del nuevo Parnaso el margen.'

12. 'In divinis oraculis [quinque] . . . praeclarae dignitatis est, quia praecipuorum Domini nostri Iesu Christi vulnerum per nostra redemptione acceptorum est designitivus, quorum signa et cicatrices triumphata morte redivivus dignatus est in suo corpore tam glorioso conservare, ad comprobandam discipulis fidem suae resurrectionis. Sane ex his tanquam quinque fontibus vivis effluxit largiter sanguis ille preciosus, qui emundat conscientias nostras ab operibus mortuis, . . . qui pretium est nostrae redemptionis, qui sanctificationis nostrae est lavacrum. Unde in mysteriis Missae et augustissimi sacramenti altaris, pleraque quinquies fieri debere instituta sunt, ut conversio sacerdotis ad populum, signorum crucis efformatio, et quintuplex . . . oratio sive collecta, ad repraesentandam nobis hanc quintuplicem Christi passionem, quae in sacratissimum quinque principalium suorum vulnerum inflictione peracta est' (258). Of course, Bongus's treatise is in no way original. The early mediaeval Hrabanus Maurus, for example, explains the numbers in another fashion, but relevant to this context: 'Quinarius ergo legem signat, et quaternarius Evangelium, ut quatuor pentagoni cum adhaerentibus sibi quatuor unitatibus quatuor cornua complent, quia passione Christi et resurrectione completa lex simul et Evangelium.' (*De laudibus*, I, p. 24; *Migne P.L.* CVII, col. 246).

13. Augustine argues from the fact that we prefer to see windows in a building matching if side by side, but not necessarily so if one above the other, in *De vera religione:* '. . . Porro ipsa vera aequalitas ac similitudo, atque ipsa vera et prima unitas, non oculis carneis, neque ullo tali sensu, sed mente intellecta conspicitur. Unde enim qualiscumque in corporibus appeteretur aequalitas, aut unde convinceretur longe plurimum differre a perfecta, nisi ea quae perfecta est, mente videretur? . . .' 55 (Maurist edition, Paris 1836: I, p. 1236).

14. The Seventeenth Century handbook to information about the Sibyls was that of Baltasar Porreño, *Oráculos de las doçe sibilas, profetisas de Christo nuestro Señor entre los Gentiles.* (Cuenca 1621). He distinguishes between the Cuman Sibyl, who prophesied the era of peace at the Nativity, and the Cumaean Sibyl, she of Virgil's *Eclogue IV* (and of Augustine's *Epistola ad Romanos inchoata*, which 'Christianised' her). Calderón continues what Porreño sees as a confusion.

15. The nine Muses corresponded to a *numerus imperfectionis*, associated with the nine prophetic books of the Hebrews (Isidore) and the nine ungrateful lepers of the Gospel (Augustine), cf. Jacques Fontaine, *Isidore de Séville et la culture classique* (Paris 1959), I, p. 382–3 and 388.

16. Regocijo's play on the two meanings of *gracia:* '. . . aquella fuente/cuyo cristal elocuente/mayor gracia le dará/para escribir al certamen,/ . . .' (789a) recalls rather the topography of Mount Helicon, where the Cassotis was said to flow beneath the ground and appear in the adyton of Apollo's temple, conferring sacred enthusiasm on those who drank it; cf. Walter Otto, *Die Musen* (Düsseldorf 1955), p. 65.

17. This passage interprets one of the most striking poetic irruptions into the *Confessions*, on the force of memory: '. . . et tanquam de abstrusioribus

quibusdam receptaculis eruuntur; quaedam catervatim se proruunt, et dum aliud petitur et quaeritur, prosiliunt in medium quasi dicentia: "Ne forte nos sumus?" Et abigo ea manu cordis a facie recordationis meae, donec enubiletur quod volo, atque in conspectum prodeat ex abditis.' X, 12 (Maurist edition, I, p. 297).

18. Cf. the modern judgment of Romano Guardini: 'For Augustine, Monica seems to have been the representative, the living embodiment of the Church . . . the images of the two mothers permeate each other.' *The Conversion of Augustine* (London 1960), p. 150. Augustine himself equates Monica's tears and his own baptism (ibid., p. 151). As the ingenuous Fifteenth Century sequence has it: '*Augustinus dum sophiae/mundi servit, matrix piae/sacra spernit monita./Mundi rhetor parvipendet/Christi fidem, nec adtendit/quae sit Christi semita.*' *Analecta hymnica M. A.*, IX, no. 109, strophe 3b.

19. 'The primary theme of Augustinian becoming: that this powerful sensuousness be elevated to the realm of the spirit' (Guardini, p. 135).

Essay 15

1. *Un tal Lucas* (Buenos Aires 1979), p. 176–83.

2. *Presencia,* published under the pseudonym Julio Denis in Buenos Aires in 1938 is a volume of sonnets. *Pameos y meopas,* published in Barcelona in 1971 but written apparently between 1951 and 1958, contains fifteen sonnets. *Ultimo Round* (Mexico City 1974) contains two sonnets: vol. I, p. 245 and vol. II, p. 92–3. 'Cinco sonetos eróticos' were published in *Point of Contact/Punto de contacto* (April–May 1978), p. 42–44.

3. *Ultimo round,* II (Mexico City 1974) p. 16.

4. *Octaedro* (Buenos Aires 1974), p. 51.

Essay 16

1. I have relied upon Brian Dutton's valuable work of coordination and research in establishing a chronology for the major manuscript collections of early fifteenth-century love lyric, 'Spanish Fifteenth-Century *Cancioneros:* A General Survey to 1465', *KRQ* 26 (1979), 445–60. His dating of the *Cancionero de Baena* has to be revised in accordance with the findings of Barclay Tittmann, 'A Contribution to the Study of the *Cancionero de Baena* Manuscript', *Aquila* 1 (1968), p. 190–203, and Alberto Blecua, '"Perdióse un quaderno . . .": sobre los cancioneros de Baena', *AEM* 9 (1974–79), 229–66.

   I shall make reference to the following *cancioneros* by an italicized short title and, unless otherwise stated, take my texts from the modern editions given below. Where necessary, I have added accents and modernized punctuation. The parenthetical abbreviations after each manuscript callmark refer to the *sigla* devised by Brian Dutton, Stephen Fleming, Jineen Krogstad, Francisco Santoyo Vásquez and Joaquín González Cuenca for the *Catálogo-índice de la poesía cancioneril del siglo XV* (Madison 1982).

Baena: Paris, Bibliothèque Nationale anc. fonds esp. 37 (PN1), ed. José María Azáceta, *El cancionero de Juan Alfonso de Baena,* 3 vols (Madrid 1966).

Herberay: London, British Library Add. MS 33383 (LB2), ed. Charles V. Aubrun, *Le Chansonnier espagnol d'Herberay des Essarts (XVᵉ siècle),* Bibliothèque de l'École des Hautes Études Hispaniques 25 (Bordeaux 1951).

Palacio: Salamanca, Biblioteca Universitaria MS 2653 (SA7), ed. Francisca Vendrell de Millás, *El cancionero de Palacio (manuscrito no. 594)* (Barcelona 1945).

Gallardo: Madrid, Real Academia de la Historia 2-7-2, MS 2 (MH1), description only by José María Azáceta, 'El cancionero de Gallardo de la Real Academia de la Historia', *RLit* 5–6 (1954), 239–70; 7–8 (1955), 134–80 and 271–94, who follows the modern foliation.

Reference will also be made to the following *cancioneros* without consulting modern editions, where any exists: *Modena* (ME1), *Roma* (RC1), *Stúñiga* (MN54), *Paris A, E* and *H* (PN4, PN8, PN12), *Palermo* (PM1) and *Marciana* (VM1).

2. 'Baena, Santillana, Resende and the Silent Century of Portuguese Court Poetry', *BHS* 59 (1982), 198–210, p. 204.

3. 'Fifteenth-Century *Cancioneros'*, p. 456.

4. Alberto Blecua, '"Perdióse un quaderno"', has shown that some of the earliest lyrics in the extant manuscript, those by Pero González de Mendoza (d. 1385) and Garcí Fernández de Jerena (fl. 1385–1400), were added to the original *cancionero* after it was complete, presumably from written sources that Baena might have had at his disposal. Other evidence of lost fourteenth-century lyric would include some of the poems cited by *cancionero* poets which remain unidentified today.

5. Vivienne Richardson's research suggests that both literary dialects were used indiscriminately from about the middle of the fourteenth century, except by Pero Ferrús who wrote in Castilian only. See 'Five Early Poets of the *Cancionero de Baena:* Their Development of the Castilian Lyric and Interpretation of the Courtly Ideal', MA dissertation, Centre for Medieval Studies, University of Leeds, 1981.

6. A complementary view of the lady as a sparring partner in courtly games is given by debate poems. For examples see note 9, below.

7. I have made a separate study, as yet unpublished, of the traces of traditional lyric in the early *cancioneros*.

8. *Herberay* 9 and 19 respectively. Dolly Lucero del Padrón discusses 'Soy garridilla' in 'En torno al romance de *La bella mal maridada'*, *BBMP* 43 (1967), 307–54, p. 311–12.

9. These poems include *Baena* 537 and 538, by Fernán Sánchez Talavera; *Palacio* 104, by Juan de Dueñas; *Palacio* 119, by Estamaríu, is a *Debat d'una senyora et de su voluntat; Gallardo* (MH1 117) contains a *Pleyto que ovo Juan de Duennas con su amiga* which is printed by Francisca Vendrell, 'Las poesías inéditas de Juan de Dueñas', *RABM* 64 (1958), 149–237, p. 182.

10. For example, *Baena* 101, by Pedro Morrera, and *Baena* 105, by Francisco de Baena.

11. Alan Deyermond, 'The Worm and the Partridge: Reflections on the Poetry of Florencia Pinar', *Mester* 7 (1978), 3–8, p. 3. One female poet of the period, Vayona, is credited with only a short *respuesta*, *Herberay* 2, in praise of her mistress, Leonor de Foix. See Aubrun, p. lxii–iii.

12. *Gallardo*, f. 315 (modern foliation), 'El conde de Mayorga para los días de la semana de amores: "Quieres saber commo va" '. The *Catálogo-índice* follows the original foliation of the manuscript, and this poem is entered as MH1 145 (389r).

13. There are other cases of poems being linguistically updated in this way. Azáceta draws attention to the practice in his notes to *Baena* 16 and 18. For a different interpretation of the evidence, involving the restoration of Galician forms to a quotation by Santillana, see Dutton, 'Fifteenth-Century *Cancioneros*', p. 450–51.

14. *Palacio* 190, 'Piérdesse quien esperança'; also *Herberay* 106 and *Modena*, ME1 35. 'Ay, señora en quien fiança' is a well-known and much quoted poem by Macías.

15. 'Cancionero de Baena No. 237: *Cativa muy triste*', *MLN*, 76 (1961), 29–34. She argues that Francisco Imperial could have seen Angelina of Greece when she was brought to Seville in 1403. See also María Rosa Lida de Malkiel and Renée Toole Kahane, 'Doña Angelina de Grecia', *NRFH* 14 (1960), 89–97.

16. Colbert I. Nepaulsingh, *Micer Francisco Imperial: 'El dezir a las syete virtudes' y otros poemas*, Clásicos Castellanos 221 (Madrid 1977), p. 39–44.

17. *Palacio* 103 (SA7 103bis). In the notes to her edition Vendrell acknowledges the hiatus and loss of leaves at this point but does not assign a new number to the feminine lyric. The host poem, 'Senyora, fablar querría', occurs in full in *Herberay*, 115, and *Modena*, ME1 47.

18. *Herberay* 128 and *Modena*, ME1 60.

19. Six of these are the closely related *cancioneros* of *Roma* (RC1 43), *Stúñiga* (MN54 45), *Paris A, E* and *H* (PN4 32, PN8 28 and PN12 23) and *Palermo* (SM1 8). Parts of the *Planto* were also copied into two different places in *Gallardo* (MH1 74 and 256).

20. For the date of *Paris A, E* and *H* see Alberto Várvaro, *Premesse ad un' edizione critica delle poesie minori di Juan de Mena* (Naples 1964), and Brian Dutton, 'Fifteenth-Century *Cancioneros*', p. 458. It is without attribution in all the manuscripts except *Palermo:* see Alessandra Bartolini, 'Il canzoniere castigliano di San Martino delle Scale (Palermo)', *Bollettino del Centro di Studi Filologici e Linguistici Siciliani* 4 (1956), 147–87. The poem had previously been thought to be the work of Santillana, but its new attribution is defended by Rafael Lapesa in *La obra literaria del Marqués de Santillana* (Madrid 1957), p. 90–94, and Arnold G. Reichenberger, 'The Marqués de Santillana and the Classical Tradition', *Iberoromania* 1 (1969), 5–34, p. 32–34.

21. I have used the most accessible but far from satisfactory text of the poem given in Vicente García de Diego (ed.), *Marqués de Santillana: Canciones y decires*, Clásicos Castellanos 18 (1913; repr. Madrid 1968), p. 114–23.

22. *Carvajal: Poesie*, Officina Romanica 9 (Rome 1967), p. 101–05. The *romance* occurs in *Roma* (RC1 92), *Stúñiga* (MN54 115) and *Marciana* (VM1 21).

23. For a discussion of the different dates that have been suggested see Scoles, p. 25–29. Her own hypothesis, that the queen's death, a year after Alfonso died, was the occasion for the composition of the poem and letter is commended by A. J. Foreman in his review-article, *RPh* 27 (1973–4), 125–28.

24. *Poesie*, ed. Scoles, p. 96–100.

25. Apart from poems I may have overlooked, I have deliberately disregarded three: *Palacio* 300, 'Ya non sé nada que diga', by Pedro de la Caltraviesa, seems to be a complaint by an abandoned girl, but the printed text is very defective; in *Palacio* 334, 'Amigo, si goçedes' (anonymous), the girl speaks the *estribillo* and her lover's answer forms the *glosa; Modena* (ME1 6a) f. 19v, 'Por la vuestra departida', is a complete feminine *despedida* but a later addition to the manuscript.

26. See Ramón Menéndez Pidal, *Reliquias de la poesía épica española* (Madrid 1951), p. 246: ' "¡Mezquina! ¿qué faré o qué será de my? Non oviera de ser naçida!" '. In the *Corbacho* the speech illustrates 'la segunda manera de matrimonio o amor reprobado, quando el viejo casa o ama la moça', and includes the lines: '¡O triste de mí! que en ora mala nascí! ¡Y para mí fueron guardadas, cuytada, estas fadas malas!' See J. González Muela (ed.), *Arcipreste de Talavera o Corbacho*, Clásicos Castalia 24 (Madrid 1970), p. 201. Nepaulsingh. *Micer Francisco Imperial*, p. lxxix, cites similar passages from the *Libro del Cabellero Zifar* (lament by the Empress Nobleza) and *Amadís* (lament by Oriana).

27. *Palacio* 292, 'Pues mi triste corazón' (I emend l. 3, 'careza'). It ends with a complaint quoted from an old song: 'Ay, ¿a quién diré, a quién,/mi tristura?/Pues de mí qui es mi bien/non ha cura'.

28. From the *Passión trobada*, stanza 212. See Dorothy S. Severin and Keith Whinnom (eds), *Diego de San Pedro: Obras completas*, III: *Poesías*, Clásicos Castalia 98 (Madrid 1979), p. 202. For the relevant part of the *Siete angustias* see *Obras completas*, I, ed. Whinnom (1973), p. 158.

29. See Dorothy S. Vivian [Severin], 'La *Passión trobada* de Diego de San Pedro y sus relaciones con el drama medieval de la Pasión', AEM 1 (1964), 451–70.

30. See James T. Monroe, 'Formulaic Diction and the Common Origins of Romance Lyric Traditions', *AR* 43 (1975), 341–50.

31. *MHRA Annual Bulletin* 32 (1960), p. 17–34.

32. I owe my knowledge of the manuscript to its inclusion in the *Catálogo-índice de la poesía cancioneril del siglo XV*, but texts of the two poems were first published by Morel-Fatio in *RABM* 6 (1876), p. 292–93. Francisco López Estrada reprinted them with other material taken from Morel-Fatio in his edition of *La embajada a Tamorlán* (Madrid 1943), p. lxxii–lxxvi, and it is from this work that I take all references to the poems.

33. For the lady's name, see López Estrada, *La embajada a Tamorlán*, p. lxxxi. It is not given in the rubric to the poem.

34. According to Jose María Alín, *El cancionero español de tipo tradicional* (Madrid 1968), no. 611 is taken from MS 17698 (ca 1560–70) of the Biblioteca Nacional. He refers also to the version in a *pliego suelto* of 1594–8, published by R. Foulché-Delbosc, 'Les Romancerillos de Pise', *RHi* 65 (1925), 160–263, p. 187–88.

35. *Gallardo*, f. 275 (modern foliation), 'al cantar antiguo que dizen *Alta mar esquiva*', MH1 90 (347r-v) (see note 12, above). It is printed by Eloy Benito Ruano in 'Lope de Stúñiga, vida y cancionero', *RFE* 51 (1968), 17–109, p. 81.

36. 'Poys me boy sin falimento' starts off with a predominance of Galician forms, including several pairs of rhymes that would be impossible in Castilian. As the poem progresses, however, the author's resolution seems to falter and by the fifth and final stanza the language is entirely Castilian.

37. I am grateful to Professor Alan Deyermond for his helpful comments on the final draft of this article.

Tabula Gratulatoria

His students:

Algeo, Tricia (now Marnham)
Anderson, Janet (now Trotman)
Andrews, Alison (now Slade)
Armstrong, Gwennie
Atkinson, Sue
Baird-Fraser, Bob
Balfour-Paul, Ann
Barker, Catherine
Barlow, Juliet (née Molony)
Begg, Fiona
Bells from Belfast
Bentley, Bernard P. E.
Bergh, Sonia L.
Berner, Eileen E. H.
Blair, Susan
Boulter, Mary (now Miller)
Boyd, Stephen
Brenchley, Hilary
Buckley, Wendy
Bumpus, Judith (née Collison)
Butler, Claire
Calcraft, Ray
Cameron, Mary (née Ransom)
Carmichael, Patricia (now Richer)
Carter, Robin & Valerie
Chadwick, Susan
Clifford, John
Connolly, Claire Marie
Constance, Graham
Corbett, Anne F. (née Cameron)
Cotter, Helen (now Stell)
Coupar, Alice (née Tully)
Craig, Anita Nieves
Cummings, Peter
Cummins, John G.
Cuthbert, Sandy

Davies, Howard
Davis, Sue & Paul
Dazeley, Lulu
Docherty, Pat
Drysdale, John & Carol (née Mackenzie)
Dugan, Mary B.
Dunkley, Caroline (now Sellick)
Durante, Charles & Barbara (née McDowell)
Edwards, Carole
Emerson, Carole (now Edlmann)
Eustace, Katharine
Evans, Peter
Fallaw, Shirley
Ferguson, Keith & Elspeth M. (née McKechnie)
Finnegan, Anne-Marie (now Hiddleston)
Fodor, Karen
Fortes, Robert A.
Fry, Derek B.
Gale, Valerie (née McGregor)
Gallone, Deborah
Galloway, Gillian
Gentilli, N. C.
George, Carmel
Gledson, John
Glen, Jonathan K.
Gomme, Katherine
Goodwin, Andrew
Greening, Nicola
Gregorson, Marilyn
Gurney, Bob
Guy, John
Haidinger, Brigitta (now Farmer)
Hardie, Katriona (now Persson)

Hartle, Sharon
Hawken, Kathryn
Haworth, Amanda
Hawtrey, Anne
Henderson, Ruth
Hitchcock, Richard
Hopkins, L. J. M.
Hoystead, Rosemary (now Fraser)
Hunt, Rosemary (now Senior)
Hunter, John
Jolly, Anne (now Anderson)
Jones, E. Y. Miranda
Jones, Olwen (née Meek)
Jones, Warwick L.
Jordan, Deborah M.
Kiely, Michèle (née Parzy)
Lancaster, Elizabeth
Lanham, Jean
Lauber, Ruth
Legg, Christopher & Christine
Leslie, Marion (née Serjeant)
Lewis, Christine
Lindsay, Niobe (now O'Connor)
Lofting, Sally
Loryman, Deidre A. (now Anderson)
Louden, Wendy (née Loudon)
Lucas, Carolyn
Lush, Eleanor (now Nightingale)
Lutley, Margaret
McAllister, Colin
McAndrew, Diane
McAweaney, Stephen
Macdonald, Ian R.
McDonald, Kate
McFarlane, Elspeth
McIlroy, Heather
McIntyre, Doreen M.
McIvor, Eelin (née Emmerson)
Mackenzie, Sheila C.

Mackie, Maddy
Mackie-Robertson, Margaret
Maguire, Elaine
Malcolm, Jennifer (now McGregor)
Mallard, Sheila (née Fraser)
Margey, Alice
Maynard, Gabrielle (now Robertson)
Melville, Mary
Millar, Marilyn (now Cuthbert)
Miller, Ann (née Craig-McQuaide)
Mitchell, Kathryn
Moir, Lyn (née Ross)
Montgomery, Susan V.
Morgan, Christabel (née Bartlett)
Morson, Caroline
Muir, Mary (now Baker)
Nimmo, Gibby
Noble, Alison
O'Connor, Cornelius
Pearson, Kate (now Steer)
Philpot, Christine M. (now Steele)
Piercy, Henrietta
Plumpton, Jill
Poole, Kate
Porter, Sallie (now Bryson)
Reid, Caroline Ann
Reilly, Rosina (now Kettle-Williams)
Richterich, Daniel
Ridsdill-Smith family
Ritchie, Fiona (née McCracken)
Romyn, Christine (now Willis)
Rutherford, Margaret (now Hill)
Ryan, Paul M.
Schimmer, Elizabeth A. (now Pedersen)

Selka, Helen
Simpson, Margaret (née Shannon)
Simpson, William
Skinner, Judy
Sleeman, Margaret
Smart, Kay (now Welsh)
Smith, Catriona
Staveley Taylor, Victoria
Stewart, Sheila M. I.
Strathairn, Deidre
Syme, Anne T.
Szepesi, Jane (née Pentland)
Tarbet, Nick
Turnbull, Andrew J.
Turner, John H.
Urquhart, Lesley
Vazquez-Azpiri, A. J.

Vincent, Sarah
Waddell, Heather
Walker, Lorna (now Thomson)
Wands, T. Anthony
Ward, Anita
Watson, Fiona
Webb, Marie-Elaine (now de Rafael)
Wedderburn, Frances
Welsh, Paul F.
Whetnall, Jane (née Glass)
Whitworth, Paul
Wilkie, Malcolm
Williams, Dr. and Mrs. P. V. A.
Williams, Bill
Wilson, Barbara M.

Tabula Gratulatoria

His friends and colleagues:

Amherst College
Salvador and Pamela Bacarisse
John Beverley
Blackwell's of Oxford
Elizabeth Boyce
Peter Branscombe
E. V. K. Brill
J. H. Brumfitt
A. R. Butler
H. G. Callan
Ronald G. Cant
R. Cardona
Chris Carter
R. F. Christian
R. M. Cormack
R. M. M. and B. Crawford
J. S. Cummins
Catherine Davies
Gareth Davies
John Devereux
Victor Dixon
Alexander F. Falconer
Isobel Fraser
Douglas Gifford
Nigel Glendinning
C. P. Gordon
H. F. Grant
J. Gray
John C. Hall
Vernon and Marion Harward
Michael Herbert
Sándor Hervey
L. Hoggarth
J. M. Howie
Tony Hunt
C. and J. E. A. Husband
Alicia Jackson
D. E. P. Jackson
Ron Keightley

H. P. King
Ruth Leslie
A. H. T. Levi
Douglas and Lydia Lloyd
D. W. Lomax
Catherine McCallun
K. M. MacIver
T. E. May
B. Mayo
I. D. L. Michael
E. W. T. Morris
H. C. T. and M. J. Morris
Mount Holyoke College Library
Margot G. Munro
Terence O'Reilly
R. J. Oakley
D. D. R. Owen
Arsenio Pacheco-Ransanz
A. A. Parker
A. K. G. Paterson
Frank Pierce
R. D. F. Pring-Mill
R. V. Pringle
Kenneth S. Reid
G. W. Ribbans
G. E. Rickman
E. C. Riley
E. J. Rodgers
St. Catherine's, Oxford
D. S. Severin
Hilary S. D. Smith
J. D. Smith
C. Alan Soons
George Spater
Geoffrey Stagg
Susanna Stuart-Smith
Sam Taylor
J. E. Varey
D. R. Wagg

179

Pamela Waley
L. E. M. Walker
R. M. Walker
Bruce W. Wardropper
J. Steven Watson
D. E. R. Watt

Jenny A. Woodward
Arne Worren
Crispin Wright
P. A. H. Wyatt
C. M. Zsuppán